School Education in India

Quality Improvement Techniques

School Education in India

Quality Improvement Techniques

Edited by

S. Kumar
Dean, Faculty of Education and Psychology,
The Maharaja Sayajirao University of Baroda, Vadodara.

Sujata Srivastava
Senior Faculty Member, Department of Education,
The Maharaja Sayajirao University of Baroda, Vadodara.

NEW NC CENTURY
New Century Publications
New Delhi, India

NEW CENTURY PUBLICATIONS
4800/24, Bharat Ram Road,
Ansari Road, Daryaganj,
New Delhi – 110 002 (India)

Tel.: 011-2324 7798, 4358 7398, 6539 6605
Fax: 011-4101 7798
E-mail: indiatax@vsnl.com • info@newcenturypublications.com
www.newcenturypublications.com

Editorial office:
LG–7, Aakarshan Bhawan,
4754-57/23, Ansari Road, Daryaganj,
New Delhi – 110 002

Tel.: 011-4356 0919

First Published: **2010**

ISBN: **978-81-7708-226-5**

Published by New Century Publications and printed at Salasar Imaging Systems, New Delhi.

Designs: Patch Creative Unit, New Delhi.

PRINTED IN INDIA

Contents

About the Book

Since Independence in 1947, there has been an enormous expansion of school education in India. The school segment has adopted and integrated Information and Communication Technology (ICT) to improve quality and productivity in education. However, the existing inequalities prevailing in school education system have led to *digital divide*. Other problems and challenges facing the system include outdated curriculum, pedagogy, lack of infrastructure, dropouts, teachers' absenteeism, unequal access, lax administration and slow speed of vocationalization of education.

This volume contains 31 papers, authored by the scholars in the field of education, which focus on various dimensions of school education in India. It is designed to act as a reference book for students of Bachelors in Education (B.Ed.), Masters in Education (M.Ed.), Post-graduate diploma in Education, Masters in Educational Management and other related courses. The contents of this volume would also give a deep insight to school teachers, school principals, college and university teachers, educational administrators, policy-makers, policy-planners, scholars, academicians, trainers, field-workers and all those who are related to the spread and improvement in educational standards.

The volume is organized into 3 theme parts, each part containing papers related to a particular theme.

About the Editors

Professor S. Kumar is Head, Centre of Advanced Study in Education and Dean, Faculty of Education and Psychology, The Maharaja Sayajirao (M.S.) University of Baroda, Vadodara. He did his M.A in Economics from Meerut University and M.Ed. and Ph.D. from The M.S. University of Baroda, Vadodara. He has been the recipient of the National Scholarship of the University Grants Commission (U.G.C.), New Delhi at the M.Ed. level and the U.G.C Junior Research Fellowship.

He has published 2 books and 60 research papers in journals of National and International repute. Considering his performance and contribution in the field of education, Professor Kumar was conferred in 2007 the Life-Time Education Achievement Award by the Health and Education Development Association of India.

Dr. Sujata Srivastava is a senior faculty member in the Department of Education, Faculty of Education and Psychology, The M.S. University of Baroda, Vadodara. She completed her B.Sc. from Miranda House, University of Delhi and her B.Ed. from Dev Samaj College of Education, Punjab University, Ferozepur. She did her M.Ed. and Ph.D. from The M.S. University of Baroda, Vadodara. She has been the recipient of the U.G.C. scholarship at the M.Ed. level and was awarded the S.N. Mukherjee gold medal in M.Ed.

She has authored and co-authored 30 articles, research papers, reviews and book chapters in the areas of education. She is an academic counsellor at Baroda study centre for B.Ed. programme of Indira Gandhi National Open University (IGNOU), New Delhi.

Acknowledgements

We place on record our deep sense of gratitude to all the scholars who have contributed their papers to the present volume. We are thankful to Dr. Manoj Soni, formerly Vice-Chancellor of The Maharaja Sayajirao University of Baroda, Vadodara for his encouragement and administrative support. We are indebted to Professor R.G. Kothari, formerly Vice-Chancellor, Veer Narmad South Gujarat University, Surat for inspiring us to undertake this work. The co-operation received from all the faculty members of the Faculty of Education and Psychology, The Maharaja Sayajirao University of Baroda, is gratefully acknowledged.

We take this opportunity to express our deep gratitude to our parents who have always been a source of inspiration and moral support in all our academic endeavours.

S. Kumar
Sujata Srivastava

Contributors and Their Affiliations

S. Kumar
Head, Centre of Advanced Study in Education,
Department of Education,
Faculty of Education and Psychology,
The M.S. University of Baroda,
Vadodara.

R.G. Kothari
Centre of Advanced Study in Education,
Department of Education,
Faculty of Education and Psychology,
The M.S. University of Baroda,
Vadodara.

S.C. Panigrahi
Centre of Advanced Study in Education,
Department of Education,
Faculty of Education and Psychology,
The M.S. University of Baroda,
Vadodara.

R.C. Patel
Reader, Centre of Advanced Study in Education,
Department of Education,
Faculty of Education and Psychology,
The M.S. University of Baroda,
Vadodara.

Satish Pathak
Reader, Centre of Advanced Study in Education,
Department of Education,
Faculty of Education and Psychology,
The M.S. University of Baroda,
Vadodara.

R.S. Mani
Reader, Centre of Advanced Study in Education,
Department of Education,
Faculty of Education and Psychology,
The M.S. University of Baroda,
Vadodara.

Sujata Srivastava
Senior Lecturer, Centre of Advanced Study in Education,
Department of Education,
Faculty of Education and Psychology,
The M.S. University of Baroda,
Vadodara.

Ashutosh Biswal
Senior Lecturer, Centre of Advanced Study in Education,
Department of Education,
Faculty of Education and Psychology,
The M.S. University of Baroda,
Vadodara.

Jayshree Das
Senior Lecturer, Centre of Advanced Study in Education,
Department of Education,
Faculty of Education and Psychology,
The M.S. University of Baroda,
Vadodara.

Anjali Khirwadkar
Lecturer, Centre of Advanced Study in Education,
Department of Education,
Faculty of Education and Psychology,
The M.S. University of Baroda,
Vadodara.

Preeti Chowdhary
Lecturer, Centre of Advanced Study in Education,
Department of Education,
Faculty of Education and Psychology,
The M.S. University of Baroda,
Vadodara.

R.L. Madhavi
Lecturer, Centre of Advanced Study in Education,
Department of Education,
Faculty of Education and Psychology,
The M.S. University of Baroda,
Vadodara.

Geetha Dinkar
Lecturer, Centre of Advanced Study in Education,
Department of Education,
Faculty of Education and Psychology,
The M.S. University of Baroda,
Vadodara.

Rina Choudhary
Lecturer, Centre of Advanced Study in Education,
Department of Education,
Faculty of Education and Psychology,
The M.S. University of Baroda,
Vadodara.

Mario Xavier
Reader, Department of Psychology,
Faculty of Education and Psychology,
The M.S. University of Baroda,
Vadodara.

Priya Nair
Lecturer, Department of Psychology,
The M.S. University of Baroda,
Faculty of Education and Psychology,
Vadodara.

Priyanka Beharani
Lecturer, Department of Psychology,
Faculty of Education and Psychology,
The M.S. University of Baroda,
Vadodara.

Sudipta Roy
Lecturer, Department of Psychology,
Faculty of Education and Psychology,
The M.S. University of Baroda,
Vadodara.

Sarita Agrawal
Reader, Department of Business Economics,
Faculty of Commerce,
The M.S. University of Baroda,
Vadodara.

Jyoti Achanta
Lecturer, Department of Business Economics,
Faculty of Commerce,
The M.S. University of Baroda,
Vadodara.

A. Ramachary
Research Scholar, Centre of Advanced Study in Education,
Department of Education,
The M.S. University of Baroda,
Vadodara.

M. Rajendran
Research Scholar, Centre of Advanced Study in Education,
Department of Education,
The M.S. University of Baroda,
Vadodara.

Vishal Mohandas
Research scholar, Department of Education,
Faculty of Education and Psychology,
The M.S. University of Baroda,
Vadodara.

Vandana Talegaonkar
Lecturer, Navarachana College of Education,
New Sama Road,
Vadodara.

Archana Tomar
Lecturer, Navrachana College of Education,
New Sama Road,
Vadodara.

Mandira Sikdar
Lecturer, Navrachana College of Education,
New Sama Road,
Vadodara.

Leena Bhojwani
Lecturer, Navrachana College of Education,
New Sama Road,
Vadodara.

Jignasa Prajapati
Lecturer, S.R. College of Education,
Makarpura,
Vadodara.

Lakshmi Shah
Lecturer, S.R. College of Education,
Makarpura,
Vadodara.

Lakshmi Venugopal
Lecturer, S.R. College of Education,
Makarpura,
Vadodara.

Indu Kataria
Lecturer, S.R. College of Education,
Makarpura,
Vadodara.

Pradeep Patel
Educational Counsellor,
62, Balajinagar Society
Kareli Baug, Near Amit Nagar Circle
Vadodara.

Priyadarshini S. Kelkar
Principal, New Era Senior Secondary School,
Nizampura,
Vadodara.

Anitha D. Shetty
Principal, Ambe Vidyalaya,
Sama-Savli Road,
Vadodara.

Sejal Dave
Teacher, Bright School,
Vadodara.

Pallavi D. Khedkar
Teacher, Bright School,
Vadodara.

D. Sarangi
Lecturer, DAV College of Teacher Education,
Koraput.

Manoranjan Pradhan
Research Scholar, DAV College of Education,
Koraput.

Mahesh Narayan Dixit
Shikshan Mahavidalaya, Gujarat Vidyapeeth,
Ahmedabad.

Bharti Rathore
Lecturer, WayMade College of Education,
Vallabh Vidyanagar,
Anand.

Namita Sahoo
Lecturer, K.P. Training College,
University of Allahabad,
Allahabad.

B.C. Das
Lecturer, Department of B.Ed.,
RBD Women's College,
Bijnor.

Vaya K. Bharat
Lecturer, Shree Mahavir B.Ed College,
Dhrangadhra,
Surendranagar.

Omprakash Purohit
Lecturer, Shree Mahavir B.Ed College,
Dhrangadhra,
Surendranagar

P.K. Sahoo
Professor of Education and Director of Institute of
Correspondence Course and Continuing Education,
University of Allahabad,
Allahabad.

Dinesh Kumar
UGC-SRF, Department of Education,
University of Allahabad,
Allahabad.

Sona Ahuja
Lecturer, Faculty of Education,
Dayalbagh Educational Institute,
Dayalbagh, Agra.

Preface

Education has always played a vital role in the nation building process. It acts as an agent of social change and reflects the ethos, culture, aspirations and concerns of any society. School education is an important segment of the total education system and contributes significantly to the development of the individual and the nation. It lays the foundation of a knowledge-based society. It is widely accepted that school education, of enhanced quality is the most powerful tool for the overall improvement of the system.

Since Independence in 1947, there has been an enormous expansion of school education in India. The school system is reeling under the impact of the changes which need to be accommodated. The school segment has adopted and integrated Information and Communication Technology (ICT) to improve quality and productivity in education. However the existing inequalities prevailing in education have led to the issue of *digital divide*. Other problems and challenges are related to curriculum, pedagogy, infrastructure, dropouts, access, inequity, administration, vocationalization etc.

Serious attempts have been made to take care of these concerns. Innovations have led to new pathways resulting in improved education. Alternative schooling initiatives have further contributed to the system. During the past several decades constant, deliberate and sustained efforts have been made for qualitative improvement of the primary, secondary and higher secondary system. Though the achievements have been substantial in quantitative terms, a lot still remains to be done. The quest for quality never ends. It is the compelling force behind all human endeavours. It is imperative that improvement in the quality of school education becomes the major focus of all reform initiatives.

This volume contains papers which focus on various dimensions of school education in India. This volume has been produced to act as a reference book for students of Bachelors in Education (B.Ed.), Masters in Education (M.Ed.), Post-graduate diploma in Education, Masters in Educational Management etc. The content of this volume would also give a deep insight to school teachers, school principals, college and university teachers, educational administrators, policy-makers, policy-planners, scholars, academicians, trainers, field-workers and all those who are related to the spread and improvement in educational standards.

This volume presents a critical review of the work done on various aspects of quality improvement in school education in India. The papers have been contributed by academicians, scholars, research workers, school teachers, educational administrators, counsellors, and other agents of change. The editors have woven the papers together to give them the present form.

The volume is organized into 3 theme parts, each part containing papers related to a particular theme.

Part I: School Education: Issues and Concerns

Over the last decade, changes in every walk of human endeavour have been much greater as compared to earlier times. The educational and social demands have changed. Education has undergone a major transformation. The goal of universalization of elementary education still remains elusive. Researches have revealed that this goal cannot be achieved without addressing to the socio-economic issues.

A large number of children dropout because of reasons related to the school environment. These include attitude of teachers, irrelevant curriculum, sub-standard and uninteresting teaching, teacher absenteeism, corporal punishment, poor school infrastructure, inability to cope with the pace of learning, lack of parental support in the case of first generation learners, maladjustment, etc. Girls form the majority of the dropouts in all categories.

A recent disturbing trend has been the exodus of children from free State-managed schools to privately-managed institutions. This trend is likely to lead to further increase in inequity. The male-female disparity at all levels of school education still exists. School education has to devise strategies to bridge this gap between boys and girls. India is struggling to cope with the problem of child labour. A large number of children exit from school at an early stage and join the world of work. In this context the school curriculum has to be made more need-based, differentiated, and vocationalization has to be given impetus. And interface between cognition, emotion and action is essential.

India being a land of paradoxes has elite schools which have adequate infrastructural facilities and have been able to cope with the ICT wave. On the other hand, the public education system which is not so well endowed has no place for ICT in its school education programme. The tremendous potential of ICT needs to be explored to improve the quality of the school system.

A qualitative improvement in the content and processes of school education, in order to make them more responsive to learner needs and the development needs of different socio-economic sectors, continues to be a major challenge today.

The authors in this section have highlighted various issues and a concern being faced by school education in India today. A critical issue concerning the education of the urban disadvantaged has been brought to light. The need for specialization at an early stage of schooling, vocationalizaion of education stimulates readers to think in a different direction. The rapidly emerging problems of mental health and the reflections of psychologists to enhance quality through counselling and inclusive schooling offer a new perspective to the readers.

The concept of instructional supervision and organizational development has been introduced to improve quality. The relevance of Women Rights Education for girls at the secondary school stage and education for creating a knowledge-based society has been emphasized upon. The policies and programmes for the achievement of universalizaton of elementary education in India have been written about and the academic achievement of tribal students of Ashram Schools have been studied. The problems faced by NIOS learners with respect to gender, stream and support-services have been studied and suggestions offered. Different authors have analyzed other diverse issues like the growing need for emphasizing on regional languages, lack of infrastructure, sub-standard teaching, irrelevant curriculum, teacher attitude, improper home support, socio-economic issues, unfriendly school environment, assessment practices, declining attendance in the classroom apathy towards the teaching profession etc.

Part II: Innovations in School Education

Innovative practices in school education have led to its improved quality. Innovation is the key driver which seeks to discover new approaches and methodologies. Innovative means of raising standards and promoting excellence in different key areas needs to be explored further. No country can afford to ignore the curriculum development process. Curriculum development which includes components such as formulation of curriculum policy, curriculum research, curriculum planning, curriculum design, its implementation and evaluation play an important role in determining quality. Reforms in pedagogical techniques need to cater to the current needs of the learner. Today the constructivist movement has re-emphasized the active role children play in acquiring knowledge.

Across the country Information and Communication Technology is revolutionizing the school education sector in a way as never seen before. Innovative technologies available to the administrators, teachers and students may steadily develop various skills required today. Administrators are responsible for managing the course of their institutions through sound management practices, creative administrative tools and balanced partnerships. Innovative pathways in school leadership would lead to quality institutions. Schools need to be supported by policies that encourage innovation. The meaningful innovation in education is possible only by bringing together administrators, policy-makers, teachers, parents, children and other professionals. It is through innovation that education keeps putting forward new initiatives, adapting to changing needs.

The papers in this section focus on various areas of innovation. They include grass-root innovations at the primary level, innovative methodologies like the value integrated approach for the teaching of Mathematics, interventions for student achievement in Mathematics and the role of language teaching in preventing value erosion. Acquisition of process skills using the constructivist approach and the role of technology in constructivist classrooms have been detailed out. The domains of the educational system have been visualized using the Zach man's frame work and the Deep Approach of learning has been explained. The role of non-verbal communication in improving quality of the teaching –learning process and quality enhancement through student's feedback has been addressed. A new line of innovation in school education called Entrepreneurial Education has been recommended. The need and scope of different investigatory projects at different school levels has been emphasized .Other papers on innovation and change in school education for quality enhancement and curriculum change for quality also find a place here.

Part III: Alternative Schooling in Education

Alternative schooling includes non-formal modes such as correspondence education, open schooling and other flexible systems of education run by the government and non-government agencies. The non-government organizations deserve a special mention in this regard. Many of them are actively involved in providing school education in rural and urban areas Alternative schooling today caters to a large number of students who have either not enrolled in schools or dropped out due to social, economic or geographical disadvantages. The students who are in the age group of 6-14 and 15-35 learn in a system that provides autonomy, flexibility and enables learning to take place according to learner convenience. Alternative schools go a long way in meeting the national goals of UEE. They are the means of universalizing access to schooling, particularly among marginalized communities in far-flung locations.

Open schooling has now come of age in India. National Institute of Open schooling in New Delhi and open schools in different states of India provide education at elementary, secondary and higher secondary levels. Mobile schools in rural India also contribute their bit providing education to rural children. Under innovations and experiments in education government of India has launched Education Guarantee Scheme and Alternative and Innovative Education scheme (EGS and AIE) to achieve goals of UEE. EGS and AIE aims to provide quality educational opportunities with the help of diverse strategies and approaches to the millions of children who today remain out of school for various reasons. It is expected that such schemes would give momentum to the non-formal education in the country.

However a mere increase in the enrolment numbers is not enough. It is crucial to retain these students and provide them with constructive and meaningful learning experiences. Therefore, more quality initiatives need to be undertaken in curriculum design, instructional materials, transactional strategies, contact programmes, etc. which would result in quality improvement.

The papers contributed in this section focus on alternative schooling as a solution to the threats and challenges being faced by are school education today. Home schooling is slowly emerging as an option today. Case studies of alternative schools have been highlighted. The relevance of alternative schooling with innovations and experiments in education have been addressed to in depth.

The contribution of the faculties, experts and scholars from all over the country has helped to sketch a nation-wide scenario of quality school education in India. We sincerely hope that this volume will make an impact in the area of quality school education in the Indian context.

Vadodara
October 2009

S. Kumar
Sujata Srivastava

Part I
School Education: Issues and Concerns

1

Education of the Urban Disadvantaged

D. Sarangi and Manoranjan Pradhan

Introduction

In the midst of urban affluence, a group of young population continues to remain far from the main streams of the contemporary life. They are the urban disadvantaged comprising of the slum children, street children, children of sex workers, children on the construction sites, bonded labourers, the runaways, the orphans and those in the remand centres. In spite of our constitutional declaration and commitment to ensure basic education as fundamental right, the issues of access, affordability, equity and equality could have not been addressed for these people. The problem has been escalating due to rising population and increasing urbanization. In the two weak areas of habitations- the newly coming up urban conglomeration and the slums the problems are different. The slums are the headache as they come up without any plan and lack in the basic civil amenities and schooling facilities.

This paper overviews the generic profiles of the urban disadvantaged such as disabling home environment, negative socio-cultural impact of slum environment, the effects of poor child-grooming practices already built into their behaviour, expressed or latent engagement in child labour, increased vulnerability to sexual activity/child abuse, perforce structured juvenile delinquency and trap in the underworld of crimes. On the contrary most of them are bilingual and are having parents well exposed to outside influence as compared to their rural counter parts.

On this back drop the paper critically examines four basic

issues pertaining to the education the urban disadvantaged group namely:

- Goals and objectives of education of the urban disadvantaged.
- Curriculum focus and emphasis.
- Pedagogy.
- Policy and strategy.

Each of the above issues is discussed in the light of available research reports current practices of humanitarian organizations offering education for the group and the common observations and experiences.

Generic Profile of Urban Disadvantaged

The urban disadvantaged children are heterogeneous population comprising of slum children, street children, children of sex workers, children on the constructive sites, bonded labourers, the run away, the orphans and those in the remand centres. These people live in improved neighbourhoods with no or little access to amenities of life. The slum habitations are characterized with:

- Predominantly very poor housing structures.
- Very high housing density.
- Poor sewage and drainage or even no such facilities.
- Inadequate, unhealthy drinking water supply.
- Unhealthy atmosphere.
- Little/no paved road.
- Inhabited by poor, uneducated and below poverty lined.

"Slums are usually characterized by urban blight and by high rates of poverty and unemployment. They tend to be breeding centres for many social problems such as crimes, drug addiction, alcoholism, and prostitution, high rates of mental illness and suicide and despair. In many poor countries they exhibit high rates of diseases due to poor sanitary conditions, malnutrition, and lack of basic health services." WIKIPEDIA

The slum dwellers are mostly immigrants from rural areas

and are victims of processes of pauperization. The following factors contribute for slum settlements:

- Rural push-Urban pull effect.
- Large scale migration in search of employment, economic opportunities & better equality of life from rural areas to urban areas, & from small towns to big cities.
- Concentration of urban population in one or few large cities (primary city syndrome).
- Unauthorized squatting on marginal lands.
- Social factors: uprooted , driven out, abandoned etc.
- Natural disasters.

Most of the slum dwellers employ themselves in informal economy, largely depend upon low income livelihoods and work as

- Rickshaw puller.
- Industrial labourer.
- Construction labourer.
- Peddler.
- Housemaid.
- Porter.
- Other similar work.

In some slums people make their livelihood by collecting and selling recyclable trash of different kinds, drugs dealing sometimes prostitution.

The major problems of slum population are lack of security of land tenure, potable drinking water, sanitations, employment economic opportunities, health facilities, hygiene, child care, education, skills acquisition, access to credit, proximity of shelter to jobs and affordable and acceptable shelter.

Issues in Education of the Urban Deprived

What arrests school enrolment and school completion of slum children? The roots are traced to the systematic inefficiency, slum environment and economic positions of slum population

1. Blocking of Developmental Milestones Disables a Slum Child in Coping with Schooling: The slum children are the most vulnerable sections of the society who suffer from human deprivations of all forms. Their economic situations cumulatively impact their health, development and ability to successfully complete their primary education since the very inception of their life.

Health nutrition and education no doubt the three main sectors that impact on a child's development. In different stages of life of the slum children non-attachment of the developmental milestones in respect of health, nutrition , learning out comes has been observed by research studies.(Ramachandran, 2003), The non-attainment of the developmental milestones is carried over additively to the successive stages of life and sometimes to the next generations and impacts negatively their education.

The study also mentioned that "despite the potential, the current social policy is unable to effectively capture and tap the positive synergy of the different sectoral interventions (Health, Education and Livelihood). It is also unable to proactively harness the family and the community in meeting its objectives of reaching the child, especially the poorest child and creating a supportive environment for its development".

2. Participation and Successful School Completion is Delimited by Economic Situation: Some of the slum parents are engaged in such livelihood activities that shuts the scope for school participation of their children. Many of the slum children are urged to for engagement in child labour. For these children bread is the warranted priority over education, Even though some are enrolled very soon they discontinue their schooling as they become regularly irregular, acquire learning difficulties resulting in academic backwardness, truancy, despair and finally drop out from schools.

3. Teachers' Negative Attitude and Low Expectations Create Low Self-esteem in Slum Children: Teachers' attitude towards and expectations of slum pupils affect their learning and development to greater extent. The teaching communities who are mostly in the mid hierarchy perceive the slum children as children of low cognitive ability, uneducable, low morale and repository of nuisance value. As such explicitly, implicitly teachers deal the slum children in such ways which plant a sense of rejection, low self esteem, limited aspirations and motivation for schooling. Teachers' common explanation for the low performance of slum children as one as is "these children are not interested in studies, they are irregular, and they come from families which do not value education" speaks a lot. Teachers do not understand the life situation/setting in which the slum children struggle to live.

4. Negative Impact of Slum Environment: Most of the slum children grow up in disabled home environment and neighbourhood since early part of their life. Synthesizing 99 research reports Mccloskey (2000) concluded that "such children live in a world of isolation, limited experience, rejection, a demoralizing neighbourhood and a disorganized family life- all contribute to the disadvantaged child's general impoverishment. The environment affects health, attitude and values of the child. These attitudes are carried into the classroom and affects school performance". The slum children are vulnerable to the derogating contact and influence of delinquents, antisocial, drug addicts and criminals, sex workers and sex Dalals, Which gradually is built into their behaviour. The slum society systematically criminalizes the child mind, propels him away from the mainstreams of life and sinks in the darker side.

5. Non-productive and Irrelevant Education Strengthens Aversion and Divorce to School: Education in the conventional slum schools is mostly non productive and irrelevant to the slum children. Sole thrust upon the liberal subjects, educational success in terms of grade achievement instead of facilitating a child's school completion make him school apartheid. Such education no way helps the child to liberate from the distressed situations of life and assures a sustainable development. Besides literacy and numeracy acquisition of life skills and critical information on life resources is indispensable for the urban disadvantaged. The common perception of slum people about the worth of education depicts deep apartheid and rejection. This behaviour of slum parents impedes enrolment, attendance, academic performance in Schools & overall development of slum children and consequently breeds the group across generations

6. Non-accountability of Schools: One of the painful truths is that slum schools (Also many of the schools in other areas) do not have accountability to the students and the community. The pressures of enrolment drives, MDM has raised the quantum of records in various platforms rather than teachers' responsibility and effort to bring the children to school and involve them in education. Genuine efforts on part teachers to promote positive self-concept, motivation and life ambitions among the slum children are little visible. Teachers perceive their work just as routines devoid of heart.

7. Poor Quality of Instruction Induces Non-completion of Basic Education: SSA efforts although have improved school building to some extent in different areas but the same have little moved the instructional setting and procedure in most schools. Teachers' capacity building efforts are yet to yield its impact in the class rooms. Long standing issues of teacher absenteeism, low commitment and non-performance among teachers compound with schools' isolation and lack of community involvement in school management. These add to the complexity of the instructional and organizational issues. Although efforts are on, Education has yet not become a co-operative and collaborative effort of the primary stakeholders-teachers, parents and community. Large number of the slum children does not attain the minimum standards.

Day by day the issue of quality divide is outweighing many of the SSA efforts and inputs. Even the slum community fingers to this issue and show craziness for quality education for their children. Media observes, "a growing number of slum dwellers and lower middle class parents are going beyond their means to ensure 'good' private education for their children" (Mukherje, 2006). Over the last 10-15 years there has been a sharp decline in the number of students in the municipal and government own and managed schools in favour of the private schools for which accessibility and affordability by the slum children is difficult. Thus the equity issues in respect of right to quality education remains stand by unresolved.

Ramachandran (2006), a known columnist reported similar issues which affect universal elementary education in urban areas:

Firstly, access to good quality and relevant education remains a big issue in urban areas. While children may technically have access to primary and secondary schools, these do not function effectively. The time spent in teaching-learning is cause for concern. As the government essentially monitors enrolment rates, dysfunctional or poorly functioning schools are not noticed in official monitoring reports.

Secondly, while broad policies and programmes are certainly important, they fail to capture the specific situations of urban children. Organizations working in urban areas repeatedly point out that there are systematic and schematic barriers to access, continuation and transition. Given the steady immigration into cities and cross-migration within cities, problems faced by children who migrate with their families are rarely factored into planning. Persistent demand for identity proof, birth certificate and transfer certificate continue to block easy access. The specific problems of child workers, street children (who have run away from home) and children in difficult circumstances are not factored into schematic patterns. While political leaders talk about the complicated situation in urban areas, administrators are not willing to mould or adapt schemes and programmes for the urban poor. For example, in Mumbai six wards account for 70 percent of out-of-school children (Survey by Pratham 2004). The ongoing Sarva Shiksha Abhiyan (SSA) is yet another example of how planning in broad strokes leaves huge gaps on the ground.

The third issue pertains to defining a community around a school—who are the stakeholders? Are they the parents, neighbourhood leaders, local voluntary groups or social action groups? People working in urban areas point out parents have little time to come to school and they may be away from their locality all day. Children are often left at home with elders or with siblings. Social workers working in the area see themselves as the primary stakeholders. Again, the concept of School Education Committee (SEC) and Village Education Committee (VEC) were designed for rural areas and do fit into the urban context.

The fourth big issue is one of quality. It is now widely acknowledged that quality education is not only about learning outcomes, it has to do with relevance, happiness index and what the child takes away from the school other than just reading and writing. But even if we were to limit the quality discourse to learning, evidence from across the country shows that there is very little learning in urban municipal schools. But to emphasize a point, even if we are to keep quality education value-neutral, we still need concrete measures to see whether we are making progress on holistic development of children.

Fifth, attitude of teachers in urban areas remains a big issue. The social distance between teachers (who are middle class) and vast majority of children (who come from extremely poor families) reveals vast and abusive behaviour, derogatory language and punishment which in turn affect the self-esteem and confidence of children. The government has to acknowledge that quality is not just about buildings and toilets. Education is about building capacities, confidence and concrete skills.

Objectives of Slum Education

What education would bring to the slum children a secured survival and sustainable life? For these children shelter, health and education are equally warranted needs. The issue of slum education cannot be viewed as a mere matter of education rather to be seen as a serious concern of total human development. Isolated efforts to promote education among the deprived sections of the population have not reaped satisfactorily in the past .Therefore most of the current development plans and programmes have been favouring convergence of health, livelihood and educational upliftment among the weaker masses.

Holistic development of the slum population in general and the children in particular is very often jeopardized for lack of critical information. To quote Ahamad (2003) "Information is the critical missing link between ignorance and enlightenment, between poverty and prosperity, between dehumanization and empowerment. A well planed effort encompassing collection, processing and dissemination of information would help in attaining the required level of awareness in society and in turn would accelerate the process of empowerment of the people by reducing knowledge gap." Hence education for the slum children must essentially make aware them about the vital information on availability of and access to life resources.

Two goal options are open for education of the slum children—liberal knowledge and knowledge and skills for sustainable life. The conventional schooling purporting liberal would not be of any sense and would not attract the slum population. For this population food, security and sustainability is the need of the highest order. Therefore knowledge for knowledge sake would not serve any purpose. 'On the other hand the kind of education offered by the humanitarian agencies, NGOs and developmental bodies back up their evolution, thus of the two options.

One has the conventional schooling for personal enlightenment through NCERT recommended curriculum frame work and the other achieving secured survival and sustainability through specialized intervention, the latter would be more pragmatic. Setting goals for mainstreaming and upward social mobility education must enable slum children for a healthy departure from their parental platforms through appropriate educational interventions.

Education of the slum children has to counter act against two strong forces which sizes their scope for school completion. First the negative social environment in slum areas fosters unhealthy attitude, values and beliefs towards the life perspectives and the children are captured by dehumanizing forces. The disabling home environment and the poor child grooming practices further aggravate the issue. Many of the slum children are perforce structured for vulnerability to child labour, sexual abuse, juvenile crimes and underworld of crimes. The slum education needs to be a shield against these devastating forces.

Curriculum Focus and Emphasis

Is it the same curriculum as run in the conventional schools be suitable for this clientele group? For a holistic development of the slum children the curriculum should not be broken into subjects. Appropriate dose of literacy, numeracy, Socio-cultural information, Life skills and prevocational skills may be fused to constitute an integrative whole. Since an urban school will have children of different background—never enrolled, drop out, backward learners and of different age groups modular approaches to curriculum organization would be a pragmatic approach. A slum child on the basis of his/her background as said will start school education with an appropriate module and not necessarily with the first level. Such a curriculum will have to balance, the cognitive, affective and psychomotor inputs having enough opportunities for exposure to the critical life resources, critical awareness and sensitivity to the developmental issues in the slum society. Adequate number of projects for life skills building should be important elements of the curriculum for slum children.

What emphasis is to be put to each of the curricular areas—literacy, numeracy, socio-culture information life skills and pre-vocational skills? The specific features of slum children would determine the curricular focus and emphasis for each part. The literacy, numeracy and the life skills components may have common elements across all regions and should draw upon heavily from the National School Curriculum Framework proposed by NCERT. This is essential for linkage between the schools for slum children and those in the normal areas and for continuation of education into secondary stage on part of the slum children.

Pedagogical Contours

A class room of the urban deprives may embrace the over-aged children, having or not having earlier school experience. Children of school age group the, drop-outs, the never enrolled ones. They have different history, varied exposure and experience. Unlike the rural counterparts many of the urban deprived have bilingual background ands are less shy and shrunk. They are better exposed to the modern life in the non-slum areas. All plans of school organization, instructional setting and curriculum transaction should be in synchrony with the proposed development oriented curriculum. Teaching and learning therefore be essentially a process of life skills building.

Instead of the conventional school pedagogy the classes for slum children should stretch far beyond the schools. Critical information on life resources can be imparted through involvement or engagement in health, hygiene and livelihood linked sectors. Actual work plans can be evolved in relation to slum specific issues. A modular curriculum is proposed. After entry into a slum school a child's learning and progresses can be decided on basis of completion of a module and related projects. In respect of literacy, numeracy and environmental studies learner centric participatory approaches crass age tutoring, co-operative learning, peer-group activity would be more yielding.

Policy and Strategy

1. Inter-sectoral Interface and Synergy: The universalization of primary education in urban slums requires distinctive policy and strategic decisions. The educational issues as discussed before indicate to an integrated development paradigm for the education of the urban disadvantaged. Education for slum children has to be rehabilitational in character guarantying shelter, security, health and learning opportunities. A number of development and welfare programmes are in operation in the country such as ICDS, RCH, ECCE, DPEP/SSA. The programmes require more synergy in the urban areas to minimize the developmental blockades among slum children. ECCE is to be intensified. Inter-sectonal interface had also been emphasized at the government level earlier. To quote Joshi (2001): "We could not see the problems in society in overall context .The population problem is related to education, health and sanitation is also related to education and are related to each other. The highly compartmentalized approach, dividing developmental issues into various segments, as it is happening now, is detrimental to progress. So we should adopt integrated and holistic approach to synergize, co-ordinate and converge all the programmes of different social sectors to achieve better success."

2. Special Schools: Slum education in the country has not received as much due attention as in the rural and tribal areas. Special residential schools on the patterns of Navodaya and other welfare schools of rural and tribal areas may be setup. Special schools will rescue the slum children from the negative impact of the society; ensure smooth child development, reduce the social distance between the teachers and the pupils and would facilitate school completion. Unlike the conventional schools these schools will have to focus more on the demands of the slum life. So many non-educational foundations in the country have come up with very good curriculum models, which provide shelter, health, education and livelihood and life skills. The most effective models may be synthesized to formulate slum specific working models.

3. Sharing the Burden of Special Schools with Other Sectors: The corporate sector, philanthropic organizations have been extending their assistance in the extension of education. Policy & directives encouraging these sectors to share the responsibilities and burden of special school system in slum areas are the need of the hour in the country. Strong political will and bold decisions allowing the proposed multipurpose development oriented schools in urban areas as some autonomous foundations providing alternative education to this population of the country is a prerequisite. The ministry of urban development and the ministry of education will have to workout common goals and strategy.

4. Allowing Market Forces in Education: Government efforts alone have been proved inadequate to take up the challenges UEE in slum areas. We have to allow market forces to education which would open avenues of school choice from different school systems providing options to slum communities to choose a suitable form of schooling. The existing municipal schools are to tie up with local NGOs, charity foundations and developmental organizations to improve/ strengthen current inputs and services for slum areas. The joint efforts would better mobilize the slum communities for enrolment, retention and primary school completion.

5. Empower Mothers, Educate Children: It has already been pointed out that low community involvement is a major obstacle in the UEE of education in slum areas. Therefore community mobilization operations should be more rigorous and forceful. Besides this adult non-formal education programmes need to be designed to sensitize the slum parents. "Empower mothers and Educate children" can be the work strategy.

6. Multiple Entry Options: The slum schools will have to accommodate learners of diverse profiles. Therefore slum schools at the primary level need to have flexibility in enrolment with provision of multiple entry points into the proposed modular curriculum. Children who earlier dropped out should be allowed to continue their education from a level where (s)he discontinued. There is no rational for rigid admission regulation refusing direct admission into a higher grade level for learners who discontinued for some reasons.

7. Teachers' Compatibility: Teachers are the real fulcrum for success of UEE. Appropriate mechanisms need to be devised to promote commitment and dedication among the slum teachers. Teachers require a changed attitude towards the slum children in terms of their positive capabilities. As teacher is a major element in the internal system efficiency, slum schools require better qualified and skilled staff. Low paid teachers can not be expected of devotion and sincerity. The issue of unskilled teachers and low salary has wider ramifications not only for UEE also for supply of skilled manpower for the growing completive world in the urban areas. Pre-service as well as in-service teacher training programmes be tailored to prepare teachers who are compatible to slum environment and slum children.

References

Ahmad, M(2003), Community Development Library Annual Activity Report 2003. Dhaka.

Chattopadhyay, S.S (2001), "Population problem in urban slums". Paper presented in the conference on convergence of social sector programmes for population stabilization held in 4th October 2001 at Hotel Kaniska, Ashoka Road, New Delhi. (Source: http://populationcommission.nic.in/conf4oct.htm)

Joshi, M.M. (2001) Presentation made in the conference on convergence of social sector programmes for population stabilization held in 4th October 2001 at Hotel Kaniska, Ashoka Road, New Delhi. (http://populationcommission.nic.in/conf4oct.htm)

MC Closky, ELINOR F: "Urban disadvantaged pupils, A synthesis of 1999 research reports". ERIC. ED015228

Mukherje, A. (2006). Your BAI's Kids are going to private schools too. Times of India , Mumbai, 20 Feb 2006.

2

Problems of Learners of National Institute of Open Schooling (NIOS)

P.K. Sahoo and Dinesh Kumar

Introduction

Open schooling system is one of the examples of alternative schooling at secondary and higher secondary stage. Since its inception i.e. November 1989 the National Open School now renamed as National Institute of Open Schooling (NIOS) has been functioning as a pioneering institution of distance education at school stage. The priority of the NIOS is to provide opportunity continuing and developmental education at the school stage with special emphasis on rural people/urban poor, Girls, under privileged (SC/ST), unemployed and post employed school dropouts and people with special need, i.e. physically and mentally challenged persons. Different kinds of courses are provided at secondary stage as well as elementary stage. However the major emphasis has been laid on academic and vocational courses at secondary/higher secondary stage. Because of flexibilities in entrance policy, course combination, instructional system and evaluation procedures diversified groups of learners keep on pouring into different streams of programmes offered by the NIOS.

As a major feature of distance education teaching learning activities are carried out with the help of guided self instructional system as well as provision for face to face interaction with tutors/counsellors and practicals for development of required knowledge and skills in different curricular areas. At field level the study centres are located in different kinds of institutions like central schools, government aided schools, private schools, NGOs and a number of technical and vocational institutions either managed privately or by the government. The distance learners, because of their diversified socio-cultural and academic background are the key elements of distance education programme. The extent to which their needs, expectations and problems are kept in the forefront of teaching learning system reflects on the success of any distance education programme. The NIOS which has created a large number of accreditation institutions in different nooks and corners of the country aims at catering to various kinds of academic and non- academic needs of the distance learners.

More specifically, the problems accrued in the context of students support services (SSS) provided in the accreditation centres at field level must give feedback to the system to make the system effective and accountable to the stakeholders. In this context, it has been thought appropriate to explore empirical evidences concerning the problems faced by NIOS learners in availing opportunities at study centre level and their expectations from the study centres. Moreover, an analysis of the learner's problems in the context of gender and nature of courses shall throw light on specific steps to be taken in strengthening the students support services of the NIOS.

Objectives

The objectives of the present study are:

- To explore problems faced by the NIOS learners in the context of students support services, gender and stream wise.
- To explore suggestions of the NIOS learners in the context of students support services, gender and stream wise.

Methods and Procedures

The population of the study covered distance learners of all the NIOS study centres in the U.P. state. For the present study one hundred students, 50 each from general stream at class X stage and vocational stream were selected from 20 study centres of UP. Data were collected with the help of a self made questionnaire with three point scale. The questionnaire covered the items concerning academic and non-academic support services, resource management and teaching learning strategies adopted in distance learning system. Data were analyzed descriptively.

Analysis and Interpretation of Data

Problems of NIOS Learners: Stream-wise

It was observed that majority of distance learners (50 to 58 percent) faced different problems to a large extent concerning:

- Distant location of study centres (56 percent).
- Lack of timely communication of the academic schedule (56 percent).
- Non-availability of appropriate study materials in the study centres (52 percent).
- Less number of classes as a major hindrance for clarification of doubts (50 percent).
- Lack of necessary equipments/apparatus in the laboratories (50 percent).
- Higher price of audio-video learning cassettes than of printed on the cover page (58 percent).

Other problems faced by majority of general course students—either to large/some extent (total range 78 percent to 88 percent)—were related to:

- Lack of timely availability of the co-coordinator in the study centre.
- Indifferent behaviour of the counsellors.
- Non-availability of audio video cassettes in the study centres.
- Non-supply of library books to the students.
- Less interaction with colleagues.
- No audio-video conferencing facility.
- Higher fee structure.
- No Edu-Sat based educational programmes at study centre

level.

The vocational stream students faced major problems (50 to 62 percent) concerning the following:

- No provision for interactive instruction by audio-video conferencing (62 percent).
- No provision for supply of library books to learners carrying home (50 percent).
- Higher price of audio-video lessons than that printed on the cover (52 percent).

There are other kinds of problems faced by vocational stream learners either to a large/sine extent (total range 58-82 percent) was related to:

- Distant location of study centres.
- Lack of appropriate study materials in the study centre library.
- Less number of periods taught during the contact sessions.
- Higher fee structure.
- No Edu-Sat based educational programmes.

Problems of Students: Gender and Stream-wise

It was observed that the boy students of general streams faced major problems (52 percent to 68 percent) concerning the following areas:

- Distant location of study centres (56 percent).
- Problems encountered in understanding print based materials (52 percent).
- Less number of periods taught during the contact sessions (52 percent).
- Lack of timely communication regarding the schedule (64 percent).
- Higher rate of audio-video lessons (68 percent).
- No provision of supply of library books to student's home (60 percent).
- No Edu-Sat based educational programmes (52 percent).

The girl students of general stream faced major problems regarding:

- Far distance of study centres from their residences (56

percent).

- No provision of appropriate study materials in the study centres (60 percent).
- Lack of required apparatus in the laboratories (52 percent).

The boy students of vocational stream faced major problems on the areas of:

- Higher price of audio-video cassettes (64 percent).
- No provision of supply of library books to students residence (68 percent).
- No provision of interactive audio-video conferencing (64 percent).

Major problems faced by the girl students of vocational stream were:

- No provision of interactive audio-video conferencing (60 percent).
- No provision of Edu-Sat based teaching learning activities (60 percent).

Major Problems of NIOS Learners: Gender-wise

It was observed that major problems faced by the boys in general as well as vocational streams (50 to 66 percent) were identified as:

- Distant location of study centres (50 percent).
- Higher price of audio-video lesson cassettes (66 percent).
- No provision of supply of library books to student's home (60 percent).
- No provision of interactive audio-video conferencing (54 percent).

It was noticed that the major problems faced by girl students of general as well as vocational streams were non availability of appropriate number of study materials in the study centre library (54 percent).

The content analyses of open responses of students reveal that:

- Students could not get English medium study materials.
- Late delivery of admit cards and examination schedule.
- Least opportunity for use of laboratory and laboratory

based experiments.

- Less number of computers and limited training in computer programming.
- Lack of availability of text books of different writers.
- Problems of audio-video conferencing.
- Problems of availability of operators.
- Problems of lack of maintenance of apparatus and
- Outdated curriculum

Suggestions of NIOS Students

Suggestions given by the NIOS students indicate expectations of students on academic, administrative and other areas of student support services. Table 4 reveals that the stream wise response of students did not differ much from each other. The prominent areas of expectations which were common to general and vocational stream students read as follows:

- The libraries of study centres should be equipped with more number of printed materials (74 percent).
- Creation of new study centres in the locality of students (54-66 percent).
- Increasing the duration of personal contact sessions (54-68 percent).
- Presentation of content in clear and simple languages (62-66 percent)
- Information to students be given on time (54-66 percent)
- Enhancement of facilities in the laboratories located in the study centres (58 percent)
- Provision of audio-video lesson cassettes for students at nominal cost (64-68 percent)
- Provision of issuing books to distance learners, home without extra charges (52-68 percent).
- Provision of hostel accommodation to participants coming from distance localities (54-64 percent).
- Increasing the scope of Gyan Darshan programmes for NIOS (58-68 percent).
- Provision of e-learning courses (62-68 percent)

Besides these, the general course students suggested for

availability of study centre co-coordinators more frequently for NIOS learners (68 percent) and increasing the duration of radio programmes/Gyan Vani for NIOS students (58 percent) and enhancement of quality of sitting arrangement of students during contact classes (72 percent).

The response pattern of boys and girls of vocational and general streams remained almost same with regard to their suggestions. Majority of boys (60-88 percent) agreed on all the statements in the questionnaire. The girls students (56 to 84 percent) also expressed most positive opinion on all the areas except one item on increasing the duration of PCP and issue of books to home. The vocational stream boys and girls students gave major suggestions regarding:

- Creation of study centres in students localities (52-56 percent).
- Enhancement of more print based study materials in the study centres (64-84 percent).
- Increasing the duration of PCP classes in different subjects. (60-76 percent).
- Presentation of content of study materials in simple and clear languages (64-68 percent).
- Provision of issue of library books to students (64-72 percent).
- Provision of low cost audio-video lessons cassettes to learners (64-72 percent).
- Provision of hostel accommodation to distance students (52-56 percent).
- Increasing Gyan Darshan programme for NIOS (60-76 percent).
- Provision of e-learning courses (80-88 percent).
- Communication of special information to students through mobile phones (64-72 percent).

The open-ended suggestions read as:

- Updating the curriculum.
- Ensure monthly attendance of students in the study centre counselling.

- Facility for games and sports.
- Increase the number of study centres.
- Increase the computer facilities in the study centres.
- Proper repair and maintenance of equipments.
- Increase the duration of different vocational programmes.
- Introduction of diploma level courses in vocational subjects.

Conclusion

The empirical evidences concerning the problems of NIOS students are mostly genuine from the point of view of management of Student Support Services. The problem areas covering manpower and physical resources must be taken care of by the NIOS. Moreover, the academic inputs and process mechanisms must be streamlined keeping in view the course requirements and expectations of learners. Proper arrangement should be made for monitoring and supervision of academic activities through involvement of the academic facilitators at local level. In this context empowerment of counsellors is most essential to deal with various inputs and processes of SSS. The regional centres need to be vigilant about ensuring proper supply of study materials, leadership of co-coordinators, performance of counsellors and co-operation from the host institutions regarding library services, laboratory based experiments and other physical supports.

Moreover, the students demand better functionality of interactive radio and TV programmes in the study centres. Student's suggestions concerning better opportunity for computer based learning and increasing contact class durations are most genuine in nature. The NIOS must adopt explore alternative designs and systematic procedures for extending relevant support to the distance learners of different streams.

References

Deshpande, Prakash M. (1995). "Student Support Services in Dual-Mode Correspondence/Distance Institutions" in Bakhsish Singh (Ed.), New Horizons in Distance Education. New Delhi: Uppal.

Hand Book for Academic facilitators, NIOS, New Delhi (2004)

Kaushal, S. (2002), Functioning of Distance Education Institutions in Delhi, An Unpublished Ph.D. Thesis, Delhi: University of Delhi.

Koul, P. (2003) A Study of Effectiveness of Distance Education Programme in Nursing, An unpublished Ph.D. Thesis, New Delhi: Jamia Millia Islamia.

Muchhal, M.K. (2001) "A Study of Effectiveness of Instructional Strategies of Social Science and Science at Class X level of NOS" Unpublished Ph.D. Thesis, Indore: DAVV, Indore.

Negi, U.R. (2003). Student Support Services in Correspondence Course Institutes in University, New Delhi: AIU.

NIOS At A glance, New Delhi, (2004)

Patri, K. (1996), A Study of Future Expansion and Instructional System of Distance Education in Orissa at Higher Education Stage Towards 2000. Unpublished Ph.D. Education Thesis, DAVV, Indore.

Sahoo, P.K. (1985). A Study of Correspondence Education in an Indian University, unpublished Ph.D. Education, Thesis, MSU, Baroda.

Sahoo, P.K. (1994). "Teleconferencing in Distance Education: IGNOU Experiment", Indian journal of Open Learning, 3(1).

Sahoo, P.K. (1994). Open Learning System, New Delhi: Uppal.

Sahoo, P.K. and Kumar, A. (2006) Study of networking of Institutions in Promoting Quality of Students Support Services in Open Universities, The UPRTOU Journal of Research and ODL studies, Vol. I

Tripathi, A.K. (2002), A study of SSS of UPRTOU unpublished M.Ed. Dissertation: University of Allahabad, Allahabad.

Tyagi, P. and Sahoo, P.K. (1992), "IGNOU Students' Perception of its Instructional System", Media and Technology for Human Resource Development, 4 (4).

3

Early Stage of Schooling: Need for Specialization

Ashutosh Biswal and Jaishree Das

Introduction

School is a sub -system of the society, where it is empowered to mould the children through education in order to make them fit for the society, to make them productive citizens and to develop their innate potentials to the maximum. The basic concerns of the school is to enable children to make sense of life and develop their own potential, to define and pursue an aim of life and purpose, to do the needful for the upliftment of the society and recognize and respect others. The school fulfils these aspirations of the society with the help of education. A good education system leads a society in the positive direction making children fit for the society and prepares them for the betterment of the nation as a whole. Education provides knowledge, skills, craftsmanship and values to the children through a well structured curriculum. The curriculum is designed in the context of the society, like, an agro-based society designs an agriculture based curriculum, an industrial society needs an industrial based curriculum etc. In the preset context curriculum design is based on the changing pattern of the society.

Due to the changing global order in the context of liberalization, privatization and globalization, there is a drastic change in the education curriculum and it is a continuous process of change. For example, change in the curriculum of school education is a constant effort of the apex bodies of school education. The change of National curriculum framework in our country is done after a gap of 5 years, i.e.

NCF-2000 is replaced by the NCF-2005.

Education should be such which enables the child to discover and realize his or her talents and potential by working with others towards restructuring the society. It is done with the help of curriculum transaction.

The major purpose of the curriculum is to develop in the child social skills and to provide knowledge and skills for the future existence and development of the child. Though socialization has always been one of the major purposes of school education, now it is not realized through school education as the system is more interested towards the knowledge dimension, rote memory and passing examinations. It is dismal to note that less emphasis is given on the affective domain. `The size of textbooks has been growing over the years, even as the pressure to include new topics mount and efforts to synthesize knowledge and treat it holistically gets weaker. Flabby textbooks and the syllabi they cover symbolize a systematic failure to address children in a child-cantered manner. Those who write such encyclopaedic textbooks are guided by the popular belief that there has been an explosion of knowledge. Therefore, vast amount of knowledge should be pushed down the throats of little children in order to catch up with other countries' (NCF-2005). The impulse to teach everything arises from lack of faith in children's own creative instinct and their capacity to construct knowledge out of their experience.

Hence the system of education gives more emphasis on knowledge and skills and very less emphasis on the socialization of the child. Anyway, to some extent this part is taken care by the family and the society like, media. So we can conclude that the major purpose of school education is to provide knowledge and skill to make the child fit for the future. For that purpose it has a curriculum comprising of foundation courses or core curriculum and specializations. It is assumed that the core curriculum prepares the strong foundation on the base of which different specializations can be generated or developed. In the process, it can be seen that up to standard X (15-16 years) is meant for foundation courses and specialization starts after 10th with a few options like, arts, science, commerce or vocational courses (diploma courses). Again the specific or micro specialization starts after 12th (17-18 years).

Science is micro specialized like medicine, engineering and general science stream which is further specialized to different specific subjects. Arts is micro specialized like, performing arts, fine arts and general arts stream which is further specialized to different subjects like, history, geography, political science, economics etc. This is also the case in the specialization of commerce with even more limited micro specializations. We claim that this system of specialization is on the basis of child's need, interest and abilities. There are a large number of problems related to this pattern of specialization in school education. NCF-2005 tried to highlight few concerns that may be related to the present system in the following sentences. "There is a deep disquiet about several aspects of our educational practice: (a) the school system is characterized by a inflexibility that makes it resistant to change; (b) learning has become an isolated activity, which does not encourage children to link knowledge with their lives in any organic or vital way; (c)schools promote a regime of thought that discourages creative thinking and insights; (d) what is presented and transmitted in the name of learning in schools bypasses vital dimensions of human capacity to create new knowledge; (e) the `future' of the child has taken centre-stage to the near exclusion of the child's `present', which is detrimental to the well being of child as well as the society and the nation."

Major Concerns

Concerns related to the present system of school curriculum and the specialization patterns are highlighted as follows.

British System of Education: The British system of Education was designed to prepare clerks and other white collar jobs. To be a clerk it was essential to have a strong grip on English, the local language, Mathematics and Social Studies. For their requirement (all over the globe) the curriculum for matriculation was designed with these core components. At that time this qualification was enough to get a clerical job. They were not interested to provide specialization at an early age to restrict people for other jobs. Till date the same pattern and curriculum continues with minor modifications from time to time.

Killing of Child's Inner Potential and Interest: In the present system of education, the child is compelled or forced to go to school and to learn the standard syllabus till the age of 15 years (standard X). We do not see the interest, aptitude and other potentials of the child. After 10th, when we see the interest and aptitude of the child, most of them are either killed by the present standard curriculum or shaped according to the objectives of the standard curriculum.

Socially Accepted Specialization: Few specializations are highly accepted by the society like, medicine, engineering which is the part of the Science stream. Presently Management education is highly accepted by the society, giving more emphasis on the Commerce stream. In most of the cases irrespective of their interest and aptitude, children choose socially accepted specializations and it is not according to their abilities, leading to failures. It is also influenced by the media and socio-economic status of the people in some specific professions.

Parents Compulsion: In many cases selection of specialization is based on the desire of the parents. Some parents want their child to go into the science stream in order to become a doctor or an engineer. It may be due to the unfulfilled desire of the parents, comparing themselves with others, liking towards their own profession, looking to the socially accepted profession etc. Anyway, parents have a major impact on the child's selection of specialization.

Poor Psychological Testing: Even our highly reputed schools are lacking the minimum psychological facilities needed for school children. Due to which we are unable to measure the interest, aptitude, IQ, creativity of the children which is needed for a child to choose a specialization. In many cases we do not even have a proper counselling system at any level to guide students to choose their specialization.

Minimum Specializations in Schools: We have no specialization at the secondary level and only three major specializations like, Arts, Science and Commerce at the higher secondary level. There is no scope for further micro specialization at the higher secondary stage. There is no specialization for sports, performing arts and fine arts.

Discussion and Reflections

Considering all these concerns related to late and limited specializations in the school education, there is a felt need to discuss these concerns to suggest an early need of diversified specializations at the school stage according to the ability and interest of students. The following points need to be discussed before emphasizing on the early specialization at the level of school education.

- Is there any need for early specialization in school education?
- Is our system ready to accept such a change? Is there a need to change the total pattern of education for this purpose?
- Is our society; are parents ready to accept the required specialization according to the ability and interest of the children?
- At which stage specialization needs to be started? Should it be at the Elementary, Primary or Secondary stage?
- What type of curriculum is needed for this specialized education system?
- What type of specialization needs to be introduced?

- What will be the position of values, attitude and morals if the specialization is introduced at an early stage? Will specializations only lead to knowledge and skills?
- Whether the present structure of education would be able to bear the load of the specialized system of education? Will different schools be needed for different specializations?

There are many more issues to discuss related to the introduction of early specialization in the school education. It may help to come out as an alternative mode of education where it is possible. Navodaya Vidyalaya and the Basis Education of Dr. Zakir Hussain are some of the eye openers in this direction. The scheme of Basic Education failed as it was introduced at the wrong time, when the people were not open to change and the scheme was very limited to traditional and socially accepted specializations. Though the objective of Navodaya Vidyalaya was to offer specialization in all fields according to the need and ability of the children, it was under the same structure of education and after the passage of time it is going to be a part and parcel of the existing system of education. Hence there is a need to discuss more on this issue as the time is quite suitable for this type of change and there is a market and appreciation for every unique specialization.

Conclusion

Our school education system is doing quite well. The development and progress of the country is mainly due to the education system. Our school education system to a large extent lays the foundation of manpower development. The time is changing very fast. We need to develop and progress differently according to the changing present and future. Learning to learn and willing to unlearn and relearn are important as means of responding to new situations in a flexible and creative manner. The curriculum needs to emphasize the processes of constructing knowledge (NCF-2005) which may be possible in a new system of education.

Introducing specialization at an early stage of school education may be one of the answers in this direction. Let us hope for the best.

References

Biswal, A. and Das, J. (1996), Value Orientation in Teacher Education, Progress of Education, Pune, October.

Biswal, A., (1998), Value Orientation in Teacher Education in Venkataiah, N. (ed..), Value Education, New Delhi, APH Publishing Corporation, 1998.

Delors, J. (1996), Learning: The Treasure Within, Report of UNESCO of the International Commission on Education for Twenty-first Century, France: UNESCO Publication.

Department of Education, (1986) National Policy on Education-1986, New Delhi: MHRD.

Department of Education, (1992) Programme of Action on National Policy on Education- 1986, New Delhi: MHRD.

Government of India (2000), Quality Education in a Global Era: Challenges to Equity and Opportunities for Diversity, Country Paper, New Delhi: MHRD.

Government of India (1990), Towards an Enlightened and Humane Society: NPE, 1986- A Review, New Delhi: MHRD.

Joshi, S.M. and Biswal, A. (2002), Taming the Information and Communication Technology for Teacher Education, University News, July 15-21, 2002, Vol.40, No.28.

Ministry of Education and Youth Services (1971), Education and National Development: Report of Education Commission 1964-66, New Delhi: NCERT.

Ministry of Education, (1953), Secondary Education Commission 1952-53, New Delhi: Government of India.

NCERT (2000), National Curriculum Framework for School Education: A Framework, New Delhi: NCERT.

NCERT (2005), National Curriculum Framework, New Delhi: NCERT.

Ramsey (2000), Quality Matters: Revitalizing Teaching: Critical times, Critical choice, New South Wales: Department of Education and Training.

4

Organizational Climate for School Improvement

Priya Nair and Mario Xavier

Introduction

Efforts to recognize the importance of school climate is as old as the very existence of educational institutions. The changing times and ever growing challenges have forced the educators; the policy makers and everyone who has a stake in the educational system to explore the relevance of school climate. School climate refers to the quality and character of a school, underlying norms, goals, values, interpersonal relationships, teaching, learning and leadership practices, managing conflicts and problems, organizational structures and so on. A sustainable, positive school climate fosters an open system ensuring school effectiveness. School can also be regarded as a social system in which the stake holders, principal, staff, students and parents interact to accomplish common goals. Hence, a school could be viewed as a system which has inputs, outputs and processes.

The terms "school climate," "school culture" and "learning environment" have been used interchangeably. Researches have indicated a significant difference in student achievement between schools with a good school climate and those with a poor school climate (Bulach, Malone & Castleman, 1994). School climate is defined as the "atmosphere" of a school (Brookover et al, 1979; Edmonds, R. 1982; Lehming, R., & Kane, M., 1981; Rutter, M. et al, 1979 and Saradson, S, 1982). Rutter (1979) indicated that the climate is a product of the beliefs and values expressed by people in a school where people share common beliefs and values about school and schooling.

Robert. W.M. and Clement A.S. (1983) concluded that the climate of the school is characterized by a sense of purpose, an atmosphere of order and quiet, and a feeling of pleasure in learning. The administrative organizational climate is an important factor that influences perception and performance of staff; hence a healthy organizational climate is crucial for a good school (Hoy and Tarter, 1992). Ochitwa (2002) pointed out that organizational climate can arouse employees' motivations; conducive environment could provide warm and friendlier climate contributing to energized and satisfied staff with their job, while non-conducive climates could lead to frustration and unproductive staff. Cherniss, (2001) had indicted that a motivated and satisfied teacher would be considerate, dependable, committed to work, and induces trust and caring disposition in the organization.

The school climate refers to the unique character and a distinct identity of the school. A healthy school climate ensures that the school environment, teachers and processes are complementary, interdependent and work in consonance with each other. Organizational climate has several critical dimensions and components, which shape the climate of a school. Most important of these dimensions in an educational setting are intimacy, morale, consideration, and accountability. The classification of open and closed climate typologies is the outcome of the interplay of these dimensions of the organizational climate. The openness or closeness of any educational institution depends on whether the dimensions of organizational climate are positively or negatively demonstrated by the School Head and the staff.

The present study aims at exploring the school climate in one such school to examine the prevailing and the desired school climate so as to suggest possible changes to ensure the climate is conducive for organizational growth and effectiveness. The school climate is assessed on 13 areas of climate under 6 motivational dimensions.

Methodology

Aim: To assess the prevailing and the desired school climate and suggest appropriate changes for creating a conducive climate for school effectiveness.

Objectives

- To examine the perceived present school climate.
- To identify the desired school climate as perceived by the staff.

Sample: The sample consisted of 80 teaching and non teaching members of staff from an English medium school in Baroda.

Tools and Data Collection: The School Climate survey was carried out using a standardized instrument "Motivational Analysis of Organization - Climate" (MAO-C), designed to study organizational climate with special regard to motivation by Udai Pareek (2007). The instrument employs 13 areas of climate (Orientation, Interpersonal relationship, Supervision, Problem management, Managing mistakes, Conflict management, Communication, Decision making, Trust, Managing of rewards, Risk taking and Innovation and Change and 6 motives (Achievement-A, Expert influence-B, Control-C, Dependency-D, Extension-E and Affiliation-F). Each of the 13 areas has six statements representing the 6 motivational dimensions. The respondent had to work individually to rank order the six statements for each dimension according to their perception of how much each statement describes their institution, where rank 1 is the most prevalent and 6 is the least.

For the present study, the respondents were also requested to rank order the statements for each dimension in terms of the desired climate for identifying better conducive working environment. The ranks were then assigned weightage to arrive at respondent's index, thus for each of the motivational dimension the index could vary from 0 to 100 and for each of the 13 climate areas the index could vary from 0 to 10. The index number shows the relative strength of the climate with regard to the motives where the cut of point is 50. If the index number for a particular motive is greater than 50, the climate is relatively strong for that motive. The index also helps in comparing organizations or units or sections within an organization. The data was collected in a class room situation.

Statistical Analyses: The data was analyzed using descriptive statistics.

Discussion

The data was analyzed collectively for all the respondents taking the school as a unit. The responses were analyzed both section wise and overall for the entire whole school. Summary of the overall results is presented in Tables 4.1 and 4.2.

Table: 4.1. Perceived Existing & Desired School Climate

Dimensions	Achievement	Expertise	Control
	Existing	Existing	Existing
Overall	40.8**	45.0*	39.5
	Desired	Desired	Desired
Overall	57.3**	56.2	24.2

Contd...

Dimensions	Dependency	Extension	Affiliation
	Existing	Existing	Existing
Overall	39.7	40.4	39.5
	Desired	Desired	Desired
Overall	50.2	66.2*	43.8

* Dominant Climate; ** Backup Climate

The results indicated that Expert Influence (Index number = 45.0) emerged as the dominant climate with Achievement (Index number = 40.8) as the Backup climate as existing at present. As mentioned earlier, the index number for each of the 6 motivational dimensions could range from 0 to 100, where 50 is the cut off score. A dominant climate is one which has the highest index number and the backup being the next highest. The dominant and the backup climate determine the character of the institution. Thus the results indicated that the overall school climate is characterized by Expertise Influence and Achievement as dominant and backup motivational dimensions, respectively.

Udai Pareek (2007) pointed out that Achievement, Expert Influence and Extension climates are functional and useful while, Control, Dependency and Affiliation climates are dysfunctional for an organization. The Expert Influence, power dominant climate indicates that experts with skill and expertise are encouraged. They are influential in decision-making, resolving conflicts and problems, and are regarded highly in the organization. Similarly, the Achievement oriented climate refers to the fact that concern for work, excellence and competition with other organizations prevail in the organization. Excellence is rewarded; information is available for those who need it for decision-making. People who achieve targets are trusted. People prefer to solve problems by themselves and learn from experience, take moderate risks and are concerned about achieving targets.

Institutions with 'Expert Influence–Achievement' climate places a high value on specialization. The specialist influences most decisions, and the organizations emphasize high quality work and unique contribution. Expert Influence dominant institutions tend to be prevalent in University departments and scientific organizations (Udai Pareek, 2007). The prevailing Expert Influence climate is a functional climate and very relevant for the school, since school and University share the same objective namely Education. However, this climate did not have a very high score (index = 45), indicating that it is not a very strong motive.

The present study also made an attempt to explore the desired climate as perceived by the staff members of the school for identifying the gap between the existing and the desired climate and to carry out the gap analysis for suggesting mechanisms for institutional change. The results of the perceived desired climate indicated that the staff members of the school would rather want to have 'Extension–Achievement' climate instead of the existing 'Expert Influence –Achievement' climate. The Achievement climate remained as the backup climate as existing and desired for future. The only change the staff members wanted was to shift the dominant climate from 'Expert Influence' to 'Extension'. An extension dominant climate indicates that there is high concern in the organization to develop people and to do group work for larger good. People are treated as human beings with a genuine concern for their welfare rather than being treated as playing certain roles. In such organizations, people help their subordinates to grow and develop; and people are encouraged to handle problems and resolve conflicts supportively (Udai Pareek, 2007).

The desired dominant climate, Extension is a functional and useful climate having relatively very high index (66.2), indicating that Extension motive ought to be imperative for the school than the other motives for its relevance and existence. The desired climate results indicated that though the school is presently characterized by 'Expert Influence' climate, which is related to strategic planning and decisions, the members of the staff were of the opinion that the school should be more humanistic in its approach towards students, teachers, parents and community at large. The perception of the teachers for a congenial and more conducive environment at the school should be characterized by service, concern for others, development of individuals and facilitate growth and development of all stake holders.

An 'Extension' dominant organization is characterized by and relevant to community service organization. The teachers' perception of the desired climate of their school is that their school should aim and function to be relevant to the society at large rather than focusing on any other issues. Though the results indicated that the gap between the existing (index = 40.4) and the desired Extension climate (index = 66.2) was a large one, Extension climate is more or less the same as Achievement, which is the backup existing climate (index = 40.8). Hence shifting from a backup climate to a dominant climate would not require a major planned organizational intervention. The study also made an attempt to explore the 13 areas of school climate in order to examine whether the teachers wanted any other motivational climates other than the 'Extension–Achievement' climate for managing any specific areas of climate. The index score for each of the area could range from 0 to 10. Higher the index score, higher the relative importance of that climate. The summary of the results is shown in Table 4.2.

The results indicated that the teachers desired that the school climate ought to be 'Extension – Achievement' oriented for conducive working environment. The results showed that of the 13 areas of climate, a majority of them namely, Inter Personal Relations (IPR), Supervision, Managing Problems, Relation with Other Sections, Decision making, Risk Taking and Innovation and Change should be managed through Extension dominant climate, while Orientation and Communication should be managed through Achievement oriented climate, which is about 9 out of 13 areas of climate have been accounted for by the 'Extension–Achievement' Climate as desired by the teachers for the school.

The results also indicated that the teachers wanted certain areas of the climate to be managed by other motivational orientations. The teachers were of the opinion that Managing Mistakes (index score = 6.8) and Trust (index score = 6.8) should be handled through Dependency oriented climate while Managing Conflicts (index score = 6.2) and Managing Rewards (index score = 6.0) ought to be through Expert Influence oriented climate.

Presently 'managing conflict' is handled with a philosophy that when people make mistakes, they are not rejected; instead, their friends show them much understanding and warmth—Affiliation-oriented climate.

Table 4.2: Summary of Perceived Dominant Motivational School Climate as Existing and Desired

(* = Dominant Climate)

	Existing Climate Areas	Existing					
		A	B	C	D	E	F
1	Orientation	8.3*	6.6	7.1	7.3	6.5	7.1
2	Inter-personal Relations	7.1	7.3	6.4	7.2	6.9	8.0*
3	Supervision	6.3	7.6	6.1	7.9*	7.7	7.4
4	Managing Problems	7.2	7.4	5.2	8.2	6.9	8.3*
5	Managing Mistakes	7.9	6.1	4.9	8.4*	8.1	7.7
6	Managing Conflicts	7.3	6.6	7.5	6.5	7.3	7.9*
7	Communication	6.6	7.8*	6.7	7.1	7.6	7.1
8	Relation with other sections	7.3	7.8	5.5	8.2*	8.2	6.6
9	Decision Making	8.2*	7.0	6.4	8.0	6.1	7.2
10	Trust	7.2	8.2*	7.1	7.2	5.9	7.3
11	Managing Rewards	7.7	8.0*	7.5	6.6	6.8	6.5
12	Risk Taking	6.0	8.7*	7.8	7.6	6.3	7.1
13	Innovation & Change	7.6	6.9	8.1	8.1*	6.3	5.9

Contd...

	Existing Climate Areas	Desired					
		A	B	C	D	E	F
1	Orientation	7.6*	4.2	2.1	3.6	7.2	5.3
2	Inter-personal Relations	4.9	3.1	2.5	7.3	8.4*	4.2
3	Supervision	6.7	6.2	0.9	3.5	8.4*	3.9
4	Managing Problems	6.9	6.5	2.3	4.2	7.0*	2.8
5	Managing Mistakes	5.7	5.1	0.8	6.8*	6.1	5.3
6	Managing Conflicts	5.3	6.2*	2.4	4.4	5.8	6.0
7	Communication	7.0*	6.2	1.4	6.1	3.8	5.4
8	Relation with Other Sections	6.8	5.7	1.6	3.7	8.0*	4.2
9	Decision Making	3.6	6.9	2.6	3.8	7.4*	5.3
10	Trust	4.7	4.8	1.4	6.8*	6.4	6.1
11	Managing Rewards	5.7	6.0*	3.4	5.6	5.5	3.3
12	Risk Taking	4.7	5.9	4.6	5.0	6.2*	3.3
13	Innovation & Change	5.3	6.5	4.2	4.8	6.5*	2.4

However, the teachers felt that it has to be replaced by Expert Influence oriented climate so that people here are able to acknowledge and analyze their mistakes because they can expect to receive help and support from others. Teachers are of the opinion that Managing of Conflict ought to be through Expert Influence oriented climate rather than the existing Affiliation oriented so that the conflicts could be effectively managed when Experts are consulted and their advice used in resolving conflicts. However, there was no shift in the existing climate orientation namely, Dependency for 'managing trust', but it ought to be a lot lesser than what exists presently now, where high value is placed on trust between supervisors and subordinates. Considering the fact that Dependency is a dysfunctional motive but having it at a lesser degree probably might not affect the school climate adversely. However, over a period of time this motive has to be shifted to Extension – Achievement oriented climate in the near future.

The teachers were of the opinion that 'Managing Rewards' should be through Expert Influence oriented climate which is also the presently existing climate but the teachers were of the opinion that this climate needs to be taken with a higher intensity and want that Expert Influence should be used for managing rewards so that knowledge and expertise are recognized and rewarded in the school.

Conclusion

The present study aimed at exploring the prevailing and the desired school climate so as to suggest appropriate interventions for school effectiveness. The results indicated that the prevailing or the existing climate is Expert Influence – Achievement oriented and the desired climate is Extension – Achievement oriented, thus indicating a change in the dominant climate from Expert Influence to Extension or from expertise to community and service oriented climate. Achievement tended to remain as the backup climate both at the existing and the desired climate. Though there is a change desired in the dominant climate, it does not warrant a major intervention since it was an emerging backup climate as well. The teachers also felt that though the school climate ought to be of Extension – Achievement oriented certain dimensions of the climate such as 'managing mistakes' and 'trust' need to be handled through Dependency oriented climate and 'managing conflicts' and 'managing rewards' to be treated with Expert Influence oriented climate. The teachers have chosen the climates which are both useful and functional in creating more conducive school environment for school effectiveness.

References

Brookover, W., Beady, C., Flood, P., Schwietzer, J., & Wisenbaker, J. (1979) School systems and student achievement. Schools can make a difference. New York: Praeger.

Burke, W.W. (2002). Organization Change: Theory and Practice. Thousand Oaks, CA: Sage

Edmonds, R. (1982) Programmes of School Improvement: An Overview. Educational Leadership, December, pp. 4-11.

Owens, R. G. (2004). Organizational behaviour in education: Adaptive leadership and school reform (8th ed.). Boston: Allyn & Bacon.

Pareek U., (2007) Training Instruments in RD and OD. Tata McGraw-Hill

Robert, W. M & Clement, A. S., (1983). School Climate and School Effectiveness: Summary of Teacher, Student and Parent Attitudes in One Rural Community. Research in Rural Education, Volume 2, Number 2, 1983

Rosenbloom, D., & Brown, J. (2002). Readiness for organizational change: A longitudinal study of workplace, psychological and behavioural consequences. Journal of Occupational and Organizational Psychology

Rutter, M., Maughan, B., Morimore, P., Ouston, J., & Smith, A. (1979) Fifteen thousand hours. Secondary schools and their effects on children. Cambridge: Harvard University Press,.

Saradson, S (1982). The culture of the school and the problem of change. Boston: Allyn and Bacon`

5

Women Rights Education for Girls at Secondary School Stage

Namita Sahoo and B.C. Das

Education seems to be presumed as one of the essential women rights. A host of studies have indicated the facts that women education is the key to demographic transition from high to low levels of fertility and mortality, improving health and nutrition, overcoming disadvantage they face in a man dominated society, enhancing economic productivity and contribution in a meaningful way for gender equality, overcoming powerlessness and availing social equality and opportunity. Women Rights Education comprises the process of comprehensive understanding, consciousness and manifested awareness of women rights as well as women empowerment activities. The present paper focuses on the relevance of women rights education for girls. The paper highlights problem mapping of issues related to girls-child and women and designing a curriculum framework of women rights education for girls at secondary school stage.

Access to Equity

Equity indicates equal opportunity for human development. The females constitute nearly half of the India's population. But in each and every walk of life they are lagging behind compared to the progress of male population. The female literacy is very low i.e. 54.16 percent as compared to the male literacy rate of 75.8 percent (Censes, 2001).The Female oppression caused by family, community and religion is one of the root reasons of low literacy among females (Saroja, 1994). Discrimination and gender bias were found in relation to nutrition, nourishment, child rearing practices and education of female children in comparison of male children (Jha, 2002). It is ground reality in the Indian context that men have dominated each and every filed of knowledge and work. To meet the existing challenges of equity of men and women the National Policy for Empowerment of Women, (2001) envisages introduction of a gender perspective in the budgeting process as an operational strategy.

In this context the Ninth Plan document (1997-02) incorporated women component plan (WCP) directing both the central and state government to ensure that not less than 30 percent of the funds/benefits are earmarked for women related sectors. The Tenth Plan document (2002-07) reinforces commitment to gender budgeting to establish gender differential impact and to translate gender commitments into budgetary commitments. The Tenth Plan proposes that both the Women Component Plan and Gender Budgeting should play a complementary role and ensure through both preventive and post facto action, that women receive their rightful share from all women related general development sectors.

Rights of Women

Rights of women can be discussed with reference to gender bias and violence against women. The UNDP Report (1997) reveals that Indian women get only 25 percent of the share in the earned income. Worked burden on them is extreme as they work 69 hours a week while men work 59 hours. The Report observes that Indian women suffer on two sides (i) because of an impoverished society (ii) because they are women. The heinous factors like gender bias, age old prejudice, blind discrimination against female children, prioritizing male children have led to million female feticides and female infanticides. For instance more than four million female children joined the rank of India's "missing women" and 1.2 million lives were snuffed out, it was either abortion or post natal murder according to an estimation made during the decade 1981-91. No doubt, the violence against women is an ever–existing phenomenon in almost all the societies either in overt or covert form. Concentrated efforts by the researchers, women organizations, academics, social workers and journalists have brought to light the women issues like wife abuses, dowry victimization, divorce, rape, burning and killing of women, community oppression on women, schooling of female children, low female literacy in rural & tribal areas as the burning social problems during last three decades.

Progressive thinkers across the ideological spectrum agree that education is one of the most significant factors to bring a paradigm shift in the status of women. The skewed sex ratio and the high infant mortality are as such a cause as an effect of the gender disparity in educational opportunity. It is recognized that in rural India, out of every 100 girls enrolled in class-I only six entered class XII. In urban areas, the situation is also similarly alarming where only fourteen girls of every 100 make it to class XII. In rural area a majority of girls drop out at primary level. Out of the 100 who enrol in class I only 40 join class V. The girls drop out rate is much higher among the disadvantaged groups, the scheduled castes and the scheduled tribes. The girls and women belonging to linguistic and religious minorities and families living in inaccessible forests and hill locked areas are also major sufferers of schooling system. If they will be deprived of seeing the light of a knowledge society the rights for women may be experienced in remote possibility. It is high time to ponder on the issue of rights of children especially of girls in getting free and compulsory education at 6-14 years of age.

Women Participation in National Development

When we talk of the concept of National Development we envisage a harmonious social order behind it. The identity of this form of society stand for the people who live with self-respect and dignity possessing the opportunity to participate equally and contribute for the progress of the society and development of the nation ignoring all sorts of threats and discrimination. The Indian society may be labelled as a developing society. A harmonious social order is a remote possibility in case of our society, which is diseased with a plethora of threats to women rights.

Education is the key to individual as well as the national development. Though the union and state governments have not accomplished a lot to bridge the gender gap, the realm of competition is open for all to participate in individual and national development. Despite a score of social threats to women rights, the Indian women have showed their excellence in different fields of work such as family & health care, education, art, literature, music, politics, science and technology, public services, private sector and self employment etc.

Problem Mapping

The prime objective of the problem mapping in relation to women rights is to explore various strategies of making young girls sensitive to women rights upholding the dignity of women in the society. This approach is very much useful for designing a curriculum framework of Women Rights Education for girls.

Co-curricular Activities

The co-curricular activities like field trips, group discussion, role playing literary activities, exhibition and displays, girls, women club seminars, awareness activities, observation of women's day AIDS day etc. must be incorporated in the present model curriculum. However, the method of adoption of this curriculum is of great importance. The authors are in favour of the principle of flexibility with regards to its adoption. If the integrated curriculum is favoured then it is wise to include all the aspect of this curriculum framework though different other subject of study. If it will be adopted as a separate subject of study for girls then the detailed aspects are to be incorporated.

Conclusions and Suggestions

The educational system must play a significant role in promoting values of an egalitarian society. The Indian society that suffers from various stigmas with regard to equal status of women in different spheres of life must be transformed into a modern and humane society. Making school curriculum more dynamic and vibrant towards women's participation and their role in social development processes must accelerate the efforts made so far in this direction. In this context the school curriculum must perceive the contextual significance of gender equity and rights of women cutting across the boundaries of subject areas and disciplines.

The paper has great deal of suggestions for the policy markers, curriculum designers, text book writer, heads of institutions, researchers, journalists, social thinkers and reformers, women organizations and various intervening government and non-government organizations.

- Policy makers should do policy-mapping exercise in relation to empowerment of women with special reference to women rights.
- Curriculum designers should incorporate the related topics in curriculum at different stages keeping in mind the problems faced by the women according to the need, age, ability and interest of the target groups.
- Textbook writers should include the qualitative topics related to women rights on the basis of the problem mapping and the model curriculum framework of the present paper.
- Researchers should take interest and patience to explore a score of unexplored threats to women rights and find out their cause, relations and effects.
- Journalists should take interest in preparing and publishing the news items and articles related to various women problems and right with a view to bring awareness

to the society.

- Social thinkers and reformers should initiate the women movement against the existing social stigmas and organize awareness activities encouraging direct participation of women.
- Women organization should express their concerns over the women issue and initiate women involvement in solving their common problem.
- Intervening government and non-government organization should invite the participation of women in identifying and preserving their right on global standard. They should integrate the income generating incentives with the awareness programme related to women rights.

References

Agrawal, H.O. (1999). International Law & Human Rights, New Delhi: Central Law Publications.

Das, B.C. (2004). Curriculum Framework for Human Rights Education, Hindustan Times, HT Allahabad Live, August 3.

Government of India (1964-66), Report of the Education Commission.

Government of India (2001), Census Report.

Government of India (2003), Selected Educational Statistics, New Delhi: MHRD.

Jha, P.K. (2002). Educating Human Rights, Agra: Bhargava.

Levin, L. (1980). Human Rights, UNESCO.

Meintjes, G. (2001). Human Rights Education as Empowerment: Reflecting on Pedagogy in Human Rights Education for the twenty fifty century.

Naseema, C. (2002). Human Rights Education, New Delhi: Kaniska.

Nirmal B.C. (1999). Human Rights Education in Universities and Colleges, paper presented in the National Seminar on Human Right Education, Varanasi: BHU.

Sahoo, P.K. and Sahoo, N, (2002). Right to Free and Compulsory Education: Challenges, Paper Presented in the National Seminar, 8th Dec., Allahabad: IRA.

Saroja, N. (1994), Gender Issues in Education, Progressive Educational Herald 8 (4).

Singh, R. (1999). Human Rights & Human Rights Education: The other Dimension: Paper Presented in the National Seminar on Human Rights, Varanasi: BHU.

Tiwari, G.N. and Das, B.C.(2002). Human Rights Education, A Curricular Aspect of the Morrow, Paper presented in National Seminar on Human Rights, 8th Dec, Allahabad: IRA.

6

Role of Non-verbal Communication in Improving Quality of Teaching and Learning

Sona Ahuja

Education, by its very nature, influences and gets influenced by the whole development process. There is hardly any field of activity or sector of development, which is not, influenced by education in some form or other. There is no sector of development, which does not have its impact on the system of education. Therefore, the dynamics of education and its role in social transformation and national development makes it essential that the content and processes of education are continuously renewed in order to make them in tune with the changing needs, aspirations and demands of the society. School education is a sector of fundamental importance to both individual and national development processes.

Quality in School Education

The quality of education is considered to be a concern of highest priority all over the world. The concern for quality in education stems from the concern for improving the efficiency of the educational system. Quantity without quality is likely to defeat the very purpose of education. In fact, quantitative expansion should simultaneously take care of quality improvement. There is no contradiction between the demands for quantity and those for quality. The two can be handled together.

It is, however, unfortunate that there exists a lot of confusion in so far as the precise meaning and connotation of the quality of education is concerned. Generally, the phrase `quality of education' implies standard and efficiency based, of course, on the context in which the term is being used. In general, quality of education is an umbrella concept, which includes all those aspects of education, which make it efficient and good. It includes availability of infrastructure such as buildings, teachers including trained teachers, and the quality of instruction, course syllabi, etc. With this perspective, one cannot refer to quality of education without looking into the availability of all these attributes of education. In the matter of qualitative improvement in education, our efforts ought to be multidimensional. We cannot, of course say, that we can achieve this by improving things only on a particular front.

In measuring the quality of a school three kinds of indicators have been used: (i) the 'inputs', the financial resources or other resources available to the school (ii) the teaching-learning process, and (iii) the output or the products. It is indeed, the classroom and what goes in classroom that can be the first and foremost concern in our crusade. In other words, the classroom interaction between teacher on one hand and students on the other, as also among students themselves, should be improved because it is this interaction which is manifestation of methodology the teacher adopts to 'teach' the students. Efforts undertaken with a view to improving 'teaching-learning' situation in classroom must, perforce, therefore there is need to concentrate on devising ways and means of identifying the factors that go to make interaction effective and fruitful.

Communication in Teaching and Learning Process

For decades discussions have occurred suggesting effective and ineffective methods of instruction. Yet despite these discussions teaching methods remain relatively unaltered from the traditional learning of reading, 'riting, and 'rithmetic. The students' job was to learn. The teachers' job was to teach. The method was of little concern provided the student did indeed learn. However, recent studies seem to illustrate that the method employed by the teacher does directly affect the learning potential of students. Throughout history the role of the teacher has changed. Early in history, the teachers' primary role was to broaden a child's knowledge. Frequently the parents lacked basic reading and writing capabilities. Even though the child attended school, the parents spent the majority of the child's growing years instructing and providing a role model. As our society has become less family oriented and more dependent on two incomes, the child's time is spent primarily without the parents and with the teacher serving as the primary role model. Certainly more time is spent with teachers than parents for students in secondary and post secondary education. It can be concluded that teachers become the only source of extended personal contact for many students (Haslett, 1977).

Given the effect teachers may have on students and their development, it is reasonable to suggest that all teachers need to evaluate the communication which occurs in their classrooms. After all, communication in the classroom defines the learning process, and it is necessary to communicate in order to influence learning. No discussion of change would be complete without a discussion of factors affecting the effectiveness of classroom communication. Problems which affect classroom communication are often unique since it is different from other formalized communication in that evaluation is integral to this form of classroom communication. Additionally, classroom communication is largely information sharing. Thus classroom communication is largely interpersonal in nature. Here, meeting the needs and goals of the individual become more relevant than meeting the needs and goals of the group.

In the teaching process, the communication techniques a teacher uses play a significant role in instructional delivery. The components of communication are a fundamental human characteristic. Simply defined, they are the use of symbols to transfer the meaning of information. Communication in general is process of sending and receiving messages that enables humans to share knowledge, attitudes, and skills. Effective communicators match their communication behaviours to their goals and monitor the effect of their communication to create the desired impressions in the minds of others. Both verbal and non-verbal aspects of communication have significant role in the process of effective communication.

Non-verbal Communication in Teaching and Learning

It is not only what you say in the classroom that is important, but it's how you say it that can make the difference to students. Nonverbal messages are an essential component of communication in the teaching process. Teachers should be aware of nonverbal behaviour in the classroom for three major reasons:

- An awareness of nonverbal behaviour will allow you to become better receivers of students' messages.
- You will become a better sender of signals that reinforce learning.
- This mode of communication increases the degree of the perceived psychological closeness between teacher and student.

A speaker can add enormously to the complexity of the verbal message through simple nonverbal signals. Given that non- verbal are such potent communicative tool, it makes sense that if we improve the way we use and read non-verbal signals, we will be better communicators. There is variety of nonverbal signals emitted from teacher in classroom which to deepest levels influence classroom atmosphere, student's moods, perception, learning and eventually attitudes towards knowledge and school generally. On the other hand teacher has powerful tool to identify what is actually going on with his class in general and each individual per se, without any word being said. This is extremely important in lecture like classes when teacher is primarily supposed to talk. The following chart shows how non verbal communication can be linked to teaching learning process.

Components of Non-verbal Communication

Non-verbal communication is a system consisting of a range of features often used together to aid expression. The combination of these features is often a subconscious choice made by native speakers or even sub-groups/sub-cultures within a language group. The following components of non verbal communication have been identified from review of studies related to non verbal communication.

Kinesics (Body Language): Kinesics is a technical term for gestures and body movement. Body motions such as, shrugs, foot tapping, drumming fingers, eye movements like, winking, facial expressions, and gestures come under these. Research also suggests that students' facial expressions are the most visible form of communication when trying to interpret their state of mind (O'Hair & Ropo, 1994). Because the face has the ability to produce over 1,000 different expressions, it is instrumental in communicating a student's state of mind (Ekman, Friesen, & Ellsworth, 1972). Teachers and students show a lot of what they are thinking and feeling in their facial expressions. Students' faces might show interest, concentration, or confusion, so observing their facial expressions can be a step towards assessing engagement and understanding. Likewise, our facial expressions might show impatience, disapproval, and irritation, all of which can confuse and discourage students, particularly since we're often not aware of what—and how much—our faces show. If our goal is to encourage and empower students, then we need to project our caring and support through our facial expressions. This doesn't mean smiling sweetly all the time, even when we are bothered by something a student does or says. It does mean letting our genuine concern for our students shine through consistently, during hard and easy moments. If we are concerned about what our facial expressions communicate, we might ask a colleague to observe and give us feedback. (Rosa, 2002).

Proxemics (Proximity): Cultural norms dictate a comfortable distance for interaction with students. You should look for signals of discomfort caused by invading students' space. Typically, in large classes space invasion is not a problem. In fact, there is usually too much distance. To counteract this, moving around the classroom may increase interaction with students. Increasing proximity enables may make better eye contact and may increase the opportunities for students to speak.

Haptics (Touch): Throughout our lives, touching communication, or haptics, is a powerful tool. Physical cues projected by the instructor communicate a message to students (Kleinfeld, 1972). Since teachers are considered superiors in the classroom, they often initiate touching behaviours. Teacher judgment is the best indicator. A teacher who grabs the arm or shoulder of an unruly student enters the student's space uninvited. Aside from embarrassment, the student may develop other negative feelings toward the teacher. More positively, however, touching can also be used as a reinforcer. At times, a teacher can develop a close relationship with students by invading their space. A simple pat on the back for a job well done is a much used and usually accepted from praise.

Oculesics (Eye Contact): Eye contact, an important channel of interpersonal communication, helps regulate the flow of communication. And it signals interest in others. Furthermore, eye contact with audiences increases the speaker's credibility. Teachers who make eye contact open the flow of communication and convey interest, concern, warmth and credibility. Making eye contact with individual students can help a teacher establish a presence in the classroom and reinforces the importance of the teacher's message. It may also assist students in their ability to recall information. In one study, students whose teacher made eye contact with them while reading a story had greater recall of details of that story than students whose teacher did not make eye contact while reading the same story (Otteson & Otteson 1980).

Chronemics: It is how we perceive and use time to define identities and relationships. One of the more important uses of time on the part of the teacher is the use of the pause. Pausing while presenting information usually emphasizes the content that has just preceded or will immediately follow. Most classrooms involve interactions between teachers and students, with the teacher asking questions to which the student is expected to respond. One of the hardest things for teachers to learn is to take sufficient time between asking the question and expecting an answer.

Paralanguage: The elements of paralanguage are pitch, resonance, articulation, rate, volume, rhythm, pause and silence and sounds such as gaps and groans. No matter what we say, we may be seen as inappropriate if we don't have the right tone. Even as adults, our impulse is to fidget, snooze, whisper, or construct our grocery lists when instructor droning away at lecture. Imagine what it's like for children when we speak in a monotone voice? Comprehensive studies indicate a relationship between paralanguage (voice tone, pitch, volume, tempo, intensity, silent pauses) and teacher effectiveness. Our voices are important instructional tools that we can learn to use in flexible ways. When we're animated and vary the way we speak, we send a message that says "Hey, this is interesting. Pay attention." For example, try varying the ways you can say that well-known story opener "Long, long ago in a place far, far away..." Stretch out the words and insert a pause: "Lonnnng, lonnnng ago (pause) in a place farrrr, farrr away..." Or use a different pitch for the first "long" versus the second "long" and the first "far" versus the second "far" for a different effect. If we would like to enliven the way in which we speak, we can check on paralanguage by tape recording oneself. As we listen to the tape, pay attention to how often and when we vary the speed of what we're saying, vary the volume, and vary the pitch and tone. Also pay attention to when and for how long we pause. Then as part of daily lesson preparation, we can practice using voice more flexibly. (Rosa, 2002)

Posture: It is the position of the body. We communicate numerous messages by the way we walk, talk, stand and sit. Standing erect, but not rigid, and leaning slightly forward may communicate to students that you are approachable, receptive and friendly. Furthermore, interpersonal closeness may result when you and your students face each other. Speaking with your back turned or looking at the floor or ceiling should be avoided; it communicates disinterest to your class.

Appearance: Height, attractiveness, body shape also accompany our communication. The physical attractiveness of students and teachers does serve to influence classroom interaction. This variable, however, is probably less deserving of attention than some others, since communicators do not easily manipulate it.

Artefacts: Yet another way we communicate is through personal objects, such as clothing, jewellery, eyeglasses. First artefacts announce professional identity.

Of the above, body language (particularly facial expressions and gestures), eye contact, proximity and posture are probably those which teachers most need to be aware of in terms of conveying meaning, avoiding misunderstandings and fitting in with the target culture. In terms of skills development, non-verbal clues should not be underestimated when developing both the listening and speaking skills. Like grammatical structures, non-verbal communication has form, function and meaning, all of which may vary from language to language.

Researches in communication suggest that many more feelings and intentions are sent and received nonverbally than verbally. Nonverbal communication in instruction incorporates behaviours that do not use words (O'Hair & Ropo, 1994). Voice tone, body posture, gestures, and eye contact are incorporated in a teacher's classroom message. Mehrabian (1967) suggested that only 7 percent of message is sent through words, with remaining 93 percent sent through nonverbal expressions. According to some scholars, verbal part goes up to 35 percent in some specific type of communication process. Also a study on communication points out that contrary to intuition, the brunt of the impact of a speaker's presentation is through nonverbal communication; it has been estimated that the meaning received by the audience is derived from approximately 1/3 verbal reception and 2/3 non-verbal reception.

When the verbal and nonverbal messages are contradictory, most people will believe the nonverbal message they are receiving, not the verbal one. Hence, the nonverbal messages, conscious or unconscious, that are being sent by the speaker through appearance, attitude, gesture, and dress, are crucial to the communication of ideas. In addition, the speaker's ability to read the audience and change speaking strategies accordingly will also impact the effectiveness of the transmission of the message. Effective teaching requires that we pay a lot of attention to our verbal teacher language, using carefully chosen words to help build a positive and productive classroom community. But the way in which we deliver these verbal messages may contribute more to student understanding than the words themselves, particularly for children over the age of eight. Young children focus on the words that teachers use; older children tend to focus more on adults' nonverbal behaviours in their attempts to understand "What does s/he really expect from me?" (Mayo and La France 1978).

Accompanied by a smile or a frown, said with a loud, scolding voice or a gentle, easy one, the contents of our communications are framed by our holistic perceptions of their context. Research has established that nonverbal cues play a significant role in classroom instruction (Arnold & Roach, 1989). Grant and Hennings' (1971) case study measuring nonverbal communication in the classroom and Henly's (1977) research into enhancing communication through nonverbal cues are just two studies that support the important influence that nonverbal cues have in instructional delivery. With Petrie et al.'s (1998) research in mind, having an understanding of nonverbal cues is very helpful in classroom instruction. It helps the instructor become a better receiver of student messages and increases the instructor's ability to send positive nonverbal messages assisting in instructional reinforcement. Nonverbal communication in the classroom can produce subtle nonverbal influences, particularly in the affective domain. Moreover, an understanding of nonverbal cues affords the instructor the ability to stay away from nonverbal cues that can hinder learning.

Therefore, in classroom instruction, the teacher needs to understand nonverbal cues to accurately and effectively deliver information (Miller, 1978). The importance of non-verbal communication is quite important in first language (native) classes to add specific meaning, feeling and environment to the content. Even it is also more important in second and third language (foreign) classes as many verbal components are not understood by a large number of students mainly classes following communicative approaches. Non-verbal communication by teachers plays an important role in these classes. It has also a significant role in the classes meant for differently able students especially for deaf and dumb students in an inclusive environment. Research suggests that educators who use nonverbal cues consciously are more effective than those who do not use nonverbal cues in their teaching (Love and Roderick, 1971). These findings make it hard to ignore the impact that nonverbal cues have on instruction delivery. When designing instruction, teachers should be aware that this high-level nonverbal communication influence is necessary for instruction to be delivered completely, concisely, consistently, and accurately.

The validity and reliability of verbal messages are checked by nonverbal actions. Again, if discrepancy exists, the nonverbal will dictate. The teachers should be aware of the non verbal cues used by them and its effect on students. Also teacher should be able to interpret the non verbal cues of students. It helps teacher to understand the learner better. The facial expressions and body posture of the student communicate their extent of attentiveness. Once the teacher has identified the inattentive spots in the class, she can catch their attention. Also teacher should evaluate ones own non verbal cues as to which non verbal behaviour of teacher distracts the learner and which non verbal behaviour helps to catch the attention of the learner.

References

Albers, D.L. (2001): Nonverbal Immediacy In The Classroom. Ph.D. Department of Psychology, Missouri Western State University

Arnold, V.D., & Roach, T.D. (1989). Teaching: A nonverbal communication event. *Business Education Forum, 44.* 18-20.

Cooper, P. (1995). Communication for the classroom teacher. 5th edition. Scottsdale AZ: Gorsuch Scarisbrick.

Ekman, Paul, and Wallace V. Friesen. 1969. "The Repertoire of Nonverbal Behaviour: Categories, Origins, Usage, and Coding." *Semiotica* 1, 49-98.

Grant, B., & Hennings, D. (1971). The teacher moves: An analysis of nonverbal activity. New York: Columbia University.

Haslett, B.J. (1977). "Dimensions of Teaching Effectiveness: A Students Perspective." *Journal of Experimental Education*, 44, 1976, pp. 5-10.

Henley, N.M. (1977). Body politics: Power, sex, and nonverbal communication. Englewood Cliffs, NJ: Prentice Hall.

Kleinfield, J. (1972). *Instructional style and the intellectual performance of Indian and Eskimo students*. Washington, DC: Office of Education, U.S. Department of Health, Education, and Welfare.

Love, A and Roderick, J. (1971). Teacher nonverbal communication: The development and field testing of an awareness unit. *Theory into Practice*, 10: 295-299.

Mayo, Clara and Marianne LaFrance. 1978. "On the Acquisition of Nonverbal Communication: A Review." *Merrill-Palmer Quarterly*. (24): 213-228.

Mehrabian, Albert, and R. Ferris. 1967. "Inference of Attitudes from Nonverbal Communication in Two Channels." *Journal of Consulting Psychology,* 31 (3), 248-252.

O' Hair, M., & Ropo, E. (1994). *Unspoken messages: Understanding diversity in the education requires emphasis on nonverbal communication.* Association of Teacher Educators, Orlando, Florida.

Otteson, J.P. and C.R. Otteson. 1980. "Effects of Teacher Gaze on Children's Story Recall." *Perceptual and Motor Skills* (50): 35-42. Petrie, G., Lindaur, P., Bennett, B., & Gibson, S. (1998). Nonverbal cues: The key to classroom management. *Principal, 77,* 34-37.

Rosa, S. (2002). Using nonverbal communication to improve teacher effectiveness. *ERIC* ED464728.

7

Enhancing Quality of School Education through Counselling and Inclusive Schooling

Sudipta Roy and Priyanka Behrani

Introduction

The professional school counsellor is trained in school counselling with unique qualification and skills to address the academic, personal, social and career development needs of students. Professional school counsellors can serve a vital role in maximizing student achievement .They support a healthy learning environment and work to safe guard human rights of all members of school community. Their job is to create a mission statement supporting the school's mission while collaborating with the individuals and organizations to promote students growth. (ASCA website).

School counsellors in the western countries have well defined roles where research based applications are being extended to different areas like integrating children with special needs e.g. autistic children (Gibbons2008), children with mental retardation (Shertzeer, B.1969) or children with learning disabilities into the main stream or to specialized services like enabling rural student for urban higher education (Guiffride2008) to name a few. While school counselling in India exists since time immemorial, as a profession it has been around for not more than 30-40 years. A dearth of trained professionals and a reluctance to induct school counsellors have dominated the Indian scene to the extent that there almost no professional bodies for school counselling and efforts are made to equip teachers in the counselling skills (Mohsin,

2007).This impedes the practice of professional counselling in the areas of integration or prevention and promotion of mental health related issues. Moreover there is limited research in the Indian scenario to support school counselling practices (Mangal, 2007).This finding is similar to observations from researches in other Asian countries like China (Thomason & Qiong, 2008).

School counselling services in India are unevenly distributed. The scene in metros is much more promising than in other large cities and rural schools. Looking at the role of school counsellors in a majority of cities of India, we are reminded of a familiar scene from the very famous novel "Alice in wonderland" by the author Lewis Carroll. In the scene of the mad tea party, Alice enters the March Hare's house to find the Hatter, March Hare and Dormouse seated at one end of a very large table. The Dormouse is asleep between the two who rest there elbows over the Dormouse to talk to each other. Seeing her Hatter and March Hare cried out "no room, no room" Alice says there is plenty of room and takes a seat at the other end of the table. Here the role of the hatter and March hare seems akin to that of educational administrators, consumers of main stream education (parents and students) and instruments of the education system teachers) while Alice appears like a representative of children with special needs trying to find her way into the education system. The sleeping Dormouse is a counsellor rendered "dormant" and bullied by a dominant system. Interestingly in this scene time stands still. To the authors this scene personifies the present dilemma of psychologists who are seeking to strengthen the societal health, at grass root through inclusion and counselling.

This paper focuses on:

- The roles of school counsellors in inclusive and regular schools.
- The problems faced by them.
- Possible suggestions for improvement in this regard.

Role of School Counsellors in Inclusive and Regular Schools

Conventionally a counsellor is expected to contribute to strengthening the schools environment by:

- Identifying areas of difficulty or children with difficulty within the school.
- Conducting formal assessment for correct diagnosis
- Planning and implementing intervention programs wherever possible.
- Make reference to an appropriate source for further management for problems that cannot be handled within the school.
- To conduct programs of life skills development or prevention of mental health programs.
- To conduct programs that lead to promoting mental health or quality of life of the users of the system.
- To assess and guide students for choice of careers and vocations.
- To conduct sex education programs where required.
- To facilitate the process of teaching learning by helping students to adapt to the curricular and co-curricular demands through optimum use of potentials.(Rao, 1991)

The above specified roles are not the only roles. There is the scope of expansion. In western countries the roles are defined according to the different developmental needs of the students for the different levels of education provided by the schools. The same may be adopted in the Indian school context where educational levels are defined as Pre-primary, Primary, Secondary and Higher Secondary.

A point that is most of the time overlooked is that the roles above mentioned are equally applicable to normal as well as schools also catering to children with special needs. Integrated education for the disabled in India is more a necessity that an option considering the huge population of disabled children.(Vijayan,Geetha2006).A school that does not pay adequate attention to these facets of the educational environment is indirectly contributing to segregation of society and leading to a society with poor mental health.

The government of India has taken many several bold steps over nearly four decades towards providing formal education for people with disabilities beginning with the Indian Education Commission (1964-1966), to the Persons with Disabilities Act: 1995 and the Sarva Shiksha Abhiyan (Santhanam, Babu and Sugandhi, 2007). Yet the ground realities show that the education system in Gujarat is still not ready or equipped to accommodate the large number of people who fall under the broad terms of persons with disabilities.

Concept of Integration

Integrated education refers to the measures taken to provide educational resources, within the regular educational system, for those children who need them. The aim of integration is to avoid or reduce restrictions on any aspect of a child's development, which might result from segregated education.

Integrated education refers to meaningful involvement of children with disabilities into ongoing regular education program to the extent feasible and beneficial in a given instance, with the ultimate goal being optimal academic and social as well as personal learning of each child.

Inclusive education in special education is a recent concept but also principally an accepted approach in general education in the Indian context. A teacher in the regular school focuses on the average learner but is also experienced in handing academically talented as well as slow learners.

Inclusion offers a different perspective on the education of child with disabilities in ordinary schools. Inclusion means all children are welcome regardless of differences. In this system the emphasis is not on treating the deficit but on adapting the environment to accommodate the disability perceiving it as a normal difference. Within inclusion model there is less emphasis on trying to make the child as much like a normal child as possible. The differences are not only to be accepted and respected but also to rejoice to the fact that no two human beings same or equal.

As an inclusive school is a place where everyone belongs, the child is accepted and is supported by peers and other members of the school in the course for training for her educational needs. Inclusive education is flexible and individualized support system and is provided in regular schools, committed to an appropriate education for all inclusive education recognized and responds to the diversity of the children's needs and abilities – including differences in their ways and pace of learning.

The general educational system acknowledges the fact that education of all types of children including that of children with disabilities should come under the mainstream education. In the special school concept, the special education component is 'APART' from the general education system, whereas in integrated approach, it is 'A PART' of the general education. Inclusive education goes one step further. In this approach, the special education is an 'Integral. PART' of the general education system.

1. Characteristics of Individual Pupils: The first perspective seeks to explain educational difficulties in terms of the characteristics of individual pupils. This remains the dominant perspective in the special needs field where the nature of educational difficulties is explained in terms of particular disabilities, social background and /or psychological attributes. The frame of reference created by this perspective is the individual child and responses are chosen that seek to change or support the child in order to facilitate participation in the process of schooling.

2. Mismatch: The second perspective explains educational difficulties in terms of a mismatch between the characteristics of a particular children and the organization and/or curriculum arrangements made for them (e.g. Weddell 1981 Dessent, 1987) here supports is directed towards helping the child to meet the demands and expectations of the system if this assumed to be fixed or for the time being at least unchangeable. It may to direct towards making modifications to the system in order to extend to range of pupils that can be accommodated.

3. Curriculum Limitations: The third perspective explains educational difficulties in terms of curriculum limitations, using the term curriculum in a broad sense to include all the planned and indeed unplanned experiences offered to pupils. Thus in this perspective there is concern with what can be learnt from the difficulties experienced by some children about limitations of provision currently made for all pupils. The assumption is that changes introduced for the benefit those experiencing difficulties can improve learning for all children. (Hart, 1992)

4. Educational Considerations: Educational considerations to be applicable to inclusive education are still a new field so there are no tested methods and techniques.

5. Encouraging Participation: Teacher must be purposeful, enthusiastic and clear in their directions and instructions to promote greater participation of student. Since the excluded are included in the classroom the teachers must make efforts to line lesson experience to the students' experience to enhance their understanding. Teacher can use specific techniques at various stages of the lesson to encourage with the content and activities. The deliberate use of group – work and collaboration learning strategies between students as they carry out their task will ensure better participation.

6. Formal Planning: Formal planning is very important in inclusive education. The formal planning has two elements. First of all there is the planning of the overall learning environment. This involves taking the programs of the study outlined national curriculum and, whilst bearing in mind the principles upon which the school attempts to operate turning these in to appropriate activities materials and classroom management. The second element is concerned with planning for individuals.

There are certain other barriers in inclusive education like attitude of teachers, physical barriers, languages & communication, socio – economic factors, funding organization of the education system to name a few. Even as we are completing a decade into the 21st century, neither the schools nor the school counsellors are well equipped to overcome the above mentioned barriers.

Problems Faced by Counsellors in Schools

As discussed earlier in the paper school counselling has been around for three to four decades in India .But not many schools are willing to accept the importance of counsellors. The reason for employing the counsellors are often unclear to the management, the role of the counsellor and the necessary infrastructure are either provided with reluctance or not at all. With the result, counsellors in the schools have at times served as store room managers, peons, clerks, typists, computer operators, and most commonly as value education teachers or proxy teachers. The salaries offered to the counsellors are often a paltry sum below the scale of qualified teachers. It is that counsellors are really not needed in school? The reluctance to induct counsellors in school is more baffling in the present context where the news is replete with frightening incidents of murder, assault, abduction, sexual misdemeneanours, occurring in the school context. The incidents are a clear indication that there are certain needs that's manifest themselves in the educational environment that is not adequately met within its present conceptualization. Let us examine some of the factors contributing to this situation from the two concerned perspectives namely 1) the psychologist's perspective and 2) the educationist perspective.

Psychologist's Perspective

Employment: The first problem a psychologist faces is seeking a job. When a counsellor seeks employment in schools they are confronted by a number of negative attributes. To quote such experiences:

Situation 1: An experienced teacher once remarked what do we need a counsellor for? A good teacher already knows how to identify and handle problems of children intuitively. That's not all; several other such statements are encountered.

Situation 2: To a counsellor a teacher once remarked" you people have no idea what it is to like to be a teacher. You have no teaching work, no evaluations, no noisy students, in fact no responsibility but a fat salary".

Such responses reveal the underlying rigidity and hostility towards differences in roles even in fellow professionals leave alone accommodating the differently-abled. Thus the sad reality remains that only a few schools acknowledge the need for a counsellor and make provisions to give them a place in the school system.

Space and infrastructure: once employed the counsellor then has the job of finding a place to do counselling in much as made in psychological literature about the environment and privacy in which counselling must be done. A separate room, noise free environment pleasant surrounding etc. yet when inducted the school counsellor often has to accommodate space constraints and use store rooms, open staff rooms, libraries to conduct counselling sessions.

A counsellor also needs certain psychological test to conduct the necessary assessments which are some what expensive. Schools do not have the instruments and often do not want to spend on their procurement. This limits the efficiency with which counselling services can be rendered.

A visiting counsellor who was invited to screen children for dyslexia, faced an interesting situation: on arriving at the school at the appointed time the principal welcomed her and informed" we have made arrangements in the sick room, you'll find a stethoscope, stretcher, and many beds to examine the students".

This reveals the confusion existing about the nature of

learning disabilities as well as the role of a counsellor. Incidentally, the principal of that school held two doctorates (one in education and the other in economics)

Overload: Another situation that counsellors often lament is an "overload". Counselling activities need several contacts with the concerned children. Each contact made lasts for thirty minutes to even an hour and a half. Given that most schools usually have at least twenty five to forty children in a class and four sessions for each grade. Schools from nursery to tenth standard would have strength of about 1000 to 1500 children. About 5 to 10 percent of school population are said to be affected by one or the other cause leading to academic difficulties or under achievement. So a counsellor may be required to deal with at least 50 to 100 children at a given point of time. This is a mammoth task for a single person. Let us not forget the value education classes and proxies. Schools of this size need to have at least two or more counsellors, but may not do so.

Some additional issues in the deliverance of counselling: these issues concern the child's world and influence the perception of school counselling by:

- **Time:** When to call out and identify child for counselling becomes another issue. Not everyone can be seen in the recess time so the option is to call out a child in music, art and craft, games period, or library periods so that study periods are not missed. In which case, the child involved stands a chance of missing some thing he or she enjoys doing. Yet it may be necessary. There are no "counselling periods" on the time table and children cannot wait after school hours, so the options are limited. The counsellor may find it difficult to maintain a describable schedule of contact with the child and the child may themselves resist given to counselling or develop hostility for the counselling.
- **Stigmatization:** once a child has to be called out of a class for counselling it becomes public knowledge and the child,

may face a labelling teasing and ridicule classmates as well as teachers. This further makes children want to resist counselling.

- **Parental Attitudes:** Many times the people, who oppose counselling, more are the parents of affected children themselves. The parents for various reasons do not like to acknowledge difficulties in their children so they may either openly reject the process of counselling or passively resist it through non corporation or non compliance with instructions or suggestions.
- **Training of Counsellors:** on the flip side of the issue lies the training of school counsellors presently counsellors would typically hold a masters degree in counselling psychology, in educational psychology or in clinical psychology. It is still a fact that many post graduates courses of psychology lack adequate practical exposure to assessment and counselling. The training provided too many fail to inculcate the professional attitude needed to fulfil the job requirements. Due to this the counsellor may feel under equipped to handle their responsibilities efficiently.

Having looked at the psychologists perspective, let us now examine issues from another perspective.

Educationist's Perspective

The educationist is schooled in a framework that had very clear cut roles. Briefly, the job of the educationalist is to inculcate knowledge into students who will turn out to be future citizens of the country. Knowledge is broken down into subjects, which have a curriculum, texts, a course plan and evaluation mechanisms. The question that now enters the educationist's mind is then - how does the counsellor fit in here? From this stand point pour forth the next set of issues, which are presented below:

- **Paradox of Cost:** Educationists often report that counselling is an expensive feature. Many schools claim that they cannot afford the salary of a counsellor and cannot afford to give them space. On the other hand education is seen as "lucrative business" bigger and better school buildings are being constructed. More over fees of the students collected from parents have sky rocketed.

- **Issue of Training:** A dilemma often encountered in education is the lack of adequately trained counsellor. The number of trained counsellor is far outweighed by the number of existing schools. Therefore, some schools who wish to induct counsellors find a dearth of good, trained counsellors. They may them have to compromise on their choices or remain without a counsellor. This too acts detrimental for educationists.
- **Interference:** The other feeling often communicated but rarely voiced is that the counsellors are a nuisance interfering with the job of imparting quality education. The counsellors are seen as trying to buffer students who actually need a strong hand and disciplining. To illustrate this we would like to quote an incident. The author of this article was working with a child who was diagnosed with severe learning disability in Maharashtra but had to move to Gujarat on account of his father's job. The child was assessed, the concerned findings were sent to the school principal to request continuance of the considerations being given to the child at his Mumbai school. The author was sent back a note by the principal, who said, "Dear Ma'am, kindly do not try to protect lazy students and lazy parents or try to tell us what to do. I would like to inform you that master X. had not been completing class work for many weeks. I caned him and made him stand in the hot sun for 5 hours. Next day he completed his work. Sincerely…"

  On a similar vein, when counsellors try to enrol the help of teachers to deal with problems in students, teachers commonly retort, "I have to handle 50 students and cannot pay special attention to any one." What escapes cognizance at that time is that needs of such children are easily accommodated if one is interested or attentive to them. They do not require too much time or energy to handle. The real barrier here is the underlying attitude of the teacher, who says, "Why should I be doing this? It is not my job."

- **Counsellors as Excess Baggage:** Sometimes a principal feels that "I am an experienced person. The counsellor can do nothing that I can't." The principal of some schools feel omnipotent and omniscient. They feel that they would adequately handle problems of students as above. However, is not true that the principal is the key administrator and seen through the eyes of whom a number of students and teachers begin to visualize their futures? With such important tasks at hand taking up counselling on oneself can only spell disaster both for the principal and the children involved. The situation is akin to that of a filmmaker who wants to produce, direct, write the script, choreograph give music, sing, and act for his or her film.

These are some of the important considerations placed by the educationists

Reviewing the above arguments one is reminded of a quarrel between siblings trying for parental attention. Perhaps the issue on hand is one of sibling rivalry, where educationists and psychologists are fighting for public attention and self importance. The question then arises that are there any solutions?

Conclusions

Having reflected on the status, expectations, difficulties in the deliverance of professional school counselling the authors would like to point out that the above discussion has been using experiences in Gujarat as a case in point. We will now deliberate on some alternatives that may be helpful in bringing about healthy changes in the educational environment:

Collaborators v/s Competitors: One attitudinal change that seems pertinent is that both professionals need to view themselves as collaborators rather than competitors with the convergent aim of contributing to a healthy and productive society by complementing each others role without pushing or shoving.

Reconceptualization of the Process of Education: Perhaps also the process of education needs to be reconceptualized within a broader framework. Being the largest single entity that reaches out to vast masses of budding members of society for a sustained development it holds potential for tremendous helpful as well as detrimental influences. All professionals contributing to the care and nurturance of children have to be considered a legitimate part of the educational environment and assigned their roles. We need to look at education as a multidisciplinary venture. So that the rights of children are adequately protected and harmful processes like abuse might be detected at the right time and addressed.

Training: A merger between concerns of educationists and psychologist is seen on the issues of training. There is clearly a need for the following change in the status of training of counsellors. Firstly, many more training programs for counselling in strategic places having widespread coverage in the country are needed to meet the increasing number of schools. Second, the training programs must adequately equip counsellors for field work. Moreover educationists in the course of their training must be adequately made familiar with different needs of children and helped to develop healthy attitudes towards fellow professionals

Re-looking at Costs: The fears that hiring of counsellors would add heavily to the financial burden of managing schools needs rethinking. A cursory look suggests that better known schools have student strength of nearly 1000 and the fees have been steadily increasing. No doubt the hiked fees are used judiciously towards the growth of the children. Nevertheless it occurs to the authors that addition of Rs. 10 to 50 to the monthly fees of each student will add an income of a minimum of Rs. 10,000 a month, which we feel is a fairly sufficient salary for counsellors in today's age. Can we not afford this facility? Especially since, the cost of ignoring problems of the users of the system is much more expensive to the families, schools and the nation at large .What needs consideration is that whether it the expense that is deterring the induction of school counsellors or is it the attitude?

The changes thus needed to make professional school counselling an effective contributor to school health seem to be needing work at different levels by different groups of people. It also seems that the nature of changes needed appear to be to an extent attitudinal implying that training programs of teachers and counsellors would be a good starting point. .A healthy dialogue between existing educationists and counsellors can go a long way in choosing appropriate content for both syllabi. Going back to where we took off from – Unless Alice is given a place along side March Hare with respect and the dormouse is allowed to keep awake and participate, time will continue to stand still.

To conclude, we would like to quote a sensitive song given by a popular Music band in America called 'Genesis'. The song is called "Land of confusion and here are the lines.

"There too many men, too many people facing/making too many problems. And not much love to go around.

This is the land of confusion.

This is the world we live in and these are the hands we're given, Use it and let's start trying to make this a place Worth fighting for/ living in."

References

Gibbsons, M. (2008) Getting to Know the Child with Aspergers Syndrome. Journal of Professional School Counselling, June (Ed.)

Guiffride, D. (2008) Preparing Rural Students for Large Colleges and Universities, Journal of School Counselling, Vol-6, (14).

Kar, C. (2004) Exceptional Children Their Psychology and Education, Sterling Publisher's, New Delhi.

Mangal, S. K. (2007), Educating Exceptional Children An Introduction to Special Education. Prentice Hall of India, Delhi.

Mohsin, M. (2007), Teacher's Handbook of Counselling, Anmol Publications, Delhi.

Olivier, M., and Williams, E. (2005), Teaching The Mentally Handicapped Child, Challenges Teachers Are Facing, International Journal of Special Education, Vol-20, No-2.

Rao, N. (1991), Counselling and Guidance, Tata McGraw Hill Publishing Com., New Delhi.

Santhanam, T., Prasad Babu B., Sungandhi, S. (2007), Children with Learning Disabilities, Sonali Publication, New Delhi.

Shertzer, B., and Jackson, R., (1969), School Counselling In America and England, Journal of Comparative Education, Vol-5, No-2 June.

Thomason, T.C., Qiong, K. (2008), School Counselling In China Today, Journal of School Counselling, Vol-6, Issue-11.

Vijayan, P., Geetha, T. (2006), Integrated and Inclusive Education. R C I & Kanishka Publication, New Delhi.

8

Changing Quality Paradigm in Languages

R.S. Mani

The school education has become more important in the twenty-first century for it has seen an unprecedented growth in terms of number, more emphasis on infrastructure development and the curriculum. The private institutions have grown in number than the government aided institutions. The successive government in the state of Gujarat has gradually trying to withdraw in terms of financing school education for expansion. The Gujarat Board of Secondary and Higher Secondary Board have more than five thousand schools in the state. The trusts are given excessive power resulting in multiplicity of structures and forms, courses and programmes leading to more variety. However, the schools are classified depending on the examining body namely the State Board of Secondary and Higher Secondary Education and Central Board of Secondary Education. The Central Board has nearly more than nine hundred central schools spread across the country and several schools affiliated to Central Board are increasing for the central board is considered as better in terms of curriculum and maintains better standard.

Some of the states have found single, central organization to manage more difficult and they have divided the state into regions(four to five units) giving autonomy for organizing examination and certification at the tenth standard level for example, Maharashtra state. This decentralization has improved the quality of services concerning examinations. The West Bengal state has recently tried to improve their curriculum by offering diversified programmes and courses.

The Orissa state is also planning similar programmes. Many schools in Gujarat conduct preliminary examinations for tenth standard at school level. Those who qualify in the examination are allowed to write the board examination. This attempt has brought a conscious attempt of preparation of students for examination.

The Karnataka Board of Secondary School Examination does not require a preliminary examination. Most of the schools in the Gujarat are offering a vocational subject namely computer education from eighth standard and at the tenth standard it becomes optional subject.

Emphasis on the Regional Language In each of the state there is an excessive emphasis on the learning of regional language compulsory up to the tenth standard level. This measure may have improved the transaction in the regional language but the overall standard has not improved. Some states have allowed more than one language as regional language for example Andhra Pradesh (Telagu and Urdu). This has promoted bilingual development. Urdu has developed in Andhra Pradesh faster than in other states. The emphasis on mother tongue has been found since fifty years. The Secondary Education Commission (1952-1953) recommended the education in mother tongue up to the tenth standard level. However, the quality of the mother tongue or the regional language has not improved over years. The NCERT at the regional level and the state level has played a major part in improving the text book presentation, editing, printing and distribution. Majority of the students do get textbooks in time and they are able to buy for use. The number of regional languages accepted by the constitution has increased to nineteen (the new languages accepted were Konkani, Manipuri, and Dongri).

There has been an attempt to produce books in more regional languages in more numbers. There are several dialects in the country that brings variety within the district or block. It is assumed that each dialect has been facilitative in learning the regional language or the mother tongue. This feature does not have more research evidence. Many dialects do not have established scripts for example Kodagu dialect. People of Kodagu use Kannada language to write and speak Kodagu as well as Kannada. In Punjab state people learn Gurmukhi as well as Punjabi. Punjabi is one of the most popular regional language. People of Jammu and Kashmir (J&K) learn Kashmiri and Urdu but Kashmiri is the most popular regional language.

The literatures available in regional languages are limited and they are general. The translations of scholarly work are less in number. The regional poets emerge slowly among their brothers and they get recognized in the state very late. The appreciation of the scholarly work gets delayed due to lack of patronage and government support. The earlier royal families have not been able to continue support by giving continuous patronage for scholarly work for example Sanskrit, Arabic. Some of the regional art, culture are gradually disappearing for example, script, painting. Tripura and Nagaland states have accepted English as the regional language.

The three language formula of the central government was not well accepted. The promotion of Hindi in recent years, in southern states has found more acceptance. However, learning of southern languages in northern states or Hindi speaking states is less promoted. The financial support from government is far less.

The private initiative is the only way to promote other languages in Hindi speaking states. The state board's jurisdiction is generally spread up to the state level. The state board has seldom made any attempt to cover other regions speaking the regional language exception being the Goa state.

The state board examination has been the most accepted standard of school education. Although, each state board accepts the another state board, there are wide diversities found in the way the examinations are conducted , weighted, and compared even with the central board or the school boards in the foreign countries. It is heartening to note that over decades gradually the state boards are also improving. The major and most acceptable way of testing has been through paper pencil test (written examinations). The oral and practical components are given lesser weight age and far less importance in terms of performance. In recent years, Gujarat board has introduced practical examinations in science subjects and it is planning to introduce oral examinations in languages.

The marking system is the most accepted way of evaluation in many state boards for example, Gujarat Secondary and Higher Secondary Board, Gandhinagar, Karnataka Secondary Education Examination Board, Bangalore. The Central board has already successfully introduced nine point grading system in all central schools in the country. There are some scholars who think grading system is better than marking system.

Introduction of Semester System The Central Board of Secondary Education is thinking of introducing semester system at the higher secondary level. The introduction of semester system involves continuous internal testing and comprehensive examination to depict the integral component of the progress in performance. Teachers and students need to be oriented to the new changes envisaged for transformation.

Use of Public Tests for Determining Standards

- CIEFL, Hyderabad has developed English Language Proficiency Tests and tested widely in the entire country for determining standard in English.
- ED CIL, New Delhi has developed tests in different subjects at first and second standard .These tests are being validated by some scholars at the M.Ed. level in The M.S. University of Baroda, Vadodara.
- Ekalavya, Ahmedabad has developed test battery in different subjects at elementary level. This needs critical examination and better use.

Science and IT

- Cyber Olympiad, New Delhi conducts examinations every year from 3rd standard to 12th standard in the knowledge of computers and IT.
- National Talent Search Examination, NCERT, New Delhi. This test is conducted nationwide at the tenth and twelfth standard to determine the quality of science in performance. The successful candidates are given scholarship up to M.Sc. level studies.
- Science Olympiads, HBCSE, tifr, Mankhurd, Mumbai The Science Olympiad examination is conducted by the HBCSE, tifr, Mumbai in subjects such as Physics, Chemistry, Mathematics, Biology, Astrophysics. The selected candidates are given one month training in problem solving by the staff of the HBCSE, Mumbai. The four selected students represent the country in the International Olympiad each year.
- The Kishore Vigyan Prothsahan Yojana. This programme started in the year 1999. The students identified under this programme are provided summer school programme in Indian Institute of Science, Bangalore. They are exposed to practical and testing in laboratory.

Hindi Language Promotion

The Dakshina Bharat Hindi Prachar Sabha has been tutoring students in Hindi and conducting examinations to determine standards in Hindi. These examinations are recognized by the central government. The other Hindi promoting departments, universities, colleges and institutes have been doing well in promoting Hindi at different levels (local, state, national and international level). Most of the schools have Hindi as one of the subject for study up to twelfth standard.

Sanskrit Language Promotion The religious institutions, public trusts, Sanskrit departments, colleges and university have made earnest efforts to promote Sanskrit through their campaign, workshop, tutorials, coaching and examination. Although, state board offers Sanskrit as one language to learn, many schools are not able to provide for Sanskrit education.

- Classical languages such as Urdu, Arabic are offered in some government high schools and higher secondary schools or some schools run by public trusts.
- Tamil, Telagu, Marathi in other states these languages exist in schools with lesser support from the government and public.

Preference for Trust run Public Schools Many parents prefer trust run public schools in comparison to the local schools. The fees in public school are relatively high. Still parents prefer public schools. Public schools such as Delhi Public School, Tejas Vidyalaya, Navrachna schools, International schools etc have maintained good standard in terms of curriculum, teaching-learning and evaluation. There are certain features that can be clearly observed such as regularity in the conduct of school activities, variety in programmes and courses, relative autonomy for teachers and students for organization of programme and participation.

The evaluation is regular, comprehensive and continuous to form an integral whole as a grade. Grading system is generally followed. There are other aspects such as co-curricular activities, health, sports and games, swimming, fine arts and crafts etc that gets emphasized and reinforced during the year to develop the child as a whole. The peer relationship in terms of pairing, team and houses facilitate for adequate identification with certain values for example honesty, sincerity, equality and unity in Delhi Public School, Vadodara. Healthy competition takes place among houses to build competitive spirit. Central schools are also considered as schools with standard curriculum for its facilities, staff and selection procedures.

Public schools celebrate all national festivals and national days such as Independence Day and Republic day. The laboratory are well equipped and better used such as science, computer and mathematics laboratory. There is a concern developed for humane values in school. Teachers in public school get regular in-service training and they use different methods to teach their subject. Most of the students achieve well in the public school. There are no failures. In some schools few failures are accepted. The revision of the teaching is a regular feature. Efforts are made to provide remedial instruction. Some of the public schools are residential in nature. It seems that in public schools quality and standard are synonymous. Parents and public view public schools are quality schools maintaining standards.

Feedback from Society

Certain questions arise in this context. They are:

- What is Quality School Education?
- What are the significant factors that contribute to the Quality School Education?
- How do you evaluate Quality School Education?
- How improvement in Quality could be possible in School Education?

The process of school education is highly dynamic. It has many factors that interact simultaneously to result into a complex mechanism. The development is a matter of determination and commitment to the purpose, hard work, and thinking aloud for the continuous improvement.

How Quality May be Improved in Schools?

- Students need to get personal attention and adequate freedom to participate in school activities.
- Teaching-learning need to be focused for attention of teachers and educational administrators.
- Evaluation need to be made continuous comprehensive evaluation with grading system.
- Outstanding students need to be identified and provided additional training to participate in state and national competitions and enrichment programmes.

- Peer-to-peer network needs to be improved to facilitate more communication and sharing for more educational development.
- Activities such as mathematics laboratory, science activity centre, subject rooms (for example, Tejas Vidyalaya, Vadodara), computer centre etc need to be encouraged positively.
- Counselling centre needs to be established in each school to attend to the grievances and listen to the social emotional problems of children. School may provide positive health outlook in terms of providing programmes such as meditation, doing yoga exercises such as surya namaskar, padma asana, etc. Students could be given opportunity to meet each other as a pair to discuss their problems and share their views.
- In-service training of teachers needs to be organized by schools to facilitate growth of the teachers. Universities, research centres, colleges may help teachers to get oriented in specific areas of specialization in each domain.
- Teachers must be provided required freedom and support to develop computer software, models, teaching-learning materials, equipments and other learning resources.
- A web for teachers and students may be created for active interaction and share the development.
- Students work (activity) need to be periodically displayed on select topics (every three months) to the entire school for appreciation or it may be made open for other schools to visit and view for sharing and commenting for development.
- School is a place to learn, assimilate the culture and Indian heritage to realize the self to relate more with people harmoniously for positive development.

References

Dinker, G 2002 A study of pupils understanding of basic concepts of eleventh standard physics, Vadodara: CASE, The M.S. University of Baroda, M.Ed.

Khan , A.R 1994 Issues of education and new world order , Social Science Abstracts, Vol. XVIII, 1994, Vadodara: Indian Academy of Social Sciences(Abstracts of papers presented at the XVIII Indian Social Science Congress, 12-16 November, 1994, Baroda),p.p39-40.

Kothari, R.G., Rao, Y.D. and Umasree, P.S 1994 Science-technology-society(STS) issues in secondary school science text books, social science abstracts,vol.XVIII,1994,p.p40-41.

Praseeda, V 2004 A study of implementation of swami Vivekananda educational philosophy in Ramakrishna mission school, Vadodara: CASE, The M.S. University of Baroda, M.Ed.

Rugi, P.A 2005 A study of quality teaching learning in 1st standard in Delhi Public School, Vadodara, Vadodara: CASE, The M.S. University of Baroda, M.Ed.

Sharma, S 2005 Effectiveness of an instructional package in environmental studies among students of standard VII, Vadodara: CASE, The M.S. University of Baroda, M.Ed.

Sushma,1994 Social class, creative thinking and new world order, Social Science Abstracts, Vol. XVIII, 1994, p.p44-45

Tandel, S 2004, A Study of Student's Understanding of Concepts of XI Standard Chemistry in English Medium Schools of Baroda City, Vadodara: CASE, The M.S. University of Baroda, and M.Ed.

9

Instructional Supervision for Quality Education

Rina Choudhary

Introduction

The world Conference on education for all (1990) and NPE 1986 emphasize on the quality of education imparted to the children. Schools are a major agency for imparting education. Thus Fullan (1982) considers the quality of school as important as it "influences the child's eventual occupational attainment and levels of national income." School is a complex institution (Mukhopadhaya, 2001) catering to the social, physical and psychological needs of students but with a sharp focus on academics. Teaching learning thus becomes the primary activity of school and the principal its academic leader. Subsequently in determining the quality of school, Dimmock (1995) favours the process view and opines that "the quality of a school is best judged by the quality of teaching and learning provided throughout the school and all other school activities like leadership, management, administration, are of secondary importance. The quality of instruction/teaching learning process in turn depends on quality of teachers who are at the helm of affairs at the grass root level. Though the teachers are often equipped with pre-service training, a continuous process to guide, motivate, correct, criticize and appreciate the teachers is necessary primarily to lead to an improvement of teaching learning process. Instructional supervision, encompassing all these, is one of the key tasks of the head of the school.

School is a major agency of education and the basic purpose of school as an institution is instruction or teaching learning, so any supervision by authorities in school directly or indirectly relates to the supervision of teaching-learning process. The term supervision essentially means superior vision. Instructional supervision deals with the attempts and activities related to direct supervision to enhance the teaching learning process. Thus, supervision is the process by which some person or group of people is responsible for providing a link between individual teacher needs and organizational goals so that individuals within the school can work in harmony towards their vision of what school should be" (Glickman, 1990).

Instructional supervision can be defined as the activities undertaken to enhance the teaching-learning process. The focus is basically on the learners for which the teacher's performance needs to be made effective.

Need for Instructional Supervision

It is observed that most of the schools are not staffed with well-trained teachers, either due to lack on the part of the leader or because of inability or unwillingness of the school management to pay salaries to secure well trained teachers. Some school teachers do not possess the bachelor's degree in education. It can be said that these teachers do not have sufficient training. All teachers need assistance in reaching the highest level of professional development that it is possible for them to attain. Certainly no one questions the advisability of wise and competent supervisory help for beginning teachers. If they do not receive any help, they are compelled to muddle through as best they can.

Teachers who are new to a particular school need help in becoming oriented to an unfamiliar situation. Some teachers may need "developmental" supervision in order to arrive at their full potentialities.

In addition to new teachers who need orienting to a school situation, the experienced teachers also need supervisory help. Competent teacher who wishes to increase her scope of professional activity, may wish to try a method of teaching which is entirely new, she may also wish to prepare supplementary material to enrich the curriculum or to help in the reorganization of the entire curriculum. For this the teacher need and should receive aid when they undertake projects which aim to improve the teaching process. Such aid may be provided through variety of supervisory procedures or techniques which are discussed further in this paper.

To make Instructional supervision effective it should be properly planned. Instructional Supervisors should be democratic, cooperative and creative. Unfortunately, principals have not felt competent or comfortable in the area of improvement of instruction. Consequently, the problem of supervision has gone by default while the principal busied himself with the routine administrative work. Instructional supervisor should work as educational leaders and guide by virtue of the position, knowledge and skills. They should possess special expertise for improving the total teaching-learning process. The teacher's performance depends on factors like: their content knowledge, instructional skills, preparation of lessons, human relations skills especially interaction with students, parents and colleagues.

Practices for Instructional Supervision

Instructional supervision is an ongoing assistance to teachers by school authorities in order that successful teaching strategies are practiced to the teachers in terms of material help, like updated reading material, suggestions on improvement of teaching skills, and inputs on bettering human relations. This facilitation can be provided on daily basis or on periodic basis, by adoption of certain practices. Instructional supervisory practices on daily basis are related to preparation done by teachers and on execution of the teaching in the classroom. Practices on periodic basis can be like organizing workshops, symposium, seminars on the current and emerging aspects of teaching learning like instructional methodology, technology, innovative practices related to teaching and evaluation. Instructional supervision is a multi dimensional activity with improvement of classroom teaching and learning at its core.

The aim of Instructional supervision is to maintain a judicious mix of reinforcing specific prescribed teacher behaviours and skills and adaptation and adoption of innovation. In this the focus again is on facilitation for improvement of teaching-learning process, which is not to be achieved by means of fault finding. It is not an exercise in attempting to improve through principals/supervisors superior hierarchical power. This way it is certainly not 'inspection'. Instructional supervision thus calls for actually Instructional Leadership displayed by principal and supervisors.

The author of the paper is making an attempt to discuss certain strategies which can be adopted for instructional supervision to improve the quality of education.

Classroom Visits

Classroom visitation has been closely associated with supervision in such a way that both the terms are synonymous for the teachers as well as principals. This is a common practice done by most of the instructional supervisors, but what is lacking in most of the schools is that it is not followed with the conference and teachers meeting. Even the classroom visits are not planned properly. Classroom visitation should have a broad outlook which includes demonstration teaching, directed visitation, testing, research and curriculum development in supervision. In many cases, the classroom visits results only in inspection and rating rather than in the analysis of the learning situations or the diagnosis of pupil difficulties and follow up remedial instruction. Teachers do not get the benefit of classroom visits chiefly because they are unplanned. In this technique of supervision, a great deal of sensitivity is attached as the teachers might feel insulting when the supervisor visits their class for observation, it also may indicate loss of faith in the teachers. There is no doubt that classroom visits are desirable if it helps improve the teaching.

Classroom visits can be of use to both the instructional supervisor and the teacher if it is properly employed. To make this strategy effective it is very essential that the supervisor establishes a rapport with teachers and develop a relation of mutual trust and faith. It should be properly planned and the purpose of the same should be clarified, as it will not be same for a new teacher and for an experienced teacher. In no sense it should be to rate the teachers for purposes of determining salary or for continuing the employment.

To make the classroom visits effective, the instructional supervisor should plan the schedules and frequency if visits. A record of each visit should be made so that the instructional supervisors have pertinent data for the subsequent conferences. The supervisor while visiting the classrooms has also to follow certain etiquettes, he should not make any derogatory remarks in front of students, should make sure that he is not interrupting the classes, should not create disturbance on entering or leaving.

Individual Conference

Individual conferences should be followed by class room visits in which teachers and supervisors meet face to face. This is mainly to give feedback on the teacher's performance. Here the individual discuss the personal-professional problem with the supervisor. The topics for discussion in the individual conferences should generally be materials of instruction and classroom procedures in which the teacher needs improvement. This individual conference should be a part of planned total programme of supervision. The supervisors should keep brief records of these individual conferences also. These conferences should be held for all the teachers without any discrimination so that no teacher, even those considered the most competent, are overlooked, and the less competent do not feel that they are alone subjects of personal interviews.

This will in turn also help in developing good human relations. These conferences should be held regularly and in sequence and needs to be scheduled and should be adhered to for its achievement.

The conferences can be vital force in the improvement of instruction, if the instructional supervisor takes the time and effort to make it so. To make the conferences to be helpful, the relation between the teachers and the instructional supervisors should be democratic and impersonal. While one is speaking of the activities of the children or of the common purposes of the supervisory plan, one should avoid saying, "I think..." Or "you did..." this will help to avoid frictions and increase the possibility of improvement of instruction. The conference allows opportunity for the principal to become better acquainted with the teacher's professional ambitions and to encourage them. Perhaps he can help the teacher whose ambitions are not clear to formulate and to realize them. In the conference, misunderstandings or misconceptions which have arisen in faculty or group meetings may be smoothed out or doubtful points may be cleared up.

Conference should be held at a time which is convenient to both teachers and instructional supervisors. Usually the best time is the unassigned period in the teacher's schedule or after school. To make the conference effective, the teacher should be led to do most of the talking. If the teacher can be induced to analyze strengths and weaknesses in procedures, she will be much more receptive to change. Before closing the conference, it is advisable to summarize what has been said or agreed upon. Having the teacher summarize will often prove helpful. Conferences should be carefully planned and carried out.

Group Meetings

Group meetings of the teachers of a particular subject field or grade may be profitable supervisory technique. Planning these meetings is difficult as it may coincide with routine matters. It may so happen that teachers have poor opinion about such meetings. Any supervisor who has a planned program for supervision dealing with such vital matters as curriculum revision and methods of teaching can organize group meetings. To make these meetings effective it should deal with topics which aim to improve instruction in particular subject or grade and which interests teachers. The teachers from the same field can share their knowledge and experiences of teaching and come out with a better teaching style. They can also share the new developments taking place in their field. Even the problems of students may be discussed. If some student is facing a problem in a particular subject then the teachers together can try to analyze the problem and think of helping the child to learn better.

General Faculty Meetings

General teachers' meeting has long been mentioned as one of the instructional supervisory technique. These general meetings are held in low esteem by teachers as the principal tend to use the time for dealing with administrative routine, which could more satisfactorily have been placed in bulletin rather than read or recounted to the entire faculty. Administrative meetings should not be held frequently. No doubt the main reason why teachers have been lukewarm to general meetings is that problems which they recognize as important are frequently not dealt with. A committee of teachers, representatives of every department or grade in the school, should be appointed to plan a series of meetings, and if the meetings are related to a supervisory program which the teachers have helped to plan they will be surely interested. And finally, the teachers should be made to participate in the meetings, either as the speakers or in the discussion which follows. The general meetings can also be used effectively to give feedback on the performance of teachers. It should mainly be used for appreciation. If some negative feedback to be given then the supervisor should not discuss it in the general meeting but can be discussed in individual conference. If at all the point has to be made then it should be made as a general remark rather than specific to any teacher.

Demonstration Teaching

All teachers can profit from and enjoy well-planned and well executed demonstration lessons. The instructional supervisor should plan for superior demonstrations of teaching and see that they are carried out. Demonstration teaching is very helpful to the teachers, especially for the beginners, in practice it is almost non existent.

We all know that in teaching a new procedure or skill, the presentation of a concrete illustration will be more effective than an abstract explanation. Demonstrations are particularly valuable for:

- beginning teachers,
- for mature teachers who are interested in new methods of teaching but are not sure how to proceed and
- for teachers who are out of touch with modern methods of teaching.

To be effective, the demonstration should be planned. The supervisor should communicate the purpose of the demonstration to the teachers who are to observe it, or they should be provided with an outline of the lesson so that no one is in doubt about the purpose and proposed procedure. After demonstration is completed, a question answer session should be followed so that teachers ask the questions which have emerged in their mind to the teacher who demonstrated. At times it is advisable to hold a series of demonstrations so that the whole teaching cycle may be observed.

Securing a demonstration lessons is a challenge faced by the supervisor. It is not an easy task to secure the consent of a superior teacher to prepare a demonstration lesson. Some are diffident; others fear that the unprofessional will consider them to be "showing off". Perhaps cooperation may be secured from the shy or reluctant teacher by bringing in one or few teachers at first and then increasing the number of observers.

Probably the best effects are secured when teachers see demonstration which they recognize as being vital importance to them. Certainly any instructional supervisor, who is concerned with the development of more effective teaching in his school, cannot afford to neglect demonstration teaching as an important technique.

Supervisory Bulletins

Bulletins are commonly used for written form of administrative matters. Such bulletins may also be used to improve the instructional program. Either they may be duplicated and a copy sent to each teacher, or they may be typewritten and posted on the teacher's bulletin board. For large faculty duplicated bulletin will undoubtedly prove more effective. Supervisory bulletins may summarize results of the last teachers meeting or may carry suggestions for study for the next one. They may consist of brief annotated bibliographies or the citation of a professional article which is of special interest to a group of teachers. Reports of outstanding work observed in the school, citing the name and class of the teacher, may also be used. Although the bulletin cannot be the major supervisory technique, it is one which should not be over looked by the instructional supervisor who desires to make his services maximally effective.

Workshops

Workshops are very effective medium for in-service education. The term 'workshop', as applied to education, is commonly used to denote an informal but serious study-group in which persons individually and collectively work under guidance of a director or coordinator with the aid of consultants or specialists, surrounded by a wealth of pertinent materials. One or more problems or topics may be studied; if more than one they are interrelated. Educational workshops can be conducted to create new or improve an existing curriculum, unit, test, teaching device, method of grading and marking, or other project. The workshops should be based upon the principles of learning, such as readiness, felt need and democratic procedures, and should employ new ways of working such as group methods, individual problems. Workshops provide an opportunity for participants to make a constructive contribution on the educational frontier. It also helps in providing means of supplying more practical assistance to field workers

Conclusion

It is observed that the teachers do not react favourably to supervision and to supervisors. The reason usually lies in experiences with certain supervisors, in lack of adequate preparation for using supervisory programs. The author of the paper affirms the belief that there is need for instructional supervision in true sense and that supervision can be of such nature as always to be welcomed. Every school requires instructional supervision. The supervisor in education must bring to his profession dynamic instructional leadership. He must help teachers develop superior qualifications in themselves and in their pupils. From this perspective, instructional supervisors are able to create synergy between a focus on teaching and learning on the one hand, and capacity building on the other. If we are serious about improving the teaching learning process in our schools and thus improve the quality of schools, then we need to research and develop, more than ever before, practices of instructional supervision that promote, celebrate and enhance the importance of teaching and learning and staff development.

10

Education for Knowledge-based Society

Anjali Khirwadkar

Introduction: Education is a part of the societal system and hence can't work in isolation of society. Globalization and the spread of market relation to every sphere of society have important implication for education. There has been an increase in the number of schools especially private schools due to inadequate public funding for education. As per 73rd and 74th constitutional amendments the local communities should participate in decision making in education for their children, thereby shifting the responsibility of education from state to the family and community. At the same time there is increase in competition into which schools are drawn resulting into disparity. In order to meet these challenges the share of education in the 11th plan has been proposed to increase the allocation for education from 7.7 percent to 19 percent, to build excellence in the educational system to meet the knowledge challenges of the 21st century and increase India's competitive advantage in fields of knowledge. The dynamics of education and its role in social transformation and national development makes it essential that the content and processes of education are continuously renewed in order to make them in tune with the changing needs, aspirations and demands of the society.

Studies have revealed that universalization of basic education cannot be achieved without addressing the issue of cultural and socio-economic barriers. The results of a survey conducted by the National Sample Survey Organization in 1992 revealed that school-related factors are responsible for at least 22-25 percent of non-participation of children in primary schooling. The issue of bringing all children to school cannot be tackled with proposition of opening more schools. The problem has deeper roots in the socio-cultural and economic conditions of the people and school quality.

The 11th five year plan document has envisaged development in education by addressing following reforms:

- Education and Skill Development
- Re-orienting the education system to make it responsive with the focus on ensuring employability of graduates through high-quality, relevant, need responsive curriculum and teaching.
- Initiate an intensive program of curriculum updating/development and teacher-training, to address lacunae in relevance, topicality and pedagogic methods.
- PC and Internet Penetration
- All Government schools should have basic minimum IT infrastructure and connectivity.
- Expand the Village Knowledge Centre (VKC) concept across the country to deliver citizen services.
- Focus on development of applications and content in local language and Incentives for production of multi lingual software.

Recommendations of Eleventh Five Year Plan (2007-12)

- To spread the concept of Finishing Schools/Bridge Courses in various educational institutions across the country, a programme for capacity building has to be initiated. This may include identification and supporting of Mentor Organizations for conducting teachers training programmes, identification of gap areas, development of course curricula, course material, etc; and training teachers from various educational institutions, who would subsequently go to their respective institutions and conduct Finishing Schools/Bridge courses.
- Evolving technologies for new paradigm in pedagogy, utilizing the potentials of ICT, broadcasting, Digital

Library, etc., need to be introduced to provide wider access to high quality education, to overcome the shortage of teachers and to increase capacity. In this regard e-Learning programs for higher skill generation; and setting up of a national body of e-Learning practitioners to arrive at e-Learning solutions, standards, and interoperability, R&D, Digital Library, etc., need to be taken up on mission mode projects. In this manner quality education could be made accessible to students in tier-II and III cities (i.e. other than metros). There is a need for providing broadband connectivity at concessional rate for educational purposes.

There are several issues and problems in school education in India

1. How to link school education with economic independence? School education cannot be impervious to the fast changes taking place in the economic sector through liberalization and globalization of the market. Helping students to gain confidence in what they learn and make meaning out of their education.
2. Bridging the gap between world of work and world of academics. It is high time that academicians take initiatives in making system tune to the requirement of the life outside classroom.
3. Harnessing information technology: it is the time to take advantage of the well established fact of effectiveness of IT in imparting education at different level as has been supported by various research studies. The students and teacher be well equipped with the skills of IT. The teacher preparation program should develop a concern among teacher force for using IT in imparting education.
4. Curriculum reform to face the challenges of the 21st century and to diminish the curriculum overload. And make education a pleasing experience for the students.
5. Privatization of education at school level has lead to various kinds of disparity in terms of teaching learning

practices, infrastructure and so on. These in turn affects the quality education and increases the gap of haves and have not.

6. Gender disparity at school level: still after 60 years of independence this is a burning issue that education faces.
7. School education is unable to foster skills among students for facing the challenges of the century resulting into various kinds of stress the students face.
8. School education does not help students to develop self confidence, skills of entrepreneurship.

National Knowledge Commission (NKC 2007) believes that providing universal access to quality school education is a cornerstone of development and a minimum necessary condition for any progress towards making India a knowledge society. The school education system has to become pro-active in preparing the curriculum and processes not only as a matter of social concern, but also to meet the basic needs of those entering the emerging economic framework. The curriculum framework (2005) addresses some of these issues with regard to quality education.

School education should help students to attain following attributes:

- Promoting self direction and independence
- developing responsibility for learning
- nurturing creativity
- developing curiosity
- developing affective and emotional aspects

Curriculum, in order to be realistic, relevant and meaningful, has necessarily to be in tune with the goals of education and the nature of the learner and learning process. The following criteria be given central place for planning school activities.

Education for Three Hs

- Change your Thoughts
- Change your Outlook

- Change your World.

We have been talking about the Education for three H's, in other words—physical, mental and spiritual development. The curriculum should enable students to discover their talents, realize potentialities to the fullest, develop productive and social skills, and enjoy emotional as well as physical wellbeing. The instructions planned and delivered cater to mental development of the students and there is very little scope for physical and spiritual development. How to go about spiritual and physical development? There is very little scope in the curriculum and over and above this a large number of schools are without playgrounds and other physical facilities. There is a need to find space in curriculum for developing spiritual qualities among students, which will help students to develop understanding of social dynamics and their role. Our natural state is one of pure love, truth, righteousness and peace. Our basic spiritual nature has been covered by our fear and defence mechanisms. Students should be encouraged to read the scriptures of various religions as well as the lives of people who have been living examples of strength and they can contemplate on the meaning of their teachings and how they might apply to our daily lives.

Self-learning Skills

Developing self learning skills i.e. knowing how to learn is the most important aspect of education. This attribute is required in this knowledge based society where knowledge is growing at panasonic speed. There is curriculum overload which curbs the individuality. Students spend major time in learning redundant data or the information which is available on web.

The existing teaching methods which are predominantly based on rote learning, lectures and reproduction of information needs to be replaced by interactive modes of teaching which would focus, on 'learning'. The skills like independent thinking, problem solving skills, planning and execution of projects would be fostered. The teacher's role will be one of organizing learning environment for the students. Students learn best when students need and want to know; in other words the teachers role is to generate thrust for learning. This is a big challenge in front of teachers to induce a spark in students for learning. There is need to develop repositories of learning material on web and the readily availability of the material in the form of e – libraries. This is to keep pace with the knowledge generation and its application. Classroom instruction should enable the students to develop skills of collecting information from various sources, interpreting tabulated and graphical information, testing hypotheses, drawing inferences from the data collected as these would stimulate thinking and enable the students discover knowledge.

Skills of Self-evaluation

Fostering the skill of self evaluation, would help students in developing self regulation and internal development. Giving students the guidelines and the criteria for judging their work, is how students would learn to evaluate their work. In order to over- come the burden of examination schools should adopt continuous and comprehensive evaluation that incorporates both scholastic and non-scholastic aspects of education. Apart from written test the various qualitative techniques should be adopted for evaluating student performance.

Students should be told to reflect on their written work and select the two best works from their assignments by asking questions like:

- How much time and effort did you put into this?
- What problems did you encounter?
- How did you solve them?
- What do you think your strengths and weaknesses were in this assignment?
- How could you improve your assignment?
- What are the most valuable things you learned from this assignment?

They must provide a rationale for the selection of their best work. In addition, they must explain how the most effective pieces are different from their least effective pieces and set goals for their future work. This self-assessment, then, becomes part of the teacher's assessment as well.

In order to become lifelong learners, students need to learn the importance of self-evaluation. They can do this by filling out self-evaluation forms, journalizing, taking tests, asking questions, and through discussions. When students evaluate themselves, they are assessing what they know, do not know, and what they would like to know. They begin to recognize their own strengths and weaknesses. They become more familiar with their own beliefs, and possibly their misconceptions. After they self-evaluate they will be able to set goals that they feel they can attain with the new knowledge they have about themselves.

Teachers should encourage self-evaluation because self-assessment makes the students active participants in their education (Sloan, 1996). There are a variety of ways for teachers to provide the students with self-assessments. Research suggests that the simplest tools to encourage student self-assessment are evaluative questions that force students to think about their work (Hart, 1999).

Facilitating Creative Expression

This includes freedom to work, giving room for creative expression i.e. freedom to choose activities, take decisions, plan and organize programs. Assigning group work, cooperative learning in order to develop social skills and affective skills also facilitates creative expression. Students learn best in non threatening environment, therefore providing freedom to the students is vital. The planning of activities which would give scope for self expressions, to ask questions becomes an integral part of the curriculum. The teacher's role would be to direct students and clarify the concepts.

Inculcation of the Scientific Temper

One of the major thrusts of the school curriculum should be to prepare the younger generation to respond adequately to the need of adopting scientific outlook and approach while dealing with various problems of life. The curriculum should develop abilities like spirit of inquiry, objectivity and the courage to question. There is a need to adopt problem based learning approach to enable the learner to acquire problem solving and decision making skills. In teaching of various subjects it is important to keep in mind the interdisciplinary nature of the current scientific research. Different projects should be given to students that would help students develop the skills required for inculcation of scientific temper.

Link between Education within and Outside of Classroom

Gandhiji in his Basic Education scheme had emphasized the importance of dignity of labour. This would help student to be more self regulated and organized. Acquisition of work skills, inculcation of work ethics and development of appropriate work habits are considered to be some of the important goals of school education. A well integrated program needs to be developed connecting primary to higher secondary through secondary. Projects directed to more intensive skill formation at the upper primary stage and pre-vocational courses involving production oriented projects at the secondary stage. Student will be able to link the utility of the knowledge gained in the outside world and their life. The SUPW programs at school level needs to be revised to keep in mind the changing scenario of life outside the school.

Utilization of Media and Educational Technology

Educational technology needs to be employed in the spread of useful information, to improve quality of education, to sharpen awareness of art and culture, and to train teachers. To stimulate the development and dissemination of quality Open Access (OA) materials and Open Educational Resources

(OER) through broadband internet connectivity would facilitate easy and widespread access to high quality educational resources and drastically improve the teaching paradigm.

Table 10.1: Internet Usage and Population Statistics: India Internet Usage Stats and Telecommunications Market (2007)

Years	Users	Population	Percent Pen.
1998	1,400,000	1,094,870,677	0.1
1999	2,800,000	1,094,870,677	0.3
2000	5,500,000	1,094,870,677	0.5
2001	7,000,000	1,094,870,677	0.7
2002	16,500,000	1,094,870,677	1.6
2003	22,500,000	1,094,870,677	2.1
2004	39,200,000	1,094,870,677	3.6
2005	50,600,000	1,112,225,812	4.5
2006	40,000,000	1,112,225,812	3.6
2007	42,000,000	1,129,667,528	3.7

As part of the IT Vision for India, some of the key national IT targets are as follows:

- Increase the PC penetration to 65 per 1,000 from the 11 per 1,000 PCs in 2004
- Increase the Internet penetration (subscribers) to 40 per 1,000 by 2008 from the current Schools and teachers should be equipped to be net savvy and national level bodies should take initiatives to develop programs for teachers as well as students.

Developing Positive Attitude for Environment

It is a burning issue that the world is facing today. The curriculum should focus on this issue developing related skills and understanding for tackling the problems related to environment. Schools play an important role helping students realize that they are a part and parcel of nature. The teachers should organize activities like nature trip, industrial visit, slum visit for developing concern for environmental problem as these problems need to be sensed by the students. Realistic solutions need to be suggested.

Communication and Language

This is a skill which needs to be focused at school level especially the English language. Many times it has been found that students are unable to present their ideas and lack in expression. In a technologically oriented world students should have refined communication skills in order to participate globally in dissemination, and generation of knowledge. Schools should focus on creative expression, use of language in various walks of life. National Knowledge commission also focuses on the development of English language at school level.

The National Knowledge Commission (2007) has emphasized the importance of an inclusive society as the foundation for a knowledge society. NKC has also recognized the significance of English language, not only as a medium of instruction or a means of communication but also as a determinant of access. NKC recommends that the teaching of English as a language should be introduced, along with the first language (either the mother-tongue or the regional language) of the child, starting from Class I in school. This phase of language learning should focus on using both languages to create meaningful learning experiences for the child without disproportionate emphasis on grammar and rules.

Developing a Spirit of Nationalism, Internationalism and World Citizenship

For a country like India the curriculum should provide a wide scope for the development of Nationalism. How can they contribute for the development of the country? What are the major land marks in the history of development of India? Developing the spirit of service and dedication for the country should be aim of education in present times. Without this the above mentioned development will not happen. In the age of ICT where the world has shrunk to a global village developing understanding of world citizenship is must in order to restore peace for humanity at large.

The major challenge in front of teachers is to make the present curriculum less burdened, an enjoyable experience for the students, catering to their abilities. Teachers will have to become the managers of instruction rather than delivering the instructions in the classroom. Teachers should be in a position to locate resources on web and make them available for the student and provide updated information along with the world view. This would help the students to connect their learning to the world at large.

References

Eleventh Five Year Plan, Information Technology Sector 2007 – 12,Department of Information Technology, Ministry of Communications and Information Technology, New Delhi.

Hart, D. (1999), Opening Assessment to Our Students. Social Education: Arlington. 63 (6) 343-345.
www.aare.edu.au/03pap/mun03451.pdf

National Knowledge Commission: Compilation of Recommendations on Education, Nov. 2007, Govt. of India, New Delhi

National Curriculum Frame Work (2005), National Council of Educational Research and Training, New Delhi

11

Open the Black Box

Vandana Talegaonkar and Archana Tomar

Quest for quality in education has been a concern with policy makers, teachers, parents and learners for a long time. This quest is reflected in the various Educational Reforms, School Effectiveness Programs and endeavours to measure school effectiveness. Internationally some of these programs are PISA, establishing national, state, and district standards; target setting; enhanced programs for the external testing of students' performance; surveys such as NAEP (National Assessment of Educational Progress) and TIMSS (Third International Mathematics and Science Study). In India, the attempts are observed in Operation Blackboard, DPEP Programs, the MLL initiative, the SSA etc. Various initiatives in the same pursuit are more emphasis on school planning and management; and more frequent and thorough inspection.

A common thrust of these attempts is to search for quality in the obvious and the observables, that is, the learning outcomes and achievement of the learners. A view of the inside of the school also needs to be taken as some answers may be found there. Raising the standards of learning in schools is an important step in the quest for quality. The focus needs to be on the processes that occur in the school. Hitherto not much explored, the inside of school is still a 'Black Box' (William and Black, 1998).What are the attributes of the essential teaching learning process that occurs in school and how it can be improved is the concern of the authors. Without entering into the realm of either or of the product versus process perspective, the authors present strategies for enriching the teaching learning process especially from the perspective of assessment.

Primacy of the Learner

The endeavour of the school is the development of the learner for various purposes as its primary objective. The constructivist paradigm, advocated by National Curriculum Framework, 2005, places the learner at the centre of the activities in teaching learning process. Active learning and learner as active participant in the process of learning is an integral part of the constructivist approach to learning. It is essential to note that constructivism is an approach to learning rather than a teaching theory. Learning in schools is driven by what teachers and pupils do in classrooms. The process thus, assumes greater importance than the product. How learning process should be designed so that the learner is an active participant? One of the ways is that the learner is able to identify his/her learning needs and determine the extent to which these are met with. What should the environment be for such a process, what should the role of teacher be in this process and what assessment techniques are to be employed which assures the primacy of the learner in the learning process, are some questions that need to be addressed.

Primacy of Assessment

The evolving design of the learning process, as against the pre design, accords a central place to assessment. When information is fed into the learning process and to the learners in a way that enables them to learn is formative assessment. This information can be obtained by and provided by teachers. It can also be obtained by learners themselves by engaging in self reflective process. Formative assessment thus plays a crucial role in the process as it provides a reliable data for making the learning process an informed one.

The quest for quality is seen as the quest for high-quality learning then formative assessment ought to be understood as the most important assessment practice. In view of Education for All (EFA), formative assessment assumes greater importance as effective formative assessment has its most positive effect on low achievers. Research studies have demonstrated that high quality formative assessment has a powerful impact on learning. Unfortunately, the research also shows that high-quality formative assessment is not very common (Black and William, 1998a and b). The same researchers have also stated that formative assessment practice is weak, tending to ape summative assessment practice.

Primacy of Six A in Formative Assessment

Learning can occur effectively when supported by appropriately paced, appropriate type of and appropriately delivered assessment to the learner. Black and William (1998a and b) observe that research studies have demonstrated that high quality formative assessment has a powerful impact on learning. In this context, it is essential to understand the concept of formative assessment. The terms formative and summative are used as types of assessment. The formative assessment describes classroom assessment and summative describes externally imposed assessment, e.g. examinations. However, Brookhart (2001) prefers to use the terms to describe the functions rather than the types of assessment. The 'assessment event', according to him, includes the preparation for assessment by the teacher as well as the student, the feedback offered by the teacher to the student and impact of the assessment on the subsequent learning behaviour of the student. The challenges in this respect are six As:

1. Appropriate assessment tool.
2. Appropriate time of the assessment.
3. Appropriate manner of providing feedback.
4. Appropriate environment in which the feedback is provided.
5. Appropriate persons to assess.
6. Appropriate lessons to be learned by the learner and the teacher.

1. Appropriate Assessment Tool: There are various tools that a teacher can use for formative assessment; the most popular one is the observation of facial expressions of the children. But the expressions given can also be deceptive. One needs to work on more concrete basis to clarify the misconceptions and the myths that hang around the concept being learned and its development of concept. The requirement of the evolving design of teaching learning process necessitates timely and accurate feedback for the designer to design the next phase of learning. Thus for accurate formative assessment the teaching learning environment and the assessment tool should be non judgmental and non-threatening.

Some of the ways in which formative assessment can be done are as follows:

- Passing the parcel here each student has to say something about the topic discussed; if some aspect is not clear to the child it will become clearer in the process. It is possible to diagnose common perceptions and errors.
- Reflective log It is helpful in looking at the journey the child passes through in learning a certain concept. It is also helpful to the teacher as she/ he can also trace the journey of their own development.
- One minute self check list: It is a useful tool to find out what the child has understood in a particular class. It is also a good tool for diagnosis.
- Peer explanation: Peer explanation has a good scope for the clarification of ideas in pair work. It is also revealed in the researches that children understand better in the company of friends. It also promotes social learning.
- Portfolio assessment: Various version of the process are also to be seen to see the growth and development. Various versions can be kept together and gradually how the development has taken place can be traced.
- Concept map: For individual assessment activity concept map can be used where the students can develop a concept

map depicting the concept and its inter-linkages.

- Spoof test papers: For finding out the conceptual clarity spoof test can be used, a worksheet with errors can be given to the students which they need to correct.
- Model test paper: A model answer paper can be given against which students can evaluate their own answers.
- Swapping the worksheet: This is fairly simple exercise to remove the individual bias and work on individual development of assessment skills. The students exchange the worksheet and evaluate them.

2. Appropriate Phase of the Assessment: When to assess a learner influences the benefit of assessment. Appropriate phase in the learning cycle has to be identified.

- **Learner Readiness:** The learners' readiness is primary in giving the assessment. We should develop the mind set and remove the fear of assessment by making it non judgemental and keeping in view the scope for further improvement of the performance of the student.
- **Timely Feedback:** Timely feedback is required by the learner to improve at the time of learning. Elaborate feedback after the learning phase has passed is immaterial or less effective as the learner has passed in time and space to the new zone of learning. Its like swimming, give appropriate feedback, when a person drowns in a particular concept is the feedback really needed. As one lives behind the half baked concept and moves ahead.

3. Appropriate Manner of Providing Feedback: Feedback has three aspects: the message you want to communicate with the focus of the feedback (finding faults or reminding of the missions and providing medals for tasks learned well), the manner of communicating the feedback (body language, gestures, posture, expression) and the language used in giving feedback. For this, the typology of Tunstall and Gipps (1996) may provide a guideline.

4. Appropriate Environment in which the Feedback is Provided: NCF, 2005 describes a nurture of an enabling environment. In view of providing feedback to learners it is essential to develop a nurturing environment. For this the teacher needs to avoid fear, criticism and ridicule by offering opportunity to improve and show readiness to be assessed, transparency in evaluation by presenting evaluation rubric in advance and at times developing it collaboratively with students.

5. Appropriate Lessons to be Learned by the Learner and the Teacher: The appropriate lessons refer to the medals and the missions. Medals refer to the learning achieved and missions refer to the learning yet to be mastered or accomplished. Opportunity to improve Provision for the future improvement of the child should be at the base of the assessment. The emphasis should be of proper conceptualization of the concept rather than judgement of the ability, or labelling and comparing the child's progress with others

The other lessons to be learned not to relate the outcome of the assessment with learner's or teacher's worth. A very important caution in this development oriented assessment is the "teachers worth and potential should not be judged by the number of students putting up the remark of not being able to understand or under perform" The focus need not be on judging rather the importance be accorded to the development of the learner. The learner also should not judge his/her worth based on the formative assessment. The formative assessment and its results should neither be used as a part of teacher appraisal.

6. Appropriate Persons to Assess: Teacher is generally considered as the unquestioned authority for assessment. At times, unfortunately teachers are likely to suffer from halo and shadow effect in assessment.

Multiple teacher assessment is also the need to give different perspectives of learning. It also helps in pruning the not so effective ways of conducting, delivering and assessing. (Peer- teacher feedback)

Some methods of learning in active learning approach are collaborative and co operative approach. This creates space and need for peer evaluation. Peers are equally critical in observation and when provided with an evaluation rubric they are able to assess the performance of their classmates.

No one can be a better judge than one's own self. Self assessment should be the base. An individual is most critical of one's limitations and capacities. Self assessment doesn't suffer from the halo and shadow effect.

The appropriate persons thus should belong to all the above mentioned categories to give meaningful interpretation of the school processes (black box).

Conclusion

Once again reverting to the product versus process debate but actually not venturing into it, the authors of the paper believe that the quest for quality has to begin by opening the 'Black Box' of school. Once the processes are taken care of the product will automatically be of a higher quality. NCF (2005) states, "All efforts at curriculum definition and renewal come to naught if they cannot engage with the bulwark of evaluation and examination system embedded in schooling." In order to attain this, the teacher education programs at pre-service and in-service need to focus on understanding the school and its various processes. This must not be a lip service but integrally woven into the fabric of teacher education programs. After all what is experienced will be understood better and practiced with faith.

References

Brookhart S.M. (2001) "Successful students' formative and summative uses of assessment information", Assessment in Education, 8 (2): 153-69

Dylan William and Paul Black, "Meanings and Consequences: A Basis for Distinguishing Formative and Summative Functions of Assessment," British Educational Research Journal, vol. 22, 1996, pp. 537-48.

NCERT (2005), "National Curriculum Framework 2005" published by National Council of Educational Research and Training, New Delhi.

Paul Black and Dylan William, "Assessment and Classroom Learning," Assessment in Education, March 1998, pp. 7-74.

Paul Black and Dylan William's "Inside the Black Box: Raising Standards through Classroom Assessment" (Phi Delta Kappan, October 1998)

Tomlinson, M. (2000), "Inquiry into 'A' level standards: final report (London: QCA)

Tunstall, P. & Gipps, C. (1996), Teacher feedback to young children in formative assessment: A typology, British Educational Research Journal, 22 (4).

12

Enhancing Quality of Elementary Education

Sejal Dave and Pallavi D. Khedkar

Introduction

Education shapes the destiny of any nation. The quality of human power in any country ultimately determines the sustainable well being of its people. Elementary education is one of the important phases of learning for human beings. According to our past honourable president Dr. A.P.J. Abdul Kalam, "Education makes an important contribution to the creation and formation of a new man and society based on social justice." Education provides foundation for a person to be a responsible citizen. The real process of formal education begins with the elementary education. So, it forms an important part of the entire education system.

Having realized the importance of elementary education, India has been making lots of efforts right from the time of independence, to provide education to all its citizens. The constitution of India has stipulated free and compulsory primary education for all children until they complete the age of fourteen years, without any kind of discrimination on the basis of caste, creed, sex, religion, region etc. For the development of our country, the government of India is committed to the goal of Universalisation of Elementary Education (UEE). The main goal of UEE is provision of infrastructure and access to facilities, enrolment of children in the appropriate age group, usually 6-14 years and retaining these children for a full cycle of elementary education. Tremendous progress has been achieved in the qualitative expansion of Elementary Education and there has been phenomenal increase in the number of schools and enrolment. As a result of such expansion, 94 percent of the rural population has access to primary schools with a walking distance of one kilometre along with this accessibility the coverage of children has also increased considerably (NCERT, 1986). However, there are certain problems that are still persisting and are necessary to study and to develop alternatives to achieve UEE in India.

As far as the provision of access and coverage is concerned, India boasts of its educational system being the second largest in the world. It consists of nearly 610 thousand primary and 185 thousand upper primary schools, about a quarter million non-formal education centres, about 1.87 million teachers and 110 million students study in primary classes in the recognized schools No doubt, the system can claim it to be one of the largest, but it cannot make similar claims for efficiency, quality and achievement of learners. The gap between the planned and the realized goals of education continue be so large that even the basis of educational planning and underlying assumptions can be easily challenged (Aggarwal, 2000).

Universalization of primary education is the single most crucial problem in education in developing countries. (Buch1991). India as a developing country has also experiencing the same situation. Low enrolment, high dropout and low achievement are vital challenges in the universalization of elementary education. So to achieve the objectives of UEE central and state government has started many programmes and policies for the improvement of quality in primary education. Not only central and state government but the international organizations as UNESCO, UNICEF and even NGOs (Pratham, Care) are also working to improve the quality of primary education mainly in developing and under developing countries.

"Quality" refers to the degree of excellence possessed by students, teachers and the primary schools. The effort made or interest shown by the teachers to make teaching learning a pleasurable experience is one of the important qualities of primary education. Further quality lies in the intrinsic validity of the products of primary education with regard to reach its goal and fulfilling its enrolment and retention figures, checking out the drop-out rates and the level of competency, commitment and effectiveness developed among pupils and teachers. Seeing the degradation of quality of primary education, NPE 1986 and the revised NPE 1992 reiterated the urgency to address the quality concern in priority basis.

After independence the government has implemented many programmes and policies for the development of primary education. The planning of government genuinely wishes to improve the quality of primary education, but as we know every coin has two sides same is the programmes where issues also come with it. Here, the researcher mainly focuses on the issues related to implementation of some programmes in Gujarat.

Policies and Programmes for Achieving Universalization of Elementary Education in India

The vision of education for India is contained in the Article-45 of the Constitution; " The state shall take endeavour to provide a period of ten years from commencement of this constitution, free and compulsory education for all children until they complete the age of fourteen years." Elementary education has been one of the focus areas in the successive five-year plans. Working groups of the Planning Commission targeted the goal of Universalisation of Elementary Education (UEE) and the targets were revised successively during 1960s and 1970s. The Kothari Commission (1964-66) proposed to achieve the target not later than 1986. In 1979-80, the Department of Education, Govt. of India established Non-Formal Education centres as a strategy to achieve UEE and to reach the places where elementary schools were un-reached and to reach all the children particularly millions of girls and working children whose participation in the school system is deprived by socio-economic conditions. This programme enabled the learners to learn at their place. The National Policy on Education (NPE-1986) set the platform for the central government to play a key role in achieving Universalization of Elementary Education. Para 5.12 of NPE resolves that free and compulsory education of a satisfactory quality to all children up to 14 years of age before the commencement of the 21st century needs to be achieved. The NPE also highlighted in its Para 5.5 that UEE has three aspects:

- Universal access and enrolment
- Universal retention of children up to 14 years of age and
- A substantial improvement in quality of education to enable all children to achieve essential levels of learning.

The Policy explicitly highlighted the need for intensive effort and gave priority to reduce the disparities among gender and socio-economic groups. To carry out the policy recommendations, the Department of Education under Ministry of Human Resource Development initiated a series of grant programmes to assist and support states to achieve the UEE. The following are the centrally sponsored programme, which are very famous and working in some districts of Gujarat.

Mid-day Meal Programme

Mid-day Meal scheme in this country has been regarded as a largest programme in the world. Under this the students of government primary schools get benefit of mid-day meal n all the working days of their schools. The basic purpose of this programme is that if the children from poor class can get this sort of facility, the retention rate will improve, they will feel motivated for learning, absenteeism rate will go down finally it would prove itself as two birds killing with one stone i.e. problem of low level of literacy and low quality of education. In Gujarat the Mid-day Meal scheme is there from (1961-62) and formally started in November 1985 by Madhavsingh

Solanki. The international organizations like UNICEF and CARE have come forward to strain this programme through the contribution of protective goods such as milk, butter and bread. Taluka panchayat or head teachers also decide concerning Gujarat the menu as dal-rice, and vegetable, khichadi, dal–dhokli, sweet lapsi, sprouts and so on.

District Primary Education Programme (DPEP)

DPEP emerged in 1994 as a response to various challenges in the primary education sector. DPEP adopts a holistic approach and has the essential ingredients required to universalize access, retention and improve the learning achievement and reduces disparities among social groups. The program components include construction of classrooms and new schools, setting up the BRC/CRC, teacher training, development of teaching learning materials, researched based interventions and decentralized management. The criteria for selection of districts are:

- Backward districts with female literacy below the national average.
- Districts where total literacy campaigns have generated a demand for elementary education.

Sarva Shiksha Abhiyan (SSA, 2000)

SSA is an effort to universalize elementary education by community ownership of the school system. It is response to the demand for quality basic education all over the country. The SSA programme is also an attempt to provide an opportunity for improving human capabilities to all children, through provision of community owned quality education in a mission mode. Main objectives of the SSA are as under.

- All children in school, education guarantee centre, Alternative school, Back-to-School campus.
- All children complete eight years of elementary schooling including pre-primary also.
- Focus on elementary education of satisfactory quality with

emphasis on education for life.

- Bridge all gender and social category gaps at primary stage by 2007 and at elementary education level by 2010.
- Universal retention by 2010.

National Programme for Education of Girls at Elementary Level (NPEGEL)

The Government has approved a new programme called National Program for Education of Girls at Elementary Level (NPEGEL) as an amendment to the scheme of SSA for providing additional components for education of girls at elementary level. The NPEGEL is a part of SSA and it implemented under the umbrella of SSA. NPEGEL schemes were introduced during the 10th plan period and implementation experiences have provided valuable insights and learning that are worth considering in formulating the approach to girls education during the 11th plan period.

To enhance girls' education in educationally backward areas 21 districts, 75 Talukas and 13 urban slum areas have been covered by the NPEGEL. Under this programme, at the cluster level, a modal cluster school is being established.

In order to encourage and promote girls education in the state, educationally backward area of 18 districts have been approved by the central government for starting 30 Kasturba Gandhi Balika Vidhyalaya(KGBV) in the year 2006-07. Today there are total 52 KGBV in Gujarat. Other programmes like Meena Manch and Meena Cabinet are also implemented by central government for the improvement of enrolment of girls at elementary level.

Above are the major programmes and excluding theses are Tarang ulhasmay abhyas.

Training Programme

GCERT and the district education and training institutes undertake novel experiments, exchange of experiences, discussions and contemplations; question- answer thought processes, establishment of educational processes, pleasure oriented education, problem solving processes and experience-based education. More than 35000 Principals in the state were given training in the new approach and methodology (2005-06). All teachers in PTC and DIETS in the state were given training in English, Mathematics, and Psychology subjects to strengthen their content. On the Educational Achievement Survey, more than 1 lack teachers of Std 5 to 7 were given training in problem solving of difficult points. 1,50,000 teachers of Std 1 to 4 were trained under the integrated multi-grade education. In the same way, seminars were organized with all CRC-BRC coordinators, newly appointed Vidhyasayaks, lecturers of DIETs, representatives of Primary teacher's association, and teachers. Training programme was held for improvement in reading, writing and counting. GCERT also trained 2000 teachers of the Ashramshala. Gujarat government trains the teachers twice in a year nearby 6 days each which will help to improve the quality of primary education in Gujarat.

Thoughts to Ponder

- Several research studies conducted by Gujarat Council of Educational Research and Training (GCERT) identified the following problems for achieving Universalization of Elementary Education (UEE).
    - Non-enrolment
    - High Drop–out
    - Non- attendance
    - Low Achievement
    - Seasonal Migration
    - Low Literacy Rate
    - Lack of proper Management of Schools
    - Lack of social awareness (GCERT, 2004)
- Dropout Rates at Primary and Upper Primary Levels in India, 1999-2000 TO 2004-05 (Tables 12.1 and 12.2).

Table 12.1: Class I–IV

Stage	2000-01	2001-02	2002-03	2003-04	2004-05
Boys	39.7	38.4	35.9	33.7	31.37
Girls	41.9	39.9	33.7	28.6	24.82
Total	40.7	39.0	34.9	31.5	28.49

Table 12.2: Class I–VIII

Stage	2000-01	2001-02	2002-03	2003-04	2004-05
Boys	50.3	52.9	52.3	51.8	50.10
Girls	57.7	56.9	53.4	52.9	50.76
Total	53.7	54.6	52.8	52.3	50.39

Source: SES, MHRD * Provisional (2004-05)

- The PTA, MTA, VEC have been constituted to provide management support to school but in rural and tribal areas it is rare to see the organization of PTA/ MTA or VEC meetings. But the minutes are recorded by the teacher and signed by the VEC president.
- The block resource co-coordinator over burdened with the work of cluster resource centre and other meetings so they hardly turn up to supervise the schools.
- Due to lack of frequent monitoring and supervision of the quality improvement programme like teacher training, preparation of study materials and teaching aids, student activities, activities of the parent teacher association and VEC are taken casually.
- The health observation of school students by the medical unit and personnel were found rare. However health observation and its related data were found with Anganwadi workers up to the age of 0-6 levels.
- Teachers and most of the patents of rural areas are unaware about the programmes such as Vidhyalaxmi Bond, KGBV and so on.
- Community participation in the implementation of the programme is lacking because of poor awareness of

advocacy among other things.

- Mid-day Meal doesn't satisfy the nutritional aim of the programme. Parents are bothered about the quality that either uncooked or over fried food is given to their children.
- Government does provide grants to achieve the aims of the programme but is the grant given to the proper resource person?
- Are we able to avoid the working of the children under the age of 14? Do these policies and programmes reach the grass root levels?
- Seasonal migration has become a major problem in some districts of Gujarat.
- Meena Manch, Meena Cabinet, Ramta Ramta, and the concept of Bal-mitra varg are not utilized effectively.
- Do seasonal hostels and support schools fulfil the aim of UEE?
- Now a day's teachers with the principals are overburdened with administrative work. So they cannot give enough time for teaching.
- Principals spend a lot of time in collecting information and the data required for these activities. Therefore monitoring of the daily routine work becomes difficult.

Conclusion

"A lamp can only light when lighted by other lamp." Highlighting the present scenario of primary education at the state and national level, providing primary education to all is still a major task. The lamps of programmes and policies are there but unless one lights it by proper implementation, the objectives of UEE cannot be achieved. If the community members of rural areas understand the importance of education and change their traditional mid-set then only we can achieve the goal of UEE. Now it's a crucial time for fulfilling the objectives of the existing programmes and policies instead of making new programmes and policies. We as the experts, educators and a part of community members can hold our hands together and make an effort to light the lamp effectively throughout the country.

References

Govinda & Divan (2003): Community Participation & empowerment in primary education, Sage Publication

MHRD (1986): Programme of Action 1986, Government of India, New Delhi.

MHRD (1992): National Policy on education, 1992, Government of India, New Delhi.

Success story of Education Department (2006) published by GCERT.

Sharma & Sharma (2004): Problems of Education in India, Atlantic publishers and distributors.

13

School Education and Corporal Punishment

M. Rajendran

Introduction

The prevailing educational system, which lays stress on academic excellence, not making the grade in school is considered to be a shame. That teachers, parents and grown-ups fail to realize that every child cannot be an achiever or a topper in class, but believe that a child can be made to realize its full potential through force is the root- cause of the problem, which gets compounded by the looming fear that not coming up trumps in studies will spell doom for the child's future in the dog–eat-dog job market. Corporal punishment is a method that has been implemented by schools since time immemorial to enforce discipline amongst the students and it is also used as a means to deter the students from committing similar offences in the near future. A study conducted with support from UNICEF revealed that 66 percent of children in the state of Maharashtra reported that their teacher regularly punish them in class; the figure for the state of Tamil Nadu was 87 percent (UNICEF, 2001). This paper intends to address reasons for corporal punishment in Indian school context, different ways the corporal punishment used in schools, its effect, what are the legal and international conventions against corporal punishment and what are alternative ways to avoid corporal punishment in schools.

Corporal Punishment: Definition

Corporal or physical punishment is the use of physical force intended to cause some degree of pain or discomfort for discipline, correction, and control, changing behaviour or in the belief of educating/bringing up the child.

Physical pain can be caused by different means such as hitting the child with a hand or other object, kicking, shaking or throwing the child, pinching or pulling the hair, caning or whipping. (Save the Children, 2003)

General Reasons

There is a societal demand on teachers to make the students excellent in studies, good in behaviour etc.

For ill paid teachers the rod comes first to deal with their resentment and anger against a society that is callously indifferent to their interests and betterment.

Teacher's inefficiency in terms of teaching content or method of teaching.

Some children suffer a greater risk of corporal punishment due to their ethnic, family or class background. The Public Report on Primary Education in India (PROBE), 1998, highlighted that the disparaging attitude of upper-caste teachers towards Dalit (oppressed or low caste) children is one of the most common forms of social prejudice in the classroom. This can take various forms from telling them they are 'stupid' and making them feel inferior, to using them for menial chores and giving them liberal and physical punishment. Dalit children also commonly experience harassment from upper class/caste pupils (UNICEF, 2001).

Reasons put forth by teachers:

- Teachers are often under high stresses, such as overcrowding – they argue that these stresses should be first removed.
- Children need such discipline to learn right from wrong.
- For making student to respect elders.
- To make student hard working and obedient.
- Teacher training tells us nothing about the reality of our school; all teaching methods I knew have failed with these children. The only viable method I know is indiscriminate

thrashing. (PROBE, 1999)

Varieties of Punishment

Children may suffer injuries arising from corporal punishment that need medical attention, leave permanent damage and even cause their death. This includes children being knocked unconscious, bleeding, broken limbs, damaged eyes and stitches; being beaten with implements such as canes, belts, or thorns; being whipped or slapped, punched or kicked.

Punishment in schools includes being forced to stand for hours in the sun, smoke red pepper, which causes coughing and vomiting, being made to contort the body into shapes which cause fainting and nose bleeding, pulling hair and ears, forcing pupils into humiliating and painful contortions..

Effect of Corporal Punishment

Corporal punishment leads to depression, to low self-esteem, negative psychological adjustment and poor relationships with teachers.

Educational Consequences

Children frequently cite corporal punishment as a reason for dropping out of school. The general reaction of children after corporal punishment is transferring from abusive schools, or by dropping out of school altogether.

Social Consequences

The strongest, usually unintended, message that corporal punishment sends to the mind of a child is that violence is acceptable behaviour, that it is all right for a stronger person to use force to coerce a weaker one. This helps to perpetuate a cycle of violence in the family and in society.

The use of physical force upon children can be quite dangerous as it may lead to dangerous and violent behaviour later on in life and later it may have psychological problems on the children.

Arguments against Corporal Punishment

- It perpetuates a cycle of child abuse. It teaches children to hit someone smaller and weaker when angry.
- Injuries occur. Bruises are common. Broken bones are not unusual, many deaths have occurred due to corporal punishment.
- Corporal punishment is used much more often on poor children, minorities, and children with disabilities and boys.
- Schools that use corporal punishment often have poorer academic achievement, more vandalism, truancy, pupil violence and higher drop out rates.
- Corporal punishment is often not used as a last resort. It is often the first resort for minor misbehaviours.
- Many alternatives to corporal punishment have proven their worth. Alternatives teach children to be self disciplined rather than cooperative only because of fear.

Human Rights and Corporal Punishment

Hitting children breaches human rights, in particular, to respect for every person's human dignity and physical integrity and to equal protection under the law, upheld in the Universal Declaration on Human Rights and the International Covenant on Civil and Political Rights.

The UN Convention on the Rights of the Child (UNCRC) explicitly protects children from all forms of physical violence (Article 19) and from inhuman and degrading treatment or punishment (Article 37). It requires school discipline to be "consistent with the child's human dignity and in conformity with the present Convention" (Article 28.2). In view of the damage that corporal punishment can do to children's attendance and learning experience, it can also breach Article 28, which stipulates children's right to receive primary education (Article 28.1.a) and requires States to take measures to encourage regular attendance at school and reduce drop-out rates (Article 28.1.e).

The General Principles of the CRC, which also inform this position, provide that in all actions concerning children the best interests of the child should be a primary consideration (Article 3); the inherent right of every child to life and to survival and development (Article 6); the right to non discrimination (Article 2) and the right of children to express their views freely in all matters affecting them and these views be given due weight (Article 12).

Corporal Punishment and Indian Laws

In India there is no national prohibition in law of corporal punishment in schools. Corporal punishment is lawful as a disciplinary measure in penal institutions. Government has instructed to states to stop the use of corporal punishment in educational institutions and the National Policy on Education (1986, modified 1992) states in section 5, 6 that "corporal punishment will be firmly excluded from the educational systems". A draft Free and Compulsory Education for Children Bill which proposes prohibiting corporal punishment in schools, applicable to whole o f India, is under discussion (April 2005).

Banned in Indian States

Andhra Pradesh: In 2002, the Andhra Pradesh government imposed a ban on corporal punishment in all educational institutions by amending Rule 122 of the Education Rules (1966), violations of which should be dealt with under the Penal Code.

Tamil Nadu: Corporal punishment was prohibited in Tamil Nadu in June 2003 through an amendment of Rule 51 of the Tamil Nadu Education Rules prohibiting the infliction of physical of mental and physical pain during "corrective" measures.

West Bengal: In February 2004, the Calcutta High Court ruled that canning in state schools in West Bengal was unlawful.

Chandigarh: Corporal punishment was prohibited in Chandigarh in the 1990s.

Delhi: In December 2000, the Delhi High Court ruled that provisions for corporal punishment in Delhi School Education Act (1973) were inhumane and detrimental to the dignity of children.

Goa: The Goa Children's Act 2003 bans corporal punishment in Goa.

What Needs to be Done?

- To shift practice of teachers towards non-use of corporal punishment.
- To see changes in teaching methods and introduce positive parenting/child care.
- To end social acceptance of corporal punishment by educating society that corporal punishment is a form of violence to children.
- To ensure effective legislative protection.
- To increase visibility of corporal punishment as a child rights' violation.

Alternative Ways to Avoid Corporal Punishment

- Advising
- Counselling
- Parent's Teacher meetings
- Teacher's students meetings
- Impositions
- Giving physical exercises
- Fines from the students pocket money
- Cutting off lunch time
- Cutting off play time
- Making the students learn lessons.

The Emerging Expectations from the teacher:

Teachers need to build a relationship of respect and trust with children, enabling children to question, challenge, analyze and learn for themselves and encourage equal respect for each other. Corporal punishment would be inconceivable within any education system that was genuinely based on the rights of the child.

Conclusion

Today's children are sensitive towards every aspect of life and violence is not the answer to the problem. The maximum "spare the road and spoil the child" too seems to be losing its ground. Corporal punishment is not at all applicable in today's modern world of reform, it tends to bring negativity and make the child resort to violence, the child could possibly use corporal punishment in future date because of his/her past experience.

There are many other ways to bring up a child which would produce positive results making a child understand and value human life and dignity making him/or her better individuals and humans. Corporal punishment though may sound like a better alternative and the last resort to inflict punishment but it is highly advisable not to use it either at homes or schools, there are instances to show that it has a far reaching bad effects upon the students because there has been many deaths in the past due to the use of corporal punishment. So, the government should take a strong stand to prevent its use and it should also be wiped off completely from schools. It has to be understood that corporal punishment is not the solution; actually it leads to the problem.

References

Bhutia, T,Y (2006) Corporal Punishment in Chennai Schools – A Study, Manitham – Human Rights Organization, Chennai.

Government of India (2006) Child Protection: A handbook for Panchayat Members, New Delhi: Ministry of Women and Child Development, pg 56 – 60.

PROBE Team (1999) Public Report on Basic Education In India, New Delhi: Oxford University Press, pg 75

Save the Children (2003) International Save the Children Alliance Position on Corporal Punishment

UNICEF (2001) Corporal Punishment in Schools in South Asia (http://www.crin.org/docs/resources/treaties/crc.28/UNICEF-SAsia-Subm.pdf) downloaded on 26th December 2007.

14

Problem of Mental Health and Erosion of Values among Students

Bharti Rathore

Introduction

This is the new face of Indian schools- peers killing their friends over petty issues, quarrelling, cheating, breaking school rules, disobeying the teachers, rash driving, blackmailing, kidnapping by the teenagers. These are not the news items from U.S newspapers but a harsh reality of Indian schools as well. What prompts the students of a good and reputed schools belonging to affluent families commit these horrible crimes threatening other's life as well as their own lives. In recent past there have been gruesome murders of Abhishek Tyagi, Adnan Patrawala and Lokesh Dadwani .What is so noticeable in these murders is that all are murders of teens committed by their friends who are also in teens. As incidents of childhood and teenage aggression, depression and even suicide start sounding alarmingly familiar each day a feeling of panic is clearly visible among parents. All wondering what the kids are up to, seeking reassurance that theirs are shielded from such dark thoughts and incidents like Virginia University shoot -out do not take place here. Blaming Americanization of Indian society is ridiculously inadequate. The point is that the gun culture has invaded India and we should be ready to cope with that before it is too late.

"There is lot of work needed in the area of children's mental health" says Dr Shobha Srinath, Professor Department of Psychiatry at the National Institute of Mental Health and Neuro Sciences (NIMHANS), Bangalore. This is one of the handfuls institutes in India with a full fledged child and adolescent psychiatry unit. We still seem to be unaware of the magnitude of the problem. The World Health Organization indicates that by the year 2020 childhood neuropsychiatric disorders internationally will rise proportionately by over50 percent to become one of the five most common causes of morbidity, mortality and disability among children. But there are hardly any figures in India that show mental, emotional and behavioural problems being faced by the children today. "The issue is huge, but the level of intervention is at an infantile stage," says Dr. Deepak Gupta, child and adolescent physiatrist Delhi's Shri Ganga Ram Hospital. We need to provide positive mental health to our kids at all levels. Experts agree that that academic and learning related problems need to be examined along with mental heath problems of children.

According to one report released by the Indian Council of Medical Research based on the study conducted in Bangalore and Lucknow in 1997 the prevalence of psychiatric disorders was observed to be 12.8 percent in 1-16 year olds. Though this number is less than the general figures in the West (20-30 percent) but experiences suggest a rise in the mental and emotional problems faced by the children. "I see many more cases of anxiety and panic attacks among students today." Says Geetanjali Kumar, a counsellor with Delhi's Hansraj Model School, who has been working in this field since 14 years. Dr. P.C Shastri, the Mumbai based President of the Indian Association for Child and Adolescent Mental Health (IACAM) says that in the last ten years there has been almost a 400 percent increase in mental health problems for children. Children today face stress related problems which were previously faced only by elders. A 2004 report in Lancet has stated that teenagers in Vellore in Tamil Nadu had the highest suicide rate in the world. It found that the average suicide rate for males and females aged between 15 and 19 years was almost 4 and 70 times higher respectively than that in developed western countries.

Even if we understand the disturbing scenario, we do not

have immediate remedies. We need more psychologists, psychiatrists, super specialized paediatricians and counsellors and more mental health centres but schools also have to play an important role in dealing with this type of problem. While 11th 5year plan is concentrating on mental healthcare, we need to work in more directions to cover the ground already lost.

The underlying causes are of course many. And they have more to do with the changing social norms and life styles than the mental makeup of a depressed child. "Even though children may be more genetically pre-disposed to problems like ADHD and depression, environmental factors can do much to aggravate the condition." says Dr Gupta. Dr. Shastri blames the rapid changes in society. "Parents and schools are not able to cope with it. There is a conflict whether technology is going to help or hurt." Kumar, who also counsels students in the CBSE helpline, feels part of the problem lies in weakening of our social support system around children. "Parental supervision is declining while the influence of the media and peer groups is increasing." She says.

There are no role models either. Many parents are materialistic and teachers do not have adequate training or qualifications to deal with children's problems. Parent teacher meetings are mutual blaming exercises. Peer influence is often responsible for driving the child in wrong direction. Television and video games can desensitize them towards the horrors of gore. Their skill in video games comes in destroying maximum no. of objects in the minimum time.

Role of Schools in Improving Mental Health

In this present dismal scenario schools and the teachers have a vital role to play to. Some of the suggested steps are the following:

Reviving Emotional Ties in Schools: In the changing scenario a great responsibility lies on the schools where a child spends most of his time. As Joint families are fast disappearing and in many nuclear families both the parents are working, a child is sent to school as soon as possible for the maximum time. In absence of any grand mother or an aunt telling him good stories to inculcate good values or siblings or friends to play with, the child has to often remain busy with video games computer or television. It is sad to say that television and computer both are doing more harm than good as they are spreading aggression and violence in our society. Tired, stressed, and fatigued parents are not able to cater to the emotional needs of the child and the child develops feelings of insecurity. Here it becomes the responsibility of the schools to provide that emotional security that love which is missing in homes .For that our schools have to go back to our old system of education instead of blindly following the West. In our good old system, the Gurus were like fathers or mothers whereas all the fellow students were like brothers or sisters. There was love and affection among these relations and a child's emotional need of love and affection was satisfied in schools. It is high time to revive those emotional ties once again in our schools.

Supplementing Technology with Human Relations: Now-a-days there is a false concept that technology can replace teachers. Many famous educationists say that in this age of technology teachers have become redundant and a child can learn through technology. No doubt in the age of internet, computers and television, knowledge is at our door step but knowledge learnt through these inhuman means makes a child inhuman. A child learning through this becomes devoid of warm emotional ties which comes only through face to face contact with the teacher. All human miseries and sufferings become merely a data for the child. Nothing can replace the human factor. Human feelings and sentiments can be learnt only through interaction with human beings. There is need to use technology wisely to supplement and help the teachers and not to replace them.

Having Good Teacher-Student Ratio: In all schools there should be an ideal student-teacher ratio. In the age of commercialization all schools are bent upon admitting as many students as possible. This results in over crowding of the classes where a teacher does not know even the names of all children. Therefore it becomes difficult to solve the mental or psychological problems of the children. But if any untoward incident happens, the teachers are first to be blamed. All TV channels and journalists start the blame game .A class in secondary or higher secondary should ideally not have more than 40 students.

Changing Materialistic Attitude of Society: In the changing scenario where everything is commercialized, education is also commercialized. Many rich people have tuned it into a money making business. They start schools with the sole aim of earning money and disregard all human aspects. For them a teacher is only a seller of a commodity called education whereas students are the customers. This attitude results in disrespecting or even abusing the teachers in front of the students. This also results in dismantling the teachers from the pedestal on which the students put their teachers. It is a known fact that no society can rise above the level of their teachers. If our society does not respect the teachers, the teachers are also not able to provide good climate in the schools.

Providing Good Values through Healthy Practices: Schools should not only provide information but good and positive values should be inculcated here. As values cannot be taught but imbibed in proper conducive atmosphere, schools should consciously try to provide such atmosphere where students inculcate the positive values. For that regular assembly sessions with active participation from teachers and students are a must. Assembly provides a platform where students and teachers join to pray to Almighty. Good discourses on moral values, talks by teachers and students should be like a Satsang which should start their day meaningfully. It is sad to see that in many schools assembly is a mere ritual in which even attendance of the students and the teachers is not compulsory. There is no field or ground where students can gather together. Students remain in their respective classrooms when the prayer is sung on the mike. It is needless to say that such prayers have hardly any value.

As our society is threatened with the problems of terrorism and religious fanaticism, schools can play a major role in eradicating these negative and destructive values. This is possible by providing rich exposure to all religions and telling the students that no religion teaches bigotry, intolerance and hatred. In fact all religions stand for tolerance and brotherhood. This will save the young minds from the poison of religious intolerance so prevalent these days.

Celebrations of all important festivals like Diwali, Dussehra, Id, and Christmas will expose the students to the richness of our culture and they will learn to appreciate merits of other religions. This may end their feeling of antagonism and animosity and will develop feelings of brotherhood and altruism.

Reading of excerpts of autobiographies and biographies of great persons will also encourage the students to imbibe some of these values among themselves. It will eliminate the feeling of negativity and violence from our kids.

Improving the Conditions of Teachers: It is a fact that teaching is the lowest paid job in our society. Materialistic society thinks that money spent on education does not give enough returns. They forget that teachers are the managers of the most precious resource –human resource. If they remain poorly paid, dissatisfied and dejected lot they cannot uplift the society. It is a common experience that even schools having very good infrastructure are miserly and close fisted when it comes to the payment of their teachers. At primary level a teacher starts with the meagre salary of two thousand five hundred, at the secondary level he starts from four thousand and five hundred consolidated. As this income is hardly sufficient to support a family these days, they start following illegal means like tuitions for which they are hounded and have to remain in the constant state of fear. Such teachers cannot do justice to their profession nor can they produce good citizens. A poor teacher is looked down by the society as a result he proves to be a bad role model for his students .If the society wants that teachers should play an important role in improving the society first they should be given their due.

Changing the Attitude of Children towards One Another: A 1999 CNN article claimed that most US school shootings were by boys who had been teased or rejected by others .After Littleton's Columbine High School shootout in 1999, killing 12students and a teacher, Eric, a friend of the two shooters said "They were tired of those who were insulting them, harassing them. They wanted to stop it .Unfortunately that is exactly what they did." In our country the offenders of Gurgaon incident claimed that they had been bullied by the victim, Abhishek Tyagi. Their initial definition of being bullied was being "poked and pushed around." All parents and teachers need to be a little vigilant towards signs a child is bound to exhibit when he is threatened or humiliated by peers. A reluctance to attend schools, a dropping of interest in friends and studies, sulking without reason and irritability at home are signs of feeling alienated and ostracized. This gives rise to a rage that becomes uncontrollable in time, unless the cycle is broken. It is very important to teach students love and respect each other.

Introducing Value Education as Part of the Curriculum: To inculcate positive values, it is essential that value education is introduced in our schools. Students should be told about common ideals of all religions .They should be also introduced with universal values of Love, Tolerance, Brotherhood Sympathy depicted in all religious scriptures. They should be also given real life examples of such great and saintly figures as Gandhi, Buddha, Vivekanand, Sardar Patel, Mira, Tulsi, Surdas etc.

Making Parent-Teacher Meetings Fruitful: Parent-Teacher meetings should be such a platform where both can share thoughts about the child .There should be free discussion about the child's development, his emotional and personal problems. Teachers and parents should talk cooperatively to solve the problems of the child which are proving a hindrance in his growth.

Conclusion

In this age of rapid industrialization and growing materialism, schools and teachers can play an important role in checking erosion of values and maintaining proper mental health of children provided they may have enough direction, guidance and initiative to deal with these problems. The teachers of the schools should be intimated about this vital responsibility of shaping and directing our future generations. For that we require teachers who have kindness thoughtfulness, creativity, knowledge, great warmth and endearing manner. They should be empathetic, concerned, dedicated, selfless, learned, inspiring, devoted and courageous, compassionate but humble. Our society should also learn to respect the teachers to bring a desirable change in the society. It is rightly said by Chanakya that teachers are not ordinary they have power to create and destroy mighty empires.

References

Chakrabarti, M. 2004, Value Education: Changing Perspectives, New Delhi: Kanishka Publishers.

Gandhi M.K., 1966, My Experiments with Truth .New Delhi: Navjeevan.

Gandhi, M.K. 1956. Basic Education. New Delhi: Navjeevan.

Mukael, J.C. 2003.Gandhian Education. New Delhi: Discovery Publishing House.

Sharma, R.S.2004. The Monk Who Sold His Ferrari. Mumbai: Jaico Publishing House.

Strom and Robert D. 1969. Psychology in the Classroom. New Jersey: Prentice Hall.

Thomas, B. 2004, Moral and Value Education. Jaipur: Avishkar Publishers.

15

Reconstructing School Curriculum

Jignasa Prajapati and Lakshmi Shah

Introduction

The educational process not only has a psychological side involving the educator and the educand it has a sociological aspect also. The educand has to live in and for the society he belongs to. True education comes through the stimulation of the educand's endowments by the demands of the social situation in which he finds himself. The educator is required to stimulate the educand's power in the total social setting. Thus the social aspect of the educational process becomes more important than the psychological one.

What is School Education?

Education refers to the process of qualitative change, which develops those innate specific qualities that enable an individual to lead a full and productive life as a person and as a member of the family and society.

Since Independence our country has made impressive progress in fulfilling its constitutional commitment of providing free and compulsory education to all children up to age of 14 i.e.,8 years of elementary education. Yet the goal of achieving universal elementary education seems to have receded away at a faster pace in spite of the vast efforts of the state, and thus till date has remained out of reach. The target period of ten years that lapsed in 1960 had to be continually shifted from time to time; it would be prudent to focus on the recent initiative of the Government of India, calls the SARVA SHIKSHA ABHIYAN (SSA): an initiative for Universal Elementary Education.

It should not be found surprising that because of the heterogeneity of conditions of school education in the different states there is neither uniformity in the structure of elementary school stage nor in the curriculum.

Improvement in quality of education in schools would be major objective for the next decade. A number of steps to improve quality of students have been taken. While good progress has been achieved in extending the facility of school education to all villages in Gujarat, the quality of education imparted in many school remains different.

Now days, educational and social demands have changed. A large number of children dropout of the school because of the school environment: like teacher's attitude, irrelevant curriculum, sub-standard and uninteresting teaching, teacher absenteeism, corporal punishment, poor school infrastructure, inability cope with the pace of learning, lack of parental support in the case of first generation learners, maladjustment etc. In this context, school curriculum has to be more social need-based.

About Curriculum

Curriculum deals with all meaningful real life problems of situation, which seem important for children to solve and hence covers a wide area of learning.

Curriculum can be defined as follows: "All the activities and experience in which pupil engage under the direction of the school to achieve the objective of the school."

Irrelevant Curriculum: An Irrelevant curriculum exists in schools today. The Curriculum is full of bias and errors, so people are dissatisfied with the school curriculum. Causes of dissatisfaction with existing school curriculum are mentioned below:

Recent years have witnessed a great increase in the amount of knowledge in every sphere of activity. The existing curriculum appears to be inadequate.

A rapid advancement in sciences has widened the gulf

between what is taught in school and universities. School curriculum hardly fits the school leavers for university education.

There is no provision for practical activities: rote learning and achievement of bookish knowledge are the order of the day. Useful skills are not developed. The right kind of interests, attitude and values are not emphasized. The result is that the curriculum does not make the person fit for efficient living.

There is a rethinking in educational circles regarding the nature and duration of school education. It is generally accepted that specialization should be postponed to a later period and the general education should be given.

Curriculum Full of Bias and Errors: In today's Gujarat, the textbook continues to be a medium that is subversively used to mould children's minds according to a popular ideology. Even a cursory glance of the textbooks suffices to confirm that it is full of provocative statements, slants that idolize freedom fighters who used violent methods to fight imperialism, and crude suggestions about population control and terrorism

An ongoing study of textbooks in four states in the country, Gujarat, Uttar Pradesh, Tamil Nadu and West Bengal, conducted by the Delhi-based non-government organisation (NGO) Nirantar, a resource centre for gender and education, highlights the stereotypes and biases in the Gujarat textbooks. The study is expected to be released in April this year, but initial findings, among other things, suggest that Indian tradition and culture is "depicted as Hindu in essence and practice" in the state's textbooks. An abstract of the Gujarat leg of the study says, "Present-day anxieties about identity, culture and the threats to these posed by modernity and global cultural influences surface repeatedly, and traditional practices, values and 'the wisdom of our ancient sages are emphasized as bulwark against, and antidote to, the ills of unchecked modernity."

Consider this: the Social Studies textbook for standard five has nine stories on mythology masquerading as history. One such lesson is about Appala, the well-behaved and obedient daughter of a sage whose married life suffers as the result of a skin ailment. The tale describes how the Sun God, pleased with her devotion, heals her. At the end of the chapter are suggested exercises for children that include: 'like Appala, name five daughters of sages' and a discussion about how 'the sun is not just a ball of fire but has special powers'. Later in the book, the children are encouraged to dramatize scenes from the Hindu epics Ramayana and the Mahabharata.

The abstract of the Gujarat section of Nirantar's study also notes that in "recent editions of Social Studies books, a close association is made between terrorism and Muslim identity". In history textbooks, Muslims are first identified as "outsiders", adds the abstract. Aurangzeb, for instance, is consistently depicted as a Muslim ruler who was intolerant of other faiths. As a teacher at an Urdu school in Ahmedabad's Old City area, who requested anonymity, points out, "Whenever Aurangzeb is mentioned, he is always portrayed as an intolerant Muslim ruler, and his faith is directly linked to his intolerance." For good measure, the textbook also has the story of Hindu soldiers who derived special powers while fighting Aurangzeb with the help of sacred Gangajal (water).

Even question papers are used as arenas from where communal bias can be taught. As recently as in August last year, a question paper in the Gujarat Public Service Commission examination for Ayurvedic medical officers had queries that included ones such as the following: "Which day is observed as 'Black day' by minorities and 'Victory day' by the Sangh Parivar?" The choice given is: "September 11, January 26, July 2 and December 6." The last option was the day the Babri Masjid in Ayodhya was demolished, an event that was followed by communal violence in several parts of the country.

No Place for the Mahatma

Apart from concentrating on Hindu stories and customs, the textbooks also reflect the government's preferences in the way it idolizes revolutionaries who fought for India's freedom. Nirantar's abstract has this to say about the subject: "While Gandhi emerges as the moral educator of the nation, embodying religious/moral virtue and spiritual strength, his role in positing a viable alternative to that of power and violence is not emphasized. Overall, aggressive nationalism is promoted as a model of anti-colonial resistance, as well as against terrorism in recent times."

If revolutionaries earn considerable column space in the textbooks, it is merely a reflection of the way the majority community perceives the Mahatma in his own home state. Achyut Yagnik, activist and co-author of the book The Shaping of Modern Gujarat (Plurality, Hindutva and Beyond), points out that an anti-Gandhi sentiment is being whipped up across Gujarat. Certain sects, which hold considerable influence over the Gujarati society, are against Gandhi because of his philosophy of non-violence. Population, terrorism and other issues

The textbooks echo 'population concerns'. The population growth has been considered a "national crisis", and suggestions have been made that newly married couples take a pledge not to have children before they are 25 and after they are 30. Textbooks in various standards devote paragraphs on the problem of population explosion, calling better healthcare and widow remarriages as reasons for this. The standard nine Social Science textbook, for instance, has a chapter on population, which goes thus: "The birth rate has gone higher during three decades due to several reasons, such as high level of illiteracy, child marriage, encouragement for widow remarriage, agrarian economy, ineffective attempts to reduce birth-rate, social taboos, and poverty etc."

Desirable Principles of Curriculum

Child-centred: The curriculum is based on the interests, needs and capacities of the children.

Catering to the Social Needs: The curriculum should be related to community needs. It should be based on forward looking and creative principle. It should be relevant to nation's callings and requirements.

Catering to Individual Differences: Another requirement of the curriculum is that it should cater to individual differences. It should be adaptable to individuals and that is why diversified curricula are provided to cater to individual variations.

Flexibility: The curriculum should not be rigid and fixed. It should be modified taking into consideration the special needs of the nation and also according to the changing times. In other words, it is important that the curriculum should be dynamic.

Emphasis on Cooperative Endeavour: This is vital significance in democracy. Though proper curriculum the pupils may be provided with purposeful experiences.

Continuity and Integration: The curriculum should provide continuous and cumulative experiences. There should be perfect articulation from one experience to another, from the home to the school and from one subject to other subjects. All subjects should be integrated and coordinated. Thus the curriculum should be comprehensive, articulated and continuous.

The curriculum should be so integrated that it results in an integrated personality. The whole range of educational experiences will have to be considered as a Gestalt. By "Gestalt" we mean a configuration or a pattern. Compartmentalization of subject matter is not a healthy feature. Different subjects should be correlated and integrated.

Suggestions to Reconstruct School Curriculum

The following may upgrade and reform school curriculum:

- One of the principles of curriculum-construction in the principle of flexibility. It should be flexible and dynamic. Flexibility can come through a research in curriculum – development. This research should be undertaken by University Departments of Education, State Institutes of Education, Teachers Training Colleges and Boards of Secondary School Education. Not only is there an urgent need for revision of curricular content through research, but preparation of textbooks, teaching aids and learning materials also needs research and reform.
- The curriculum is not uniform for all pupils in all states of the country. To remove this, advanced courses may be offered in various subjects like advanced course offered in mathematics, sciences and languages. Advanced courses should be provided in all specialized subject.
- Experimental schools controlled by universities and guided by training colleges should at once adopt the revised curriculum
- The state boards of education should prepare advanced curriculum in all specialized subjects and introduce them in schools in a phased manner.
- The curriculum for first 10 years of schooling should be general and only after those courses should be diversified.
- A programme of work experience should be made an integral part of education at all stages from, the primary to the secondary, so that the extremely bookish character of school education may be changed.
- Arrangement should be made for the education in social, moral and spiritual values through direct and indirect methods by assigning two periods per week in the school timetable.
- There is no need of differentiating curriculum for boys and girls.

16

Quality Concerns in School Education

Vaya Bharat K. and Purohit Om Prakash M.

Introduction

India as a signatory to the World Declaration on Basic Education made in Jomtein more than eight years ago, agreed to achieve the target of Universalization of primary education by the year 2000. Yet, the goal has remained elusive, despite the fact that there is a primary school within 1.5 kilometres for children in 95 percent of the villages. Studies have revealed that Universalization of basic education cannot be achieved without addressing the issue of cultural and socio-economic barriers. Interestingly, the results of a survey conducted by the National Sample Survey Organization (1992) revealed that school-related factors are responsible for at least 22-25 percent of non-participation of children in primary schooling. The issue of bringing all children to school cannot be tackled with the single point proposition of opening more schools. The problem has deeper roots in the socio-cultural and economic conditions of the people. Moreover, the problem of quantitative coverage cannot be solved in isolation without paying adequate attention to improving school quality.

There are some issues in the way of improving quality of school which is described below.

Problem of Slow Growth of Post-primary Education

Statistics indicate that the rate of growth of schooling beyond the lower primary stage is low. The ratio of upper primary to lower primary schools in most part of the country is still around 1:4, as against the official commitment of making it 1:2. The ratio of secondary to primary schools is around 1:6.

This is far from the norms achieved in the developed world or even with the situation in many developing countries. In India, the Gross Enrolment Ratio (GER) for the secondary stage is only 48 percent, while the figure for China is as high as 66 percent; in the developed regions of the world, secondary education has been fully universalized. While improved provision of primary education facilities in the country has to be tackled on a priority basis, it may not prove to be effective if steps are not simultaneously taken to meet the demand for further education.

Stalling the Social Divide

Low efficiency and effectiveness of the public schooling system, coupled with inadequate financial resource allocation has tended to push more and more people to seek even primary education through privately managed institutions. May one rationalize this trend as positive, as it helps to reduce dependence of those who can afford to pay on the government institutions? However, there is no reason to believe that people are voluntarily moving away from the public system which is free, towards private education. It is important to note that this trend is likely to lead to further increase in inequity.

Bridging the Male-Female Disparity

Recent statistics show that even though GER for girls has risen to more than 90 percent at the primary stage, it has remained practically static around 50 percent at the upper primary stage for the last several years. In fact, even at the primary stage, the male-female disparity remains not fully bridged. School education has to address this issue by designing special strategies to overcome the barriers and bridge the gap between boys and girls on a priority basis.

Vocationalize or Not to Vocationalize

It is a well-known fact that millions of children in the country are forced to enter the labour market instead of pursuing education in the schools. Even among those who begin attending the school, a large number as indicated by high dropout rates and low transition rates, enter the workforce at a very early stage of life. It is in this context that the school curriculum that remains academic in nature has come under repeated criticism for not being able to add any value to the lives of such children and rather making education a drudgery and burden. Notwithstanding deliberations by several Committees and Commissions, we have yet to establish a meaningful structure of schooling which can benefit both streams of students—those who terminate at elementary or secondary stage and those who continue their education to the tertiary level.

Linking School Education with Changing Scenario

School education cannot be impervious to the fast changes taking place in the economic sector through liberalization and globalization of the market. Demands on the school, particularly with regard to those who enter the production sector straight from the school are two-fold. On one hand, school education, particularly at the secondary stage has to keep pace with the needs of a competitive market, dependent on continuously improved knowledge and skill levels. On the other hand, school education has to recognize that the liberalized market framework directly affects the micro-economics of the poorer sections of the population, often corroding their fragile occupational base.

The school education system has to become pro-active in preparing the curriculum and processes not only as a matter of social concern, but also to meet the basic needs of those entering the emerging economic framework.

Interface with Technology

Information Technology (IT) presents an excellent opportunity for making a quantum jump in the provision of school education in a need-based manner. Unfortunately, very little attention has been given in the country for exploring the tremendous potential of IT in school education, both for its quantitative expansion and for improving its quality. It is, therefore, urgent that immediate attention is given in school education to imparting basic IT skills to all learners. Learning from the past efforts, it is important that adequate provisions are made for development of software and capacity-building for teachers in order that it does not remain only as an additional skill to the existing subject areas, but becomes an integral part of the learning experience of all children.

Quality is the Heart of the Matter

Examination statistics show that about 60 percent of children routinely fail in the public examination conducted at the end of the secondary school; and of those who succeed and join higher secondary; only 40 percent succeed in the higher secondary examination. Curriculum reforms, examination reforms and large scale efforts for introducing progressive pedagogy and so on, are being made in almost all the states. However, given the large size of the school education system, these system level reforms seem to be making very little impact on the functioning of the school. Direct actions for changing the functioning of people and institutions operating at the grassroots level have not received adequate attention.

The situation demands a total reversal of perspective so that school occupies the centre stage and improvement in the quality of the school becomes the major agenda of all reform processes.

Alternatives and Plural Avenues

Non-suitability of a standardized model of full-time formal schooling to create a universal mass education system in the country was emphatically pointed out by Mahatma Gandhi much before we embarked on the task, fifty years ago. It is now fully realized that a monolithic approach to delivery of school education cannot meet the legitimate demands of the people for provision of educational facilities of a reasonably acceptable quality. Yet, it has been difficult to break the monopolistic hold of full-time formal schooling on the education system. Interestingly, society has begun adjusting its expectations to the limitations of formal schooling, instead of more actively pursuing the task of designing alternatives.

Strategies

Elaboration of issues and problems of school education confronting the country should not be construed to imply that we are saddled with an impossible situation. Rather, it points to the need for acting with a sense of purpose and determination. What are the priority areas in which well-planned action holds promise for taking the school education system in a progressive direction? Some of these strategies are indicated below.

Liberalizing the Curriculum Framework

An important area that needs immediate attention is the introduction of a flexible and dynamic curriculum framework that meets the varying needs and aspirations of the diverse profiles of children entering school education. This is essential, if school education is to be made more joyful and relevant to the lives of the people. Actions have to be initiated, therefore, to avoid increased standardization of the curriculum and allow for more decentralization. This again requires curriculum development to be a participatory endeavour of the direct stakeholders replacing the high bureaucratization that characterizes the current scene.

Breaking the Monopoly of Full Time Formal School

Creating an institutional framework of delivery and organizing the inputs in meaningful learning units are relevant only to the extent that they facilitate easy and effective transaction of learning processes. But, when the format of organization begins determining and delimiting the nature and scope of education, alternative means have to be sought, in order to effectively pursue the basic purposes of organized education. In the current state of development of school education in India, this seems to be a matter for priority action.

It is not that no effort has been made in this direction, in India. Yet, one can easily see that a monolithic set- up of age-grade organization in hierarchical learning units has become the predominant means. The monopoly of this dominant mode is so powerful as to seriously jeopardize the emergence of a pluralistic framework through apparently innocuous instruments such as equivalence, comparable learning inputs, comparable length of learning, common public examinations and so on.

Harnessing Advances in Information Technology

In India, use of technology has invariably been identified with prosperity and affluence. With the relatively under-endowed state of the public education system, technology is seen as an alien element, which has no place in the school education programme. This perspective has failed to fully grasp the potential of technology to overcome some of the very barriers arising out of inadequate resources. It is important to take positive steps for building a more meaningful interface between modern developments in the field of information technology and school education programmes.

Conclusion

We have a very large army of scientifically trained manpower; we also have, perhaps, the largest number of illiterates. As many scholars have pointed out, we seem to be unwittingly nurturing a fractured system of school education. One part of the system is keeping pace with the most advanced systems of the world and the other, which serves the poorer and disempowered sections of the society, is remaining inefficient to reach out effectively and provide meaningful education.

The challenge is to invest more energy and resources to improve the system, both in its outreach capacity and quality. We have to act on this with a sense of urgency and earnestness, lest education itself becomes a means of promoting social inequality and a source of increasing chasm between those who can pay for their education and those who cannot. It is not enough to merely proliferate input-oriented programmes. It is necessary to strategize actions so as to make real improvement in the lives of the people.

References

Daswani, C.J. (1996). Total Literacy Campaign in India: Status and Issues. Paper read at World Literacy Conference. Philadelphia.

Govinda, R. and Varghese, N.V. (1993): Quality of Primary Schooling in India: A Case Study of Madhya Pradesh. International Institute of Educational Planning / UNESCO, Paris and National Institute of Educational Planning and Administration, New Delhi.

Manjrekar, N. (2003): 'Contemporary Challenges to Women's Education: towards an elusive goal', Economic and Political Weekly 38(4), pp. 4577-4582.

PROBE (1999). Public Report on Basic Education in India. The PROBE team in Association with Centre for Development Economics. New Delhi, Oxford University Press.

Ramachandran, V. (2002) Gender and Social Equity in Primary Education: Hierarchies of Access. New Delhi: The European Commission.

17

Some Student-Teacher Related Issues in Practical Learning Situation

Anitha Shetty

Schools should begin to see the children as butterflies to be nurtured and developed instead of empty pots to be filled, help our children to become idea producers, instead of idea consumers. All educators training to be trained to manage children without coercion. Parents and educators should realize that formal schooling should only start at the age of six years. Parents should be made to realize, from time to time that the modern living is causing our children to suffer countless maladies. Cognitive learning conditions are reaching epidemic proportions that our education system cannot cope with. We should have an education system which will act as a catalyst which inspires one to follow one's dreams.

The new age education system should endow with an analytical bent of mind. It should strike a perfect balance between academic and professional education. The syllabi should have life based education. Adding or deleting content from text book is not enough. We need to identify skills, talents and aptitude in a child and then help the child to develop the potential he/she possesses. Being able to distinguish between positive and negative aspects is more pertinent for a growing citizen.

Personality development is an important aspect in the modern society. It aims at an over all positive expression of an individual for a very dynamic living in the society. Here are a few issues which are commonly experienced in day to day teaching learning process.

Student-Academic Related Issues

1. Acquisition of basic skills in reading and number work..
2. Acceptance of normal standards of behaviour.
3. Co-operated living..
4. Lacking self-expression.
5. Destructive mentality.
6. Non- attentive and les receptive to learning experiences.
7. Intellectual skills–Knowing how and why, rather than knowing.
8. Cognitive strategies: the ways in which pupil is able to control and manage the mental processes involved in learning including strategies for attending, thinking, memorizing and dealing with novel problems.
9. Attitude: An attitude can be described as pupil's feelings towards some particular object or idea. Conflict in developing a positive attitude is felt in the school today.
10. Due to the pressures of heavy syllabus, lack of motor skills.

Social Issues

1. Contradiction in value system.
2. Exposure to negativism and violence in the media.
3. No "WE" feeling, self is always highlighted.
4. Not sensitive to others nature, heritage and other societal properties and issues.
5. Diminished social belongingness.
6. Lacks co–operated/co–related existence.
7. Lacks general awareness.

Teacher: Academic Related Issues

1. Clarity of teacher's explanations and directions.
2. Establishing a task oriented classroom climate.
3. Making use of a variety of learning activities.
4. Getting all pupils involved and encouraging pupil participation.
5. Monitoring pupil's progress and attending quickly to

pupil's needs.
6. Delivering a well structured and well organized lesson.
7. Providing with pupils with positive and constructive feed back.
8. Ensuring coverage of learning objectives.
9. Helping pupils to contextualize the content in terms of their own experience and knowledge.
10. Willingness of the teacher to modify the learning in the light of pupil circumstances.
11. Teacher's enthusiasm.
12. Management strategies–Human/Physical/Time.
13. Disciplinary techniques.
14. Providing a supportive social context for learning.

Social Issues

1. Co-related existence is diminishing.
2. Lack of awareness.
3. Water tight compartmentalization of teaching linking.
4. Past- present-future.
5. Learning to real life situations.
6. Academics to spiritual to self.
7. Discussion on social issues is lacking.

Concerns

1. Structured reading and writing tasks.
2. Individualized programs of work.
3. Small group work.
4. Experiential learning.
5. Constant monitoring.
6. Monitoring Individual well-being of each pupil:

- Academic progress.
- General behaviour and attitudes.
- Personal and social developments.
- Individual needs.

7. Skill development:

- Communication.

- Numerical skill.
- Study and problem solving.
- Personal and social skills.
- Information and Technology.

8. In house professional enhancement sessions.

There is a need for such a combination of head, heart and hand. For self improvement, an individual has to build a solid foundation for life with goal-setting, time management, building self-esteem, mental discipline, interpersonal relations, communication skills, leadership skills, creativity, and conflict resolving skills. These are nothing but "Life Skill".

In the words of Swami Vivekananda "personality development is self improvement, which can really help one to raise height in life especially if one is down and out." According to him an individual should be harmoniously developed, great in heart, great in mind, great in deed. A person's heart should feel intensely for the world. The person should not only feel but should also find the meaning of things, by delving deeply into the heart of nature and understanding. Also the person should work out the feeling and meaning by actual deeds.

Our educational system predominantly focuses on hard skills rather than soft skills. It is very essential to reform this to help both the teachers and students acquire the soft skills. Reforming our education system means changing our concept of education, rather than simply modernizing schools and buying more equipment. In view of their importance soft skills should be part and parcel of any course curriculum.

These life skills focus on helping young people develop positive social behaviours, establish commitments to their families, schools, peers and commitment to lead healthy, drug free lives.

Young Adult: Adolescent Age

During early adolescence, young children experience rapid physical, social and emotional growth and development while navigating a complex society under going its won dramatic shift in social norms and structures. The pressures of a rapidly changing society are taking their toll on schools, families and other institutions that formerly helped ensure the healthy growth and development of young people. Statistics indicate that, without this support, young children are increasingly at risk for problem behaviour.

Peter Scale warns in his report from the 'Centre for Early Adolescence', "A portrait of young adolescents'. "All the trends points to a growing number and proportion of young adolescents who are in fact at high risk of being unprepared and unsuccessful in the modern social economic world" (Scale 1991).

News paper survey shows

- Children of 10-17 year olds becoming delinquents, abusing drugs or becoming adolescent parents.
- By the age of 15-18 adolescents try alcohol and tobacco.
- Children are sexually active by the age 15, use contraceptives, practice homo/hetero sexual acts.
- Suicides rate increase because of pressure.
- Malpractice, forgery and robbery at all levels have been increasing.
- Unable to with stand stress due to peer pressure. Examination and social demand.
- Lack of motivation to born.
- Lack of self discipline.

This gives a very gleam picture of the future work force. Though energetic and highly talented, these young adults will enter the work force unprepared with the academic or social skills they need to be successful. In turn society will have to bear the costs for lost productivity, additional training and financial support for those who can not support themselves. Adolescents are vital and valuable resource. Their potentials are to be recognized and canalized properly. It is essential to develop effective thinking and social skills in children engage in positive social behaviours. They strengthen their bonds with their families, schools and communities.

In today's uncertain economic times, the person who has the ability to interact and connect with peoples is likely to be the one who will succeed. For an individual, the importance and value of soft skills, though hard to quantity, are immeasurable. Dealing with difficult peers, learning to be a team player, negotiating with people, ability to listen and solve problems etc. are some of the examples of life skills.

Life Skills are Important

- To handle interpersonal relations.
- To take appropriate decisions.
- To communicate effectively.
- To have good impression and impact.
- To gain professional development.

Relationships play a vita role in human life and one of the keys to successful relationships is development of soft skills. Soft skills can enhance the career mobility of a person and increase the chances of success in landing the one wants. They are essential for a student teacher to develop so that she/he can cope with different situations in the study/work place. A continuous renewal of soft skills through teaching and training of the teachers is essential. This will make their dealings effective and successful.

Conclusion

Education for a Better World: The main purpose of education is to help prepare people to live a better individual life and also to contribute to the improvement of wider society.

Fundamental Dilemmas in Education

First Dilemma: Teacher needs to be able to find some sort of balance or at last a reasonable understanding of the difference between duties and rights. What are students expected to learn, to do what they should do or to claim what is rightly theirs. Teaching for a better world is difficult but it is possible to work from a conceptual base that makes sense.

Second Dilemma: A second dilemma is concerned with the sort of teaching that should be practiced. Education needs to aim for learners to develop conceptual understanding and relevant skills as opposed to seeking to know more about specific cases.

Third Dilemma: The third fundamental dilemma relates more obviously than the points made above, to expectations for student behaviour now and in the future. Are learners expected to participate in society or to abstain?

Fourth Dilemma: The final dilemma goes to the very heart of the educational process is it possible to see society in coherent single framework or are we witnessing such extensive fragmentation of political agendas that a talk of education for a better world is unhelpful? The real nature of globalization is unclear but the numbers of references that are made to the decline of the power of the state are extensive. Teachers should feel confident about their role in society. They are burdened with goals that seem impossible to achieve but they can and must make a difference. We need to train the future teachers who are 'Humane'.

Be definite – "I know what I want.

Be calm and consistent – "I'm always polite and fair to you."

Be positive – "You're doing great."

Give them structure – "I know where we're going."

Part II
Innovations in School Education

18

Quality Enhancement in Secondary Teaching through Students' Feedback

S. Kumar, R.C. Patel and A. Ramachary

Introduction

Quality in education, the focus of contemporary interest of all, understandably concerns with teacher effectiveness. Teacher effectiveness is an issue that has received increased attention in recent years (Muijs, 2006). Teachers are expected to motivate, inspire, explain, engage, understand, and guide the students, for their all round development. Teachers need to motivate the students towards content, concepts, attitudes, values, knowledge and skills, under the set frame of pre-determined goals. Guiding and nurturing students' talents, abilities and values through pre-determined content transmission are the assigned responsibility of teachers. Teachers are expected to possess professional proficiency, educational efficiency and social sufficiency. Pre-service and in-service trainings, orientation programs continuously aim to provide required professional support to teachers, with a view to update, up-grade their knowledge, understanding and skills for efficient performance. Young generation students look out for role models and true inspirers in teachers. This is irrespective of what subject they teach, but how they teach and interact with them.

Primary and significant role of teaching a subject is very important, which also includes periodic evaluation. Teachers welcome and get rejuvenated, when their students respond respectfully and affectionately acknowledge teacher's efforts. This users' feedback automatically justifies the relevance, effectiveness and utility of students' evaluating response on teacher's performance. Teachers, desirous of knowing their professional merits also deserve to be aware of their performance rating for further growth in their professional endeavours. Considering that the consumer is the comprehensive and complementing judge, the students' evaluating response remains a vital acknowledgement in true evaluation of teacher's performance. Accordingly, this ensures teacher's greater vigilance, relevance and competency in their professional performance.

Further, educational administrators, policy makers, managerial authorities, researchers and all those working in the field of education require teacher's ratings for varied uses; like deciding promotions and transfers, assigning various tasks depending upon one's proficiency, etc. Feedback mechanism built into the secondary level teaching is likely to serve the positive and constructive role in enhancing the quality of teaching. Predetermined and prescribed curricular content evolved with set educational objectives offered to the teacher are imparted to the students through classroom teaching. Teacher's evaluation of student's performance (TESP) is built into the existing system and goes on periodically. Missing element in the existing system is the user's evaluation. That is student's evaluation of classroom teaching (SECT). This feedback element, when implemented, has the potential to enrich the teacher's competence and promote the quality in education.

Evaluation of Teachers by Students

Literature also provides alternate opinions of the student's evaluation of their teachers. Orpen's (1982) study on 630 students at medical school, evaluating 18 teachers reveals that students can distinguish between effective and ineffective lecturers. But, Spooren and Mortelmans (2006) observe: "Although student evaluations of teachers are implemented in many faculties, not every one is convinced of desirability and utility of ratings. The use of student's evaluation of teaching performance has been an important but controversial tool in the improvement of teaching quality during past few decades". On the other hand one may raise the question, how can we really evaluate teacher effectiveness? Based on international research Campbell et. al. (2004) argues that the teacher effectiveness is too narrowly conceptualized and methods of measuring it are not attuned to real contexts in which teachers work. In this regard, considering the complexity of teacher effectiveness, they proposed following three distinct aspects for comprehensive measurement of teacher effectiveness:

- Teachers may be more effective with some categories of students than with others
- Teachers may be more effective with some teaching contexts than others
- Teachers may be more effective with some subjects/components than with others.

Pimpa (2005) examined the problems related to the national teacher performance appraisal system by the Thai Ministry of Education. The findings indicate problems to three major types; problems from the mismanagement of the system; problems arising from the evaluators; and problems arising from the applicants. These problems are the major constraints in accelerating education devolution and development. On the other hand, Ministry of Education, Ontario, Canada (2007) follows teacher performance appraisal system separately one for new teachers and the other one for experienced teachers. The appraisal process for new teachers is designed to strengthen schools as learning communities. It provides a framework to encourage improvement efforts aimed at promoting student success.

Throughout the performance appraisal process, new teacher's skills, knowledge and attitudes are assessed; strengths and areas for growth identified, and next steps for improvement are planned, thereby informing the induction process. A new teacher must have two appraisals in his or her first 12 months of teaching. Teacher performance appraisal system for experienced teachers is designed to foster teacher development, provide meaningful appraisals that encourage professional learning and growth and identify opportunities for additional support where ever required. Revised appraisal process is implemented from April 2007. In Indian context, one needs to consider the volume. There are little more than 5.95 lakh secondary teachers in urban settings alone, with an average Teacher Pupil Ratio of 25 (NCERT, 2007). One can imagine the effort for measuring teacher effectiveness.

The debate on the uni-dimentionality versus multi-dimensionality of students' ratings of teaching performance, and the relationship of this dilemma to summative and formative uses of these instruments is reviewed, with special attention to the implications of their development and application in the Spanish University System by Pedro Apodaca and Hector Grad (2005). A comprehensive theoretical framework, stressing the relation between effective teaching theory and the expected construct of teaching performance in student's view, is advanced.

The discussion placed above brings out an imperative that there is a critical requirement of evaluating the teacher effectiveness, which has a potential to offer feedback from the students for some constructive interference. Students, who face, interact and experience the teachers, get affected by the efficiency of teacher's performance. This adds relevancy and aptness for rating of teachers by their students. Recognition and praise of their teachers by students make teachers happy and positively motivated. Likewise the lapses, if any, brought out by the student evaluators may act as the basis for in-service teacher training programmes, refresher courses, orientation courses to enhance the proficiency of the teachers. A continuous effort to develop, monitor and improve the teachers rating instruments remains a welcome need for quality improvement in education. Despite the acute relevance and need of measuring the teacher effectiveness, one may not find many tools to measure the teacher effectiveness, by their students. This necessitates the development of one such reliable tool to measure the teacher effectiveness, by their students. Accordingly an effort was made to develop a reliable tool, namely (PASTBTS); Performance Appraisal of School Teachers by Their Students. The tool having 20 statements was developed by focusing on the following major acts of teacher in the classroom:

- Motivating students with due understanding of their levels and needs.
- Authority on subject knowledge and the ability to explain clearly.
- Awarding of regular assignments to students and honest evaluation.
- Using appropriate teaching aids.
- Over all personality of the teacher, including punctuality.

Norms for Evaluating Performance of Teachers

Norms were also developed for evaluating the performance of teachers on different statements. For this purpose, average performance of the teachers was calculated for all the statements, for statement 1 to 20, as rated by 5370 students. Average performance of teachers on different aspects was calculated. It is also possible to find the deficiencies, if any, in the teachers, for professional up-gradation, using the scores obtained on PASTBS, for any particular aspect as contained in the twenty statements of the tool. This, not only helps the teachers to identify their areas of improvement needs, but also for the purpose of enlisting the teacher training needs, for further professional improvement.

A reliable scale for the Performance appraisal of School Teachers by Their Students (PASTBTS) was developed along with the norms, depicted in percentiles. This is done both subject wise and for total scores, for CBSE as well as for State Board Teachers. Categorization of teachers, based on the norms defined on percentiles was thus suggested.

Conclusion

The Indian society placed the teacher at a very high level. It is the teacher who comes after mother and father in the life of a student and thus epitomized as "Acharya Devo Bhava". Commanding such a respectable position in the society by a teacher was possible through sheer dedication and hard work done by the teacher, for the best development of their student. This view of the students towards their teacher placed teachers at par with the ultimate God, as "Guru Devo Maheshwara". The role of teacher, in essence, remained as high as mentioned above, in terms of the expectations from the teachers. However, the changes in society do not permit ancient conditions to continue to exist. Every aspect of life, when changed drastically, expecting ancient standards of dedication and methods of grooming the students remains unrealistic. Yet, teachers, being the important influencers and designers of student's personality and destiny, in a broader sense, are expected to be more and more vigilant of their professional responsibilities. This is more significant at school level, owing to the formative and foundational action that occurs at this stage. Further, the multi-tasking function of today's teacher also calls for multi-ability enhancement from time to time. This augments for identification of professional needs, which necessitates the teacher's performance evaluation.

The teacher, who are cognizant of their key responsibilities always aim to be aware of their own efficiencies and deficiencies. The teacher, accordingly, attempts to enrich and enhance professional efficiencies and also makes an effort to decrease and overcome the deficiencies, from time to time, for a better quality. As John Ruskin puts it, quality is never an accident. It is always the result of intelligent effort. It is the will to produce a superior thing. This process, an effort for better quality obviously, remains continuous and non-terminating. In fact summer courses, refresher courses, in-service courses of teachers are an effort in this direction. It remains a pertinent question, how do we identify the true areas of enrichment programs for school teachers?

The correct identification of relevant training needs of school teachers, from time to time, naturally becomes a very important professional requirement for teachers, educational administrators, policy makers and training institutions etc. Laying out the relevant criteria for teacher evaluation and opting for effective evaluators become subsequent and pertinent questions. Considering the notion that the users are the best judges, one may prefer to seek the rating of teacher's performance by their students. The students, being the immediate and continuous respondents involved in the teaching – learning process, are likely to offer more relevant and useful rating response about their teachers. Besides, teachers, too, are likely to feel encouraged in getting the benefits of their own student's ratings, similar to that of parents getting an affectionate response from their children for any further improvement in the common endeavours. This leads to the identification of problem of present study.

A reliable, useful and handy rating scale, "Performance Appraisal of School teachers by Their Students (PASTBTS)" is developed successfully. This rating scale can help the teachers in knowing their professional position at any given time, as assessed by their own students. Norm based ready reckoner developed in this study offers due help for relative professional positioning of teachers by their own students. Such a rating scale when used judiciously can help the teachers to upgrade, update and enrich their professional competencies, assuring quality and ensuring respect. Further, educational administrators, policy makers, managers may derive the benefit from this educational endeavour.

In conclusion one can realize that with the policies and programmes together with the societal support at hand, following the prescribed curriculum and making the best use of resources available students may get the desired quality education. However, this is possible when key manipulators like, clarity of objectives, efficient pedagogical practices, supported by efficient feedback mechanisms. Further, the feedback mechanism essentially needs to be two ways, i.e. together with the existing TESP; there is clear need of SECT, as discussed above. Such a balanced and completed circuitry ensures better quality education, as it integrates feedback from the affected (student) to affecter (Teacher). Feedback from student, in turn requires a well developed and dependable performance appraisal, which is offered here for its constructive use.

References

Apodaca., P.and Hector, G.(2005). The dimensionality of student ratings of teachings: integration of uni-and multi-dimensional models. Studies in Higher Education, Vol.30(6), p. 723-748.

Campbell., J. Kyriakides., L Mujis., D. Robinson, W. (2004). 10-Differentiated teacher effectiveness and teacher appraisal. Assessing Teacher Effectiveness, Vol.1, Part 4, p.125-135.

Kumar S. (2001). Development of Scale for Rating Teaching Performance of the University Teachers by their Students. Centre for Advanced Studies in Education, The Maharaja Sayyaji Rao University of Baroda, Vadodara.

Ministry of Education, Ontario, Canada (2007). Website. www.edu.gov.on.ca , 19th April 2007.

Mujis, D. (2006). Measuring teacher effectiveness: Some methodological reflections. Educational research and Evaluation, Vol. 12(1), p.53-74.

NCERT (2007). Seventh Educational survey. Web site: www.ncert.nic.in

Orpen, C. (1982). Student Evaluation of Effective and Ineffective Lecturers: A Validity Study. Journal of Further and higher Education, Vol.6 (2), p.54-62.

Pimpa, N. (2005). TPA in Thailand: Poison or Panacea? Educational research for policy and practice, Springer, Netherlands, Vol.4(2-3), p.115-127.

Spooren., S.and Mortelman, D. (2006). Teacher professionalism and student evaluation of teaching: Will better Teachers receive higher ratings and will better students give higher ratings? Educational Studies, Vol.32 (2), p. 201-214.

19

Value Inculcation in Teaching of Mathematics

Sujata Srivastava and Vishal Mohandas

Introduction

Since Independence, the education system in the country has expanded very rapidly. As a result of quick economic growth, influence of western culture, over mechanization, urbanization, craving for materialistic life and media explosion there has been a loss of values and the value system in the individual and in the country as a whole. This rapid decline of values is leading to a society which is steadily disintegrating. There are many scandals related to sex, there are many crimes committed by the youth. Violence, robbery and kidnapping seem to be the order of the day. The Education Commission (1964-66), the National Policy on Education (1986) and the Ramamurthy Committee (1990) recommended that imparting of value education should be an integral part of the entire educational process. In spite of these recommendations, value education is hardly visible in the State schools. Rajput (2000) remarked that values of kindness, character, achieving the ideal, service to humanity, fearlessness, purity in personal life, freedom from lust and quest for truth have been lost somewhere in the search of materialistic gains. He further adds that self-control, humility and selfless service find practically no space in school curricula. National Curriculum Framework (2005) has laid a major focus on Peace education at the school level.

Value education need not always be confined to a particular programme or course in the syllabi but an innovative integrated approach can be used where the teachers can inculcate the values through teaching various subjects. The Integrated Approach is a process by which values can be spontaneously incorporated into the various subjects of the curriculum and taught. The values are appropriately incorporated in the subjects for the students to appreciate and imbibe the practical applications of values in their day to day living. The subject of Mathematics has its own unique nature and objectives. It is a logical discipline; however value-based situations can be used to explain different Mathematical concepts. Mathematics is a subject which is well known for developing better cognitive aspect of human through its problem solving techniques and logic related concepts. These concepts can be very useful for proper inculcation of values. A process of teaching can be adopted where values can be incorporated into the context of Mathematics. Different values can be developed in students through the teaching of Mathematics.

Various researches have been undertaken in the area of value education. Kar (1985) concluded in his study that there is often dissatisfaction with education in India and elsewhere, because it lacks the provision for education in values in general and moral and specific values in particular. This is supported by Dubey (1991) who found that socially accepted values are missing from the curriculum. Value crisis is due to lack of ideal leadership, neglect of affective domain in education, and concept practices in society.

Specific human values can be suitably built in the academic curriculum of the higher secondary school (Rathnakumari 1987). Bajpai's (1990) experimental study of an educational intervention curriculum for value development and its facilitative effect upon the level of moral-judgment of children led to the result that the intervention programme greatly enhanced children's ability to judge and act as right and wrong and to understand the intention behind the act. Vaidya (1991) also found that Science subjects too helped in the moral development of students used in the experimental intervention programme was effective in bringing about desired value change among the students. The experimental subjects showed significant Dramatization method of teaching was more effective in the development of values than the traditional method in teaching of physics.

Nagar (1990) concluded that the prevention of the undesirable and approach of positive guidance are the most effective ways for teaching values. Padmanabhan's (1992) study attempted to assess the value pattern of high school pupils and the results indicated that the highest score was obtained on social values and the lowest on political values. It was also found value change instrument change in self-respect, wisdom, and a sense of accomplishment (Kapoor,1995).This is supported by Joshi's (1998) study where the value analysis technique was used and found to be effective in terms of developing democratic values among students, through teaching of civics. Joyce (2000) examined the Caldecott Medal Textbooks to determine the values expressed in the texts values and it was found that a, total of 1,592 instrumental values were expressed by 331 characters in the text.

Of the 331 characters, there were 235 humans and 96 non-humans. And the values were not equally distributed across the years, gender, and age groups. In a survey by Mehta (2003) it was found that the language structure and language of daily use have been more emphasized in the textbooks of std V and VI rather than value elements and the value based lessons on fairy tales, fables, parables, lessons regarding legendary personality etc., are found to be missing in the text books of English at upper primary school level of Gujarati medium schools .In another study by Thakkar (2005) on the values incorporated in the English textbook of class XI it was revealed among the 8 values, personal value is the highest occurring value; while environmental value was the least.

The rapidly changing social scenario has steadily led to the decline in values. Value education in schools need to be given priority. Values need to be incorporated in the various school subjects and taught by the integrated approach. This has been the inspiration for this piece of research.

Methodology

The present study is an experimental type of study where its design is of single group design is followed, where the values identified in the chapters of mathematics will be inculcated to the students through regular teaching of mathematics. Details of research methodology followed in this present study included population, sample, tools, data collection and method of data analysis are given as follows:

Statement of the Problem: A study of value inculcation in teaching of mathematics through integrated approach at secondary school level.

Objectives of the Study: The present study was realized with the help of following objectives.

- To inculcate the taken values of Equality, Co-operation and Determination with the help of regular teaching of Mathematics among students of Std. VIII.
- To study the effectiveness of the value integrated approach of teaching Mathematics in terms of value perception and conceptual knowledge along with the achievement in Mathematics.

Hypotheses: The present study was experimental in nature. The following null hypothesis was formulated to realize the present study.

- There will not be significant differences between the pre and post value conceptual knowledge of standard VIII students in the value of Equality.
- There will not be significant differences between the pre and post value conceptual knowledge of standard VIII students in the value of Co-operation.
- There will not be significant differences between the pre and post value conceptual knowledge of standard VIII students in the value of Determination.
- There will not be significant differences between the pre

and post-value perception of standard VIII students in the value of Equality.

- There will not be significant differences between the pre and post value perception knowledge of standard VIII students in the value of Co-operation.
- There will not be significant differences between the pre and post value perception knowledge of standard VIII students in the value of Determination.
- There will not be significant difference between the pre and post achievement in Mathematics of standard VIII students.

Research Design: The present study is an experimental study having single group pre test and post test research design following quasi experimental design. As per the research design, first pre test was administered on the group of students. Then two chapters of Mathematics i.e. Classification of Data and Area and Volume were taught to students along with a motive to inculcate values using integrated approach. After completion of the two chapters post test was administered to the group. The design of the study is shown graphically which is as follows.

O1 X O2

Where, O1 = Pre test, O2 = Post test and X = Experimentation

Population: The population for the present study constitute all the students of standard 8th of English Medium in Secondary Schools following the syllabus of Gujarat state Secondary and higher secondary Education Board.

Sample: The sample for the present study was selected purposively. 42 Students of standard VIII, Division C of Baroda High School, Alkapuri were selected purposively as the sample for the present study.

Tools: The following tools were constructed for the present study by the investigator.

- **Value Perception Scale:** It consisted of 15 situations having close ended items. Students had to make tick marks in one appropriate option given out of three options. The three options had positive polarity, negative polarity and neutral polarity. For each value five situations were constructed by the investigator, comprising total 15 situations. The time allotted to give the responses was 35 minutes both for pre test and post test. Scoring was done on the basis of scale product technique by giving weight to each response category in the usual Likert Fashion. This perception scale was referred to 3 experts in the field of education for suggestions on content and language appropriateness.

- **Value Questionnaire:** It consisted of open-ended items. For each value three questions were given, so there was a total of 9 questions. The value questionnaire was shown to the experts in the field of education for its validation, the responses of the students were analyzed and based on their knowledge, and they were given weights ranging from 0-3.
- **Achievement Test:** Achievement test was constructed for administering pre-test and post-test. Pre-test was administered to check the entry behaviour of the students and post test was administered to check that value inculcation through approach does not affect the achievement of students. This test was constructed keeping in mind the content of mathematics i.e. two chapters 1. Classification of Data and 2. Area and Volume. It comprised of ten objective type of questions and total items of 30 marks. The prepared tool was shown to the experts in the field of education and mathematics for its validation. The time allotted to students was 35 minutes each for pre test and post test and achievement-test.

Phases of the Study

The study was conducted in different phases. The investigator had divided the whole study into different phases like as follows.

Phase 1: Identification of values from the content of

Mathematics.

- Selection of content.
- Preparation of lesson plans:

Phase 2: Inculcation of values using Integrated Approach along with the content.

Phase 3: Data Collection.

The present study had 2 major aspects, one was to inculcate values while teaching mathematics using Integrated Approach and another was to study the effectiveness of Integrated Approach. To study the effectiveness three tools were prepared and data was collected using these three tools: value perception scale, value questionnaire.

Data Analysis

The data collected through Achievement Test was calculated mean of gain of achievement scores, standard deviation, standard error of mean, and t- value.

Correlation was used to find the correlation between inculcation of values and achievement.

Discussion

The data was analyzed using group statistics like mean, standard deviation of mean and standard error of mean, t-value, correlation t value and df.

The data collected by the investigators from the results of Pre-test and Post-test, were considered for testing the hypothesis using Correlated t-test which is presented in the following table.

Table 19.1: Mean, Standard Deviation, Standard Error of Pre-test and Post-test Experimental Group along with df, Correlation and t-value

	Mean	SD	SE of Means	Correlation	t-value	Df
Pre-test	2.85	3.05	0.45	0.0752	16.46*	46
Post-test	15.06	4.30	0.63			

* Significant at 0.05 level with 46 df

From Table 19.1, it was observed that the means of pre-test and post-test score of the group showed that there is an increase in the mean achievement of Mathematics. The values of means and standard deviations revealed that there is an increase in the mean achievement of students in Mathematics, indicates that the integrated approach does not have any negative effect on the achievement. The increase in standard deviation of post-test showed that the material was found to effective for low achievers of learners increasing the heterogeneity of the group with a positive increase in their achievement. As per t-test, the low correlation showed that the material was found to be applicable for all type of students irrespective of their individual differences. The t-value was found to be significant at 0.05 level of significance with df 46. Hence the null hypothesis Ho i.e. `There will be no significant different in the mean achievement score of Mathematics of the students in pre-test and post-test.' was rejected. So it can be said that there is significant different in the mean achievement score of Mathematics of the students in pre-test and post-test. Hence, the integrated approach was found significant to inculcate values in the teaching of mathematics to students of VIII standard as a new approach. In the other words, it can be said that the integrated approach can help to supplement or increase the achievement of VIII standard students in the respective subject with effective and interesting teaching process.

In this study there were three values taken and tables below indicates the findings of pre-test and post test scores and calculated values.

From Tables 19.2, 19.3 and 19.4, it was observed that the means of pre-test and post-test score showed that there is an increase in the mean scores of Value perception of Equality, determination and Co-operation respectively. The means and standard deviations revealed that there is an increase in the mean score of value perception of Equality Determination and Co-operation respectively, the decrease in standard deviation of post-test showed that the approach was found to effective for all type of learners increasing the homogeneity of the group with a positive increase in their perception. co-related t-test was taken, the low correlation showed that the approach was found to be applicable for all type of students irrespective of their individual differences.

Table 19.2: Mean, Standard Deviation, Standard Error of Pre-test and Post-test Experimental Group along with df, Correlation and t-value. Mean Value Perception of Equality

	Mean	SD	SE of Means	Correlation	t-value	Df
Pre-test	2.5	0.54	0.08	-0.09	2.40*	46
Post-test	2.75	0.43	0.06			

* Significant at 0.05 level with 46 df

Table 19.3: Mean, Standard Deviation, Standard Error of Pre-test and Post-test Experimental Group along with df, Correlation and t-value. Mean Value Perception for Determination

	Mean	SD	SE of Means	Correlation	t-value	Df
Pre-test	2.33	0.51	0.07	0.26	4.13*	46
Post-test	2.69	0.46	0.07			

* Significant at 0.05 level with 46 df

Table 19.4: Mean, Standard Deviation, Standard Error of Pre-test and Post-test Experimental Group along with df, Correlation and t-value. Mean Value Perception for Co-operation

	Mean	SD	SE of Means	Correlation	t-value	Df
Pre-test	2.31	0.55	0.08	0.26	3.70*	46
Post-test	2.65	0.48	0.07			

* Significant at 0.05 level with 46 df

The t-value was found to be significant at 0.05 level of significance with df 46. Hence the Ho i.e. `There will not be significant differences between the pre and post value perception of standard VIII students in the value of Equality determination and Co-operation respectively.' was rejected. So it can be said that there is significant difference in the mean of the students in pre-test and post-test.

From Tables 19.5, 19.6, and 19.7, it was observed that the means of pre-test and post-test score of the group showed that there is an increase in the mean scores of Value conceptual knowledge of Equality, Determination and Co-operation respectively.

Table 19.5: Mean, Standard Deviation, Standard Error of Pre-test and Post-test Experimental Group along with df, Correlation and t-value. Mean Value Conceptual for Equality

	Mean	SD	SE of Means	Correlation	t-value	Df
Pre-test	3.59	2.15	0.31	0.319	9.57*	46
Post-test	6.59	1.51	0.22			

* Significant at 0.05 level with 46 df

Table 19.6: Mean, Standard Deviation, Standard Error of Pre-test and Post-test Experimental Group along with df, Correlation and t-value. Mean Value Conceptual Knowledge for Determination

	Mean	SD	SE of Means	Correlation	t-value	Df
Pre-test	1.41	2.08	0.30	0.016	8.461*	46
Post-test	5.02	2.18	0.31			

* Significant at 0.05 level with 46 df

Table 19.7: Mean, Standard Deviation, Standard Error of Pre-test and Post-test Experimental Group along with df, Correlation and t-value. Mean Value Conception for Co-operation

	Mean	SD	SE of Means	Correlation	t-value	Df
Pre-test	2.20	1.73	0.25	0.18	11.02*	46
Post-test	5.88	1.91	0.27			

* Significant at 0.05 level with 46 df

Means and standard deviations revealed that there is an increase in the mean score of value conceptual knowledge of Equality, Determination and Co-operation respectively, which may be due to the effect of the integrated approach used for inculcation of values through the teaching of Mathematics. The decrease in standard deviation of post test showed that the approach was found to effective for all type of learners increasing the homogeneity of the group with a positive increase in their perception. t-test was taken and the low correlation showed that the approach was found to be applicable for all type of students irrespective of their individual differences. The t-value was found to be significant at 0.05 level of significance with df 46. Hence the Ho i.e. `There will not be significant differences between the pre and post value conceptual knowledge of standard VIII students in the value of Equality, Determination and Co-operation respectively.' was rejected. So it can be said that there is significant different in the mean of the students in pre-test and post-test.

Further it is found that every chapter has the scope for value inculcation, also, value education will be more effective in case of teaching of any subject if dealt with expertise.

The intervention programme i.e. Integrated Approach was found significantly effective in inculcating values like, equality, co-operation and determination, in term of value conceptual knowledge. This finding is supported by the research studies conducted by Bajpai (1990), Kapoor (1995) and Biswal et al (2005) to enhance values with the help of an intervention programme, though none of these studies were related the integrated approach. Hence it could be said that intervention programmes in different forms are useful to inculcate values in terms of value conceptual knowledge.

The integrated approach has dual role to impart value as well as to improve the achievement. Apart from inculcating some of the values, the intervention i.e. Integrated Approach was also found to increase the achievement of standard VIII students in Mathematics significantly. It was noted that the integrated approach did not affect negatively the achievement of students of standard VIII in the mathematics subject along with inculcating values.

Implications of the Study

1. Provision of Modification in Textbooks in Terms of Value Integration Approach: There can be a provision in which the textbook designed also bring awareness in teachers to inculcate the value through teaching of various subjects, underlining the values to be inculcated through teaching of various contents. Text books can provide scope of defining certain values in the chapters to the teachers as well as value based stories at the end of each chapter along with some proverbs based on values.

2. Provision for Developing a Better Curriculum in Teacher Training Programme: There should be an improved curriculum in teacher training programme, so that the teachers may develop this innovative approach This can be well done through a better curriculum in teacher training program.

3. Provision for Teachers in Using this Integrated Approach in Schools at all Levels: This approach could be very useful for all the teachers at all levels. This approach has significance due to its dual nature one of inculcating values and at the same time enhancing achievement levels in students. It can thus be further enhanced in schools and teachers should adapt it to improve their teaching process as well as to inculcate values in a value deteriorating society.

Conclusion

Values are deeply embedded in human thoughts and actions that it is extremely important to understand the essence underlying values. They guide us to do the right things. Hence there is a strong need to impart values among students to make them sensible and responsible future citizens. The present study is an attempt in this direction to use the integrated approach for value inculcation in order to improve the teaching-learning process and fulfil the objectives of school education. It can be concluded that this approach can develop the required conceptual as well as perceptual knowledge about values in students without affecting their achievement level, and similar attempts are needed in future in this direction.

References

Ahmad, A. (1973), A Study of Relationship between Values and Modernity with special reference to college girls, Ph.D., Psychology, Second Survey of Research in Education, New Delhi: NCERT.

Andrews, S.V (1993). 'Two Hundred Years of Values Teaching in Reading Textbooks'. In ERIC DATABASE. Washington D.C: The Department of Education.

Benerjee, P.K (1980), A Study in the Appreciation of Prose and Poetry of Secondary School Children, Ph.D. Education, Kal. University, Third Survey of Research in Education, NCERT, New Delhi.

Best, J.W.(1977)'Research in Education' New Delhi: Prentice Hall of India Pvt. Ltd.

Biswal, A .and Srivastava, S.(2005).Designing and Implementing CCA to Inculcate Social Values among B.Ed. Students Project Report. Dept of Education, The M.S University of Education Vadodara.

Biswal, A. and Dash, J. (1996) 'Value Orientation in Teacher Education' progress of Education, October.

Buddhananda, S. (1996) Values: The Key To A Meaningful Life, Sri Ramakrishna Math, Chennai.

Central Board of Secondary Education,(1997) Value Education a Handbook for Teachers, New Delhi.

Chandra Lekha, R.S. (.1995), Value education for college students, University News, New Delhi: Association of Indian Universities.

Chatterjee, P. (2000) 'Value Inculcation: Integrated Approach'. In Challenges in School Education in 2000+.Vadodara: CASE, The M.S. Univeristy of Baroda.

Choudhary, K. (1996), Value Education in India; The Socio-ideological Dimensions, Indian Journal of Social Research,

Vol.37 (i), P.1526.

Daniel, J.T.K.(1990), Value Education Today, New Delhi: AIACHE.

Das, M.(2004).'Value Education'. University News. 42, (16), pp.12-15.

Dave, I., Concept of Value Education, Rajasthan Board Journal of Education, 27(23), 1991, pp.1-6.

Dhanalakshmi, N. (2003). 'Value Inculcation among Students'. The Education Review. 46(2), pp.14-17.

Dhar, P.L.(2000), How can Values be Taught? Journal of Value Education.

Edwards, J., Poelman, K.,(1993) Developing Citizenship in the Curriculum, London,: Fulton.

Erricker, C. Erricker, J.(2000) Reconstructing Religious, Spiritual and Moral Education, New York,: Routledge Falmer.

Fernandez, P.(2002). 'Inculcating Basic Values among School Children.' Miracle of Teaching. Journal of the Teaching Profession. 2(3), pp. 99-101.

Heaman, J.(1996) Cornerstone Values- A Value Education-Curriculum, New Zealand Foundation for Value Education.

Jaila, H.L. and Kushal (1998), Parents and Value Education, Mumbai; D.A.V Centre for Creative Education.

John.(1998). Morality and Citizenship in Education, London, Willington House.

Joshi, K. (2002) Philosophy of Value Oriented Education: Theory and Practice. New Delhi: ICRA.

Joyce, M.(2003). 'Values expressed in Caldecott Medal Textbooks (1938-2002)'.In DAI- A Humanities and Social Science, 2003,64(5),1521-A.

Kalia, S., (1970), Ego Ideals and Values of Students, Ph.D., Psychology, Agra University; First Survey of Research in Education, New Delhi NCERT, New Delhi.

Kalra, R.M. (2002), Value Oriented Education in Schools, New Delhi; Shipra Publications.

Kalra, R.M.(1977) 'Curriculum Development with a Focus on Values'. Ambala: International Book Agencies.

Kalra, R.M.(2002). Teaching of Science with Focus on Values, New Delhi: Vikas Publishers.

Kapoor (1995) 'Transmission of Values through Higher Education System', University News, February 24.

Kar,(1984) Values in Education. Paper presented at the Summer

Institute of Indian Philosophy of Education, Kohima, North Eastern Hill university, Nagaland Campus, July pp.2-11.

Kishore, L. (1990) Value Oriented Education: Foundation and Frontiers-Word Overview, Delhi, Doaba House.

Mehta, M.H.(2003). 'A Study of Value Elements in English Textbooks at Upper Primary School Level of Gujarati Medium Schools'. An unpublished M.Ed. Dissertation. Vadodara: CASE, The M.S. University of Baroda.

Ministry Of Education (1964-66) Report of the Education Commission .Delhi: Govt of India.

Ministry Of Human Resources Development.(1986)National Policy on Education. New Delhi: Govt Of India.

Morrill, R.L. (1980) Teaching Values in College, San Francisco: Jossey-Bass Publishers, pp.72-73.

Nagar, D. (1990) 'Reinforcement and Inculcation of Values'. Journal of Indian Education, September pp.33-37.

National Curiculum Framework (2000), New Delhi: NCERT.

NCERT (2005) National Curriculum Framework for School Education. New Delhi: NCERT.

Padmanaban, T.(1992), A Study of values of high school pupils in relation to certain selected variables. Unpublished doctoral dissertation (Education), Annamalai University, Annamalai Nagar, Tamil Nadu.

Rathnakumari, B. (1987), A study of human values among high school students in Andhra Pradesh in relation to their socio-economic status and mass media exposure. Unpublished doctoral dissertation (Psychology), Osmania University, Hyderabad, Andhra Pradesh.

Rokeach, M. (1973). 'The Nature of Human Values'. New York: Free Press.

Seah, W and Bishop, A.(2000).'Values in Mathematics Textbooks: A View through Two Australian Regions'. In ERIC DATABASE. Washington D.C: The Department of Education.

Sheshadri, C.(1978)Moral Education in India'. Journal of Moral Education. Vadodara: CASE, The M.S. Univesity of Baroda.

Shukla, J.D. (1983). Report of the Moral Education Committee, Uttar Pradesh.

Sidhu, K.S.(1995). The Teaching of Mathematics, New Delhi: Sterling Publishers Pvt. Ltd. Shetty, A. (Dec.1997), Valuing Values, Vol.35, No.52, University news, New Delhi :A.I.U.

Thakkar, B. (2005) A Study of Value Incorporated In the English Textbook and Reflection of Teacher and Students of standard XI. An Unpublished M.Ed. Dissertation, CASE, The M.S. University of Baroda.

Venkataiah, N. (1998).'Value Education.' New Delhi: APH Publishing Corporation.

Venkataiah, N.(2002).'Researches in Value Education'. New Delhi: APH Publishing Corporation.

20

Acquisition of Science Process Skills in Constructivist Science Classroom

S.C. Panigrahi, N. Ramkumar and M. Rajendran

Introduction

The teaching learning process in the school context aims to cultivate those intellectual abilities and capacities for understanding that learners will need to continually implement throughout their lifetime. These ways of thinking, using knowledge and building understanding are at the core of current educational endeavours. This is what counts as knowledge in the knowledge society. These 'ways of thinking, knowing and building understanding' require further unpacking and application to curriculum, teaching and learning. But traditional teaching and learning is the process of the transmission of knowledge from teacher to student. It is essentially a one-way process. Most students enter into education system with an expectation of a 'mug and jug' approach to education by their teachers, i.e. the students represent empty mugs to be filled up with knowledge from the teachers' jugs. This teaching method can hinder the development of individual student's active and creative abilities, and students who experience only this model of education may no longer be considered sufficient for the needs of a future educated citizenry. In this context constructivism emerges as a ray of hope. Constructivism is basically a theory about how students learn.

Constructivism and Education

Fosnot (1996) has provided a summary of constructivist

theories and has described constructivist teaching practices. This work shows that students learn by fitting new information together with what they already know. The constructivist teaching models have been widely used in teaching and learning of sciences in particular. Constructivist teaching models not only emphasize active and collaborative learning, but also emphasize students and teachers discovering and constructing knowledge together. It presents the students with opportunities to construct new knowledge based on their prior knowledge and understanding from previous authentic experiences. Such prior knowledge is often referred to as a 'presage variable' and represents the different backgrounds, experiences and knowledge bases that students bring with them to the learning situation. This approach encourages students to confront real world problems which are within their everyday experience. The characteristics of constructivist teaching models include: prompting students to observe and formulate their own questions; allowing multiple interpretations and expressions of learning; encouraging students to work in groups; and in the use of their peers as resources to learning.

Constructivism and Science Learning

The debate on Constructivism has dominating the education system in recent times. It ranges across different aspects of learning including science. According to Asoko (2002), learning science involves learning to use ideas of science, interpret, explain and explore events and phenomena in the natural world. It involves stimulating a process of change in the thinking of the learner. The teacher therefore needs to find ways to introduce and explain ideas in a way that make sense to children. This is a long term process which can be difficult and cause misconceptions. Constructivist perspectives share two basic beliefs (Green, Susan, Gredler & Margaret, 2002): learners construct their own knowledge and to achieve this goal teaching of science must change in major ways.

Attempts to place some order into learning, and in particular, learning in science, have broken down some of the fundamental components of the learning experience into what have been termed processes (Gagne, 1963; Millar & Driver, 1987). Millar and Driver further state that in order to change learners' conceptions there is a need to bring about "a different 'way of seeing' to bear on the situation" (1987. 48). The research reported here is part of a larger study which is an attempt to determine whether this different 'way of seeing' might involve awareness and understanding of, the decisions learners make about processes. Rather than processes bringing together conceptual and procedural understanding (Gott & Duggan. 1995), it is the method of conducting business, the decisions that are made by the learner, that bring together processes and concepts. The skill of deciding what processes to use and where, when, how and why to employ them, may be the elusive, much sought after process skills, that learners use. In this context one need to understand what is process skills in science.

What Are the Science Process Skills?

Process skills in science are very important in the formal presentation of science to children. There is a strong belief that children who are properly introduced to science through Process skills will find the skills useful throughout life. While it is possible to easily forget science content learnt, process skills tend to remain with many individuals for a relatively longer period.

Science and teaching students about science means more than scientific knowledge. There are three dimensions of science that are all important. The first of these is the content of science, the basic concepts, and our scientific knowledge. This is the dimension of science that most people first think about, and it is certainly very important. The other two important dimensions of science in addition to science knowledge are processes of doing science and scientific attitudes. The processes of doing science are the science process skills that scientists use in the process of doing science.

Since science is about asking questions and finding answers to questions, these are actually the same skills that we all use in our daily lives as we try to figure out everyday questions. When we teach students to use these skills in science, we are also teaching them skills that they will use in the future in every area of their lives. The third dimension of science focuses on the characteristic attitudes and dispositions of science. These include such things as being curious and imaginative, as well as being enthusiastic about asking questions and solving problems. Another desirable scientific attitude is a respect for the methods and values of science. These scientific methods and values include seeking to answer questions using some kind of evidence, recognizing the importance of rechecking data, and understanding that scientific knowledge and theories change over time as more information is gathered.

The process skills are viewed as central to elementary school science education and important enough to be taught in their own right, they are often combined with science content, enabling children to learn both science processes and content at the same time—in a seamless learning experience. The term process skills have been used in literature on science education with three different meanings.

Thus process skills means:

- Cognitive processes involved in learning of science.
- The process scientists' use in investigating the natural world.
- The pedagogical processes taking place in classroom.

However, in the present paper process skills of the first type have been used. The process skills consist of following skills (Harlen, 1993).

- Observing

- Question raising
- Hypothesizing
- Predicting
- Finding Patterns and Relationship
- Communicating Effectively
- Designing and Making
- Devising and Planning Investigation
- Manipulating Materials and Equipment
- Measuring and Calculating.

Holistic Model Process Skills (Harlen, 1990)

In order to understand the process skill development among children two models have been proposed. The Linear model and Holistic model, in which the linear model assumes tat process skills, tend to develop in a linear sequence. In the Holistic model, the process skills were assumed to be related to each other and they tend to develop as a 'whole'. Although linear model on process skill have guided many curricular reforms but many criticisms have been labelled against its basic assumptions.

The holistic model on process skills came as a reaction to the linear model of process skills. The holistic model is derived from the development of cognitive science and constructivism. According to it, learning is a result of an interaction between new situations and present knowledge. "The process of bringing present knowledge to bear new situations and possibly extending or adopting that knowledge in the light of new experiences involves the learner in an active way in the development of his or her own understandings". From this perspective, the dichotomy between content and process in science does not exist. Learning what is considered as 'content' in any meaningful way involves the learner in an active process of knowledge construction.

Process Skills and Concept Development

We all live in a physical, biological and social

environment. In this ambience concept development takes place. In the first instance we try to develop some understanding about the situation. This understanding involves the development of ideas or concepts, which enable related situations, objects or events to be linked together, so that past experience enables us to make sense of new experience. The development of ideas or concepts depends upon the way ideas or concepts are imparted through rigorous manner with regard to available evidences. Therefore, conceptual learning is viewed as modification or expansion of existing ideas rather than the creation of new ideas (Harlen, 1993).

The concepts and process skills are independent, as concepts gradually become most sophisticated to process skills need to be refined and extended. The development of both must go hand in hand.

The emphasis on modification of pre-conceived ideas or existing ideas among children shares a constructivist view of learning, thus places the learner at the centre of learning process. Wittrock (cited in Driver, 1988) summarizes the constructivist perspectives to learning as follows:

"The key feature in this view of learning is the idea of mental constructions or schemes. Such schemes are used by learners, whether babies or adults to interpret new situations. Furthermore, it is assumed that the learners actively construct these schemes. Learners do not simply absorb what they are told or what they read. From this perspective, learning involves the learner in bringing existing schemes or ways of thinking to bear on a situation in an attempt to understand it. What is learnt thus depends not only on the characteristics of the situations presented (Whether it be text in a book or physical phenomenon), but on the 'schemes the learner has available. In other words, learning process is an interaction between the mental 'schemes' of the learner and features in the learning environment. Moreover, since making sense of any new situations requires the learner to bring his / her schemes to bear on the new situations and assess their applicability, ultimately the learner is responsible for his or her own learning".

The constructive perspective does not limit itself to knowing the children's ideas but it involves the process of changing the prior ideas (Finley 1983). It is in this context, instruction acts as facilitator in changing pupils' ideas. As ideas change so process skills as a whole also change.

Process Skill Development

The process skill development is viewed from the perspective of conceptual learning model (Harlen, 1993); learning is seen as modification or expansion of pupil's ideas. These ideas result, when pupils interact with learning experiences. These processes are initiated by the teachers to enhance the tools of thinking and are a cooperative process of engaging in mutual activities (Vygotsky cited in Howe, 1996). The co – operative learning perspective views that "one would not treat children as essentially solitary individuals trying to make meaning – instead one would treat them as participants in a joint enterprise in which meaning is derived through interactions with other pupils" (Howe, 1996). Thus in co-operative learning pupils exert efforts to achieve, learn more and build complex structures and retain information learn more accurately thereby constructing knowledge in groups. The other advantage of co-operative learning is that it can help in learning of skills as Barbules & Linn (1991) say "Cooperative learning can create a better learning environment since skills lacked by some students can be compensated by the skills of others".

The process skills which mentioned earlier in this paper are used as an indicator by researcher to plan or assess during teaching learning situation.

Methodology

The focus of the present study is an acquisition of process skills by IV standard pupils through an instructional programme in Environmental studies. The instructional programme is intended to create 'context' of scientific investigation, where pupils work in cooperative groups to interact with the learning experiences. These interactions help the pupils to modify their existing ideas through the use of process skills to develop ideas to relate and understand the surrounding environment. The sampling procedure involved was selecting all the IV standard pupils and dividing them into five cooperative groups. The data were collected through participant observation, in-depth interviews and documentary analysis. The data analysis involved the constructing the meaning on acquisition of process skill by IV standard pupil through instructional programme in environmental studies.

The meaning construction of fourth standard students about soil during their classroom and outdoor activities is described here. The activities organized in two modes namely, whole class activities, and group activities. The teaching strategy used in whole class activities are:

- Lecture/demonstration by teacher
- Single activity for entire class
- Student repeat teacher demonstration in groups

School and Garden soil activities taken as whole class activity.

The teaching strategy used for group activities is students learn in co-operative groups through discovery approach. Soil layer, Earth worm, Grass soil, Garden soil, and Ants were taken under group activities.

During these activities the pupils' ideas on soil seem to indicate the usage of following process skills.

1. Observation
2. Communicating
3. Using Materials and equipment
4. Hypothesising
5. Questioning

1. Observation: Under the skill of observation following two categories considered for meaning construction. (a)

Change in Pupils Ideas and (b) Retaining Ideas.

Change in Pupils Ideas: Before commencement of activities, pupils were asked to draw the diagram from their previous experience, which is referred to as initial observation. After the end of the activity, pupils were asked again to draw diagram based on observation, which is referred to as final observation. The change that brought in pupils ideas from initial to final observation is seen.

In the activity on school soil of group 4, initial observation shows that soil consists of dotted lines whereas final observation showed various objects like stones, leaves on the soil. In the activity on the earthworm of group 5, the initial observation showed legs where as final observation showed it as without legs. In the activity of ants of group 5, initial observation showed ants with five legs whereas the final observation on ants showed ants had 5 to 7 legs. In all these activities pupils' diagram on observation are changing from their imaginative representation of observation to scientific representation of observation.

Retaining Ideas: In the activity of Ant of group 3 and in the activity of school soil of group 5 despite the repeated observation they retain their initial ideas. The initial and final diagrams have almost remained same.

2. Communicating: The pupil's ability to express their ideas has been presented with two categories.

- Linking one idea with the other
- Systematic presentation of ideas

Linking One Idea with the Other: Pupils attempt to link one idea (derived from a previous activity) and relate to other idea of a different activity to communicate effectively.

In group 1, the pupil ideas on grass soil and school soil have been related to each other while performing the activity on grass soil. Pupil depicted the diagram of grass followed by the roots embedded in the grass soil. The representation of grass soil is similar to the representation of school soil by the pupil.

In group 2, activities related to ant and school soil, pupil attempt to show position of ants on the soil. The representation of soil resembles the representation of school soil. Similar way in group 5, while performing the activity on the soil pupils have represented ant and listed along with objects present in the school soil.

Systematic Presentation of Ideas: This refers to the systematic reporting of the activities as against to unsystematic reporting. The orderly presentation of ideas was seen in – group one in the activity on grass soil. The observation of group 1 on grass soil is presented, as it is:

- "The soil was moist, so when we poured it into the glass vessel dust did not come."
- "First soil was 'red' in colour and when water is poured into it turns into 'coffee colour."
- "The soil present below is 'rough' where as the soil present above is 'nice' ".
- "The soil in the lower layer consisted of small stones and the soil in the upper layer consisted of leaves, coal, grass roots, and froth".
- "The 'rough' soil (lower layer) goes down because of weight and the 'nice' soil (upper soil) comes up since it does not have weight".

3. Using Materials and Equipment: One of the features of the pupils is to give attention to details. The pupil's ability, to represent the specific physical features into a diagram.

The diagram on ants depicts the progressive observations made by pupils. Pupils have represented the ant by giving attention to head, abdomen and tail portions. The diagram on earthworm was shown to have the body with crest and trough. The diagram on school soil is enhanced by the usage of hand lens as pupils have given attention to various objects present on the school soil. The diagram on grass soil shows how soil particles were being clogged to the root tips.

Hypothesis: During the hypothesis pupils attempted to formulate a tentative explanation (based on certain concepts) for certain activities. Some of the explanation has been derived from the activity on grass soil and earthworm.

- **An Explanation on the Breathing of Earthworm:** Pupils explained by stating that "earthworms breathe by holding the roots of the plants, when plant shakes roots also shake resulting in getting air to earthworm".
  In this example, pupil has extended their knowledge of air and have related to earthworm breathing. Pupil's notion is that whenever wind is blown it shakes the plants, which in turn shakes turn shakes the roots, which results in creation of air, which moves through the roots and reaches earthworm (and helps it to breathe).
- **Explanations into the Layers of Garden Soil:** In the activity on the garden soil, pupils were asked to explain to find out the reasons for formation of soil layers. Pupils explained that small stones were there in the soil. It went down because of the weight. "The 'nice' soil came up because it was smooth" (less weight as compared to garden soil).
- **Explanation on the Formation of Upper Layer in the Garden Soil:** Pupils keenly observed the upper layer of the garden soil. They labelled the soil colour as that of 'coffee' colour. Given below is an interaction between teacher and pupil on the upper layer formation.
  T—I asked you why few objects are floating on the water?
  P1—They are feeling 'cold' sir.
  T—What is cold?
  P1—Cold means you put a blanket when it rains.
  Teacher repeated the questions
  T—Why objects floats on the water?
  Another pupil intervened
  P2—It is having less weight sir.

In this activity, Pupil (P1) could not understand that less weight is the reason for floating of objects. Instead, P1 tried to explain that objects feel cold inside the water so it comes out of it. This explanation shows imaginative ideas of pupils interferes in explaining the scientific activity.

Questioning: When pupils were given an opportunity to ask questions, pupils were constantly asking questions. However, these questions were asked for the clarification of procedures involved in the scientific activity. The questions were on how to proceed with the activity. Nevertheless, when asked to write questions on related to particular activity pupils faced the difficulty in formulating questions. In the activity of ants all, the questions have been presented from group 1 and group 5.

Questions from group 5 are as follows:

Q—Why do the ants stay in the soil (G5?)

However, G1 asked the questions (Q) and they themselves have answered (A) it.

Q—How do the ants run?

A—Ants run very fast.

Q—Where does ant build anthill?

A—Ant builds the anthills on the ground.

Q—Where does the ant's walk?

A—Ants walk on the ground, trees, and the body.

The pupil ideas on skill of questioning reveals that questions need to have an answer.

Conclusion

The processes used in doing scientific inquiry and the development of conceptual understanding and knowledge work in concert; they must go hand in hand. However, the seamless interweaving of process and content depends on both the teachers' and the students' experience and confidence in doing inquiry. Teachers find that they often move back and forth, emphasizing process skills and scientific content, bringing one into focus for critical examination while the other remains in the background. Teachers have to help students develop skills to be good investigators. With ample practice, these skills develop and grow over time. This way when concepts tend to develop, process skills also tend to develop.

In summary, successfully integrating the science process skills with classroom lessons and field investigations will make the learning experiences richer and more meaningful for students. Students will be learning the skills of science as well as science content. The students will be actively engaged with the science they are learning and thus reach a deeper understanding of the content. Finally active engagements with science will likely lead students to become more interested and have more positive attitudes towards science.

References

Brien, M, O (2002) New Pedagogies and the Knowledge Society: Teaching for Deep Learning, Conceptual Understanding and Generative Thinking.

Corrigan, G (1998) The Acquisition of Process Skills and the Development of conceptual Learning. A Paper presented at the Australasian Science Education Research Association, Darwin, Australia, 9-12 July 1998.

Ramkumar, N (2003) Acquisition of Process Skills by IV standard pupils through an Instructional programme in Environmental studies. An unpublished Ph.D. Thesis, CASE, The M.S. University of Baroda, Vadodara.

Rankin, L (2000) Lessons Learned: Addressing common misconceptions about Inquiry.

Shaikh, M, Hands-On Science in Elementary School: Why and How, University of Texas, Dallas.

UNESCO, Science Series – Process Skills in Science for Children: Let us Begin Science.

Zhao, Y (2003) The Use of Constructivist Teaching Model in Environmental Science at Beijing Normal University, The China Papers.

21

Role of Technology in Constructivist Classrooms

Mandira Sikdar and Leena Bhojwani

Introduction

Education is at the confluence of powerful and rapidly shifting educational, technological and political forces that will shape the structure of educational systems across the globe for the remainder of this century. Many countries are engaged in a number of efforts to effect changes in the teaching/learning process to prepare students for information and technology based society. The UNESCO World Education Report (1998) notes that the new technologies challenge traditional conceptions of both teaching and learning and, by reconfiguring how teachers and learners gain access to knowledge, have the potential to transform teaching and learning processes. Information and Communication Technology provide an array of powerful tools that may help in transforming the present isolated, teacher-cantered and text-bound classrooms into rich, student-focused, interactive knowledge environments.

To meet these challenges, schools must embrace the new technologies and the appropriate new ICT tools for learning. They must also move towards the goal of transforming the traditional paradigm of learning. To accomplish this goal requires both a change in the traditional view of the learning process and an understanding of how the new digital technologies can create new learning environments in which students are engaged learners, able to take greater responsibility for their own learning and constructing their own knowledge. Thomas Kuhn suggests that revolutions in science come about when the old theories and methods will not solve new problems. He calls these changes in theory and methods a "paradigm shift." There is a widespread concern that the educational experiences provided in many schools will not prepare students well for the future.

Many educators and business and government leaders believe that creating a paradigm shift in view of the learning process, coupled with applications of the new information technologies, may play an important role in bringing educational systems into alignment with the knowledge-based, information-rich society (UNESCO, 2002, p. 15).

Present Scenario

The general notion regarding the use of computers in education is that it may best be used as a tool for drill and practice programs supplementing the instructional process. In such instructional processes, the learner receives information already programmed inside the computer following an algorithm. Although some amount of interactivity is ensured, the general impression is that in such instructional processes, computers control the learning structure giving the learner very little room for creativity, making him a passive recipient of information.

There is a need to explore the potentials of this device beyond these traditional notions i.e. the meaningful designing of computer based instructional processes with increased student participation. Also, it is not the extended usage on the device that would ensure the desired learning rather the nature of these learning tasks, which would transform and enrich the instructional processes. Computer application programs can be used to design learning experiences to develop creative and critical thinking and be used as 'mind tools' that can be used by students to represent what they know and to engage in critical thinking about the content (Jonassen, 1997).

Use of ICT to Promote Constructivist Learning

In classrooms today, the role of the teacher needs to

change from the traditional role of prescriptor to that of orchestrator of learning – which necessitates the designing of ICT integrated classrooms promoting higher order cognitive skills. The focus ought to be more on enquiry-based approaches often going beyond the prescribed curriculum to delve and seek answers to the problem under concern but now from different perspectives. This methodology is challenging both for the teacher as well as for the learner but eventually the process of self-learning ensures a more rigorous approach and deeper understanding of facts. The focus is more on the process of information acquisition, the critical and analytical thinking involved in acquiring information from multiple sources, analyzing this information and then designing the learning outcomes in aesthetic presentations. Such a model of learning focuses more on the process over the product, acquiring information from multiple sources, analytical and critical thinking and finally a comprehensive evaluation assessing different areas of student academic growth.

One of the significant inputs to this method of studying are the periodic scaffolds provided to ensure a framework in which the discovery and investigation is conducted and while meaningful learning is the objective, certain curricular requirements cannot be compromised in the process of exploration.

Jonassen (1996) identified many different kinds of software programs that can be used by students and each different kind of tool will be suitable for different goals. He used the term "Mind tools" to describe various computer software such as spreadsheet and database applications, concept-mapping programmes, multimedia and hypermedia development software. These programmes are only considered as Mind tools when students in a learning situation use them as cognitive tools. When students are actively involved in constructing a system using the software, they are engaged in many thinking tasks. Jonassen contrasts the situation of the teacher who uses the tools themselves to illustrate a point, manipulate information, solve problems, or perform other types of operation for the students, with the situation where the students create their own illustrations and examples, manipulate their own data and other information, and generally, wrestle with the tools themselves. The first situation is what he calls instructive, but the second is highly constructive.

Role of ICT in Constructivist Classrooms

An educational portfolio is one such typical innovation that can promote constructivist learning in the otherwise traditional classroom. It is a combination of a number of learning tasks and a compilation of the outcomes achieved as a result of the processes undergone therein. A critical component is the emphasis on 'process' over 'product' and the constant reflection of the learner as he moves from one stage to another in the realization of the objectives. The other significant feature is the acquisition of information from multiple sources and the necessary component of constant data analysis before proceeding to the following stages in the development of the e-portfolio. Assessment of learning outcomes also is a comprehensive one taking into account different areas of learner academic growth as a result of the processes being carried out from identification of goals to acquisition of relevant information and finally its processing and dissemination.

Kay Burke (1999) and Robin Fogarty (1998) advocate a balanced approach to assessment, with a focus on three components:

- Traditional Assessment, with a focus on grades and rankings, knowledge, curriculum, and skills, implemented through classroom assessments (tests, quizzes, homework assignments), and standardized tests (either norm-referenced or criterion-referenced)
- Performance Assessment, with a focus on observable results and standards, application and transfer,

implemented through standards, tasks, criteria and scoring rubrics.

- Portfolio Assessment, with a focus on growth and development over time, implemented through selection, reflection and inspection of class work, along with goal setting and self-evaluation.

Portfolio assessment is a comprehensive manner of student evaluation incorporating a variety of learning tasks with appropriate and timely provision of the necessary guidelines to complete the same within accorded criteria and allotted time limits. These are performance enablers that define the acceptable standards expected from the learner and thus define the path that he needs to adopt to achieve excellence. What differentiates the e-portfolio from the traditional forms of assessment is the designing of the portfolio around a set of standards and learning goals which are not the direct outcomes of the classroom instructional processes, rather an endeavour to ensure student higher order learning as a result of these instructional processes. An electronic portfolio is not a haphazard collection of artefacts (i.e., a digital scrapbook or a multimedia presentation) but rather a reflective tool that demonstrates growth over time. (Barrett, 2000)

Designing the E-portfolio: The e-portfolio can be an effective tool to demonstrate learner academic growth and thus the designing of the portfolio can be a challenging task both for the educator as well as the learner. The different stages involved in the portfolio preparation include the following.

- **Defining Portfolio Context and Goals:** On the basis of the content taught, higher order learning objectives are designed and resources and tools identified which would enable the achievement of these objectives. On the basis of available resources and the pre-determined objectives, a design or algorithm to be designed for systematic and sequential organizing of the various components of the portfolio,
- **Working Portfolio:** Having identified the higher order

learning goals which need to be addressed, the next step involves the identification of the possible sources of information and the learning tools which need to be employed in the collection of the needed data. The selection of resources and tools should be done keeping in mind the vision envisaged for the portfolio and must demonstrate the development within the portfolio both in terms of learner development as also the achievement of the portfolio goals. This stage requires the learner to critically analyze the vast information available and classify and selectively organize the same according to portfolio requirements.

- **Reflective Portfolio:** An important aspect of this methodology is the self-learning involved in the designing of the different components of the portfolio with constant reflection at each and every stage of the learning process. With the availability of multiple sources of information and the insistence on an enquiry based approach, learner reflections are crucial to assess the progress being made as well as the implications for the future learning required. Thus, with the teacher now assuming the role of 'orchestrator of learning' the learner becomes the 'architect 'of his own learning having self-learnt through heuristic methods. Different learning resources and tools have their own potentials and need to be utilized keeping these in mind – thus, a judicious and thoughtful approach and implementation alone would enable the realization of the portfolio objectives.
- **Connected Portfolio:** The portfolio emphasizes the interconnectedness between each and every component - objectives, learning theories, learning experiences, sources of information and the designing of the learning outcomes in keeping with the vision envisaged for the portfolio. A significant learning for the learner is the understanding of the interdisciplinary nature of knowledge and the how each and every component is entwined and aimed at the

acquisition of the portfolio goals. Understanding the underlying interconnectivity and the concept of 'holistic education' is a significant learning outcome for the learner.

- **Presentation Portfolio:** This is the final stage and involves the presentation of the final outcome and is an assessment of the overall design in keeping with the pre-determined goals. The presentation is a depiction of the learner's information acquisition skills namely mode (and sources) of information acquisition, manner of processing and the skills of effective presentation. This stage reveals the understanding of the different components of the portfolio.

Conclusion

Constructivism claims that learners construct knowledge most naturally and completely while they are constructing some artefacts. Perkins (1986) argues that knowledge acquisition is a process of design that is facilitated when learners are actively engaged in designing knowledge rather than merely interpreting or encoding it i.e. Learners benefit the most from the learning process when they are the designers of the instructional experiences.

Hypermedia is a powerful design tool for learners to construct knowledge. Hypermedia composition places students in the designer's seat so that they may construct their own understandings, rather than interpreting the teacher's understanding of the world. Researching the information, organizing and designing the presentation and managing the project in its entirety, require critical, creative as well as complex thinking skills. In this context, the e-portfolio preparation incorporates several learning experiences ensuring that the learner participates actively and learns concepts through an analytico-synthetic approach. The preparation is a very useful exercise in the comprehension of both pedagogy and technology with self-learning and higher order learning being ensured as a result of the methodology. Such innovations may truly revolutionize educational systems.

References

Barrett, Helen (2000, April). Create Your Own Electronic Portfolio. Learning & Leading with Technology Vol. 27, No. 7, pp. 14-21.

Burke, K. (1999). How to Assess Authentic Learning. Arlington Heights, IL: Skylight Professional Development.

Fogarty, R. (1998). Balanced Assessment. Arlington Heights, IL: Skylight Professional Development.

Jonassen, D.H. (1996) Objectivism versus constructivism: Do we need a new philosophical paradigm? Educational Technology Research and Development, 39(3), 5-14. Website: tlcweb.np.edu.sg/lt/articles/ict.htm

Ministry of Human Resource Development (1983). The Teacher and Society, National Commission on Teachers-1 (1983-85), New Delhi.

Ministry of Human Resource Development (1986) National Policy on Education, New Delhi, Govt. of India.

Ministry of Human Resource and Development (2000) Selected Educational Statistics, Department of Secondary Education and Higher Education, Planning Monitoring and Statistics Division, New Delhi, MHRD, Govt. of India.

National Council for Teacher Education (1998) Curriculum Framework for Quality Teacher Education, New Delhi, NCTE.

National Council of Educational Research and Training (2000), National Curriculum Framework for School Education, New Delhi, NCERT.

NCERT (2005) National Curriculum Framework, New Delhi, NCERT.

Perkins, D.N. (1992) Technology meets constructivism: do they make a marriage? In Duffy, T.M. & Jonassen, D.H. (eds), Constructivism and the technology of instruction: a conversation. pp 45-55. New Jersey: Lawrence Erlbaum Associates. Website: tlcweb.np.edu.sg/lt/articles/ict.htm

UNESCO (1998) World Education Report: Teachers and Teaching in a changing World, UNESCO, Paris.

UNESCO (2002) Education, Public Awareness and Training for Sustainability: Input to the Report of the Secretary General to the Second Preparatory Session for the World Summit on Sustainable Development. UNESCO, Paris.

World Bank (2002) Constructing Knowledge Societies: New Challenges for Tertiary Education, Washington, DC.

22

Programme for Enhancing Achievement of Class X Students in Mathematics

R.G Kothari and Pradeep Patel

Introduction

Education is the process of bringing desirable changes in learners. Education makes man a right thinker and a decision maker. Education also gives worth and self–esteem so that one can see himself as a valuable person. The secondary education system serves as a bridge between the primary and higher education systems. Secondary schools provide students for universities and centres of higher education so, secondary education is very important. It is essential that secondary education should be of high quality. Mathematics is required for effective living and acquisition of important skills. Mathematics is important not only for individual but also for the progress of the nation and human civilization. Mathematics is the synthesis of all sciences and all arts. In the present technological, electronic and computer dominated age no scientific and technological advancement can be made without Mathematics."

In the present study the investigator has taken class X students because class X is the entrance of higher secondary education from where the students can select the stream like science/arts/commerce. Moreover from eleventh standard, the abstract concepts of Mathematics are introduced, so such type of enhancing programmes become helpful to the students of class X to achieve better result.

The results of S.S.C. Board Examination (Gujarat) have reduced continuously for the last three years. In March 2001 the result was 68.91 percent, in March 2002 the result was

56.92 percent and in March 2003 the result was 49.59 percent. The repeated failure and low achievement is concluded as inability, lack of interest, insufficient practice, etc. on the part of the students.

If no assistance is provided by teachers, parents or counsellors, there is the risk of the students not completing up to class X examination, drop–out rates at the higher secondary and tertiary level will be high.

In the months of examination especially in the month of board examination cases of frustration, depression, suicide and drop out increase due to lack of motivation, good study habits, reading habits and anxiety of examination. If proper guidance is provided then such type of cases will comedown. Many researches have been conducted for secondary level to find out the factors affecting achievements in different subjects but next step would be development of a sound programme to help the students.

Here the investigator has identified the factors related to low achievement from students, teachers and parents. Investigator attempted to develop a programme to enhance their achievement as to create interest in Mathematics through different remedial measures as well as through counselling and guidance. The investigator covered some new techniques also for the students to enhance their achievement like concentration techniques, deep breathing for relaxation, mini nap for effective reading, strengthening self–esteem and self–concept through powerful auto suggestions, etc. Thus, present programme has added some newness in the system of studying mathematics.

Statement of the Problem

"Development of a Programme for Enhancing Achievement of the Students of Class X in Mathematics".

Objectives of the Study

- To identify the students having low achievement in class IX in Mathematics in Baroda city.

- To identify the factors related to low achievement of identified students.
- To study the problems faced by the students who have low achievement in Mathematics.
- To study the problems in teaching and learning Mathematics from teachers, parents and students.
- To develop and tryout a programme to enhance achievement of students of class X in Mathematics.
- To study the effectiveness of the programme in terms of achievement of the students of class X in Mathematics.

Methodology: In order to achieve the objectives of the present study, survey and experimentation were adopted and two types of data were collected – qualitative and quantitative. Situation analysis was also made. Experiment was conducted on the sample students to enhance their achievement in Mathematics.

Population and Sample: In the present study investigator used multi–stage sampling technique. In the first stage out of 111 schools, thirty schools were randomly selected. This covered six different centres of Baroda city, viz. twelve schools from Alkapuri, six from Sayajigunj, two from Raopura, one from Mandvi, seven from Karelibaug and two from Makarpura. In the second stage seventy students were selected who were low achievers in Mathematics based on their achievement in class IX. In the third stage all the teachers teaching Mathematics in the selected schools were taken. In the fourth stage the parents of all the students were involved in the sample.

Tools

- Information Schedule to collect personal information and information about the marks obtained in class IX in Mathematics in the annual examination.
- Questionnaire for Students of Class X for collecting information about factors related to low achievement in Mathematics and to study the problems in teaching and learning Mathematics.

- Questionnaire for Teachers of Mathematics of Class X to study the problems related to low achievement in Mathematics.
- Questionnaire for Parents to study the factors related to low achievement of his/her child in Mathematics
- Prerequisite tests for 19 chapters to measure the basic concepts and fundamental knowledge.
- Unit tests for 19 chapters to measure the achievement in each unit taught to the students.
- Pilot test to locate the errors made by the students, question wise and to locate the chapters in which the students were facing problems.
- Final Achievement Test of hundred marks was conducted to study the effectiveness of the programme in terms of achievement of the students.

Major Findings

Findings Based on Situation Analysis:

- Ninety three percent students responded that they liked the subject mathematics.
- Sixty six percent students opined that they find it difficult to learn mathematics. Ninety one percent felt difficulty while learning mathematics in classroom. Difficulties were of following type: lack of concentration due to weak base, frequent transfer of teachers in the class, the method of explanation differs from teacher to teacher, speedy teaching, less practice in geometry, lack of proper guidance regarding preparation of the subject and less use of black board by the teachers.
- About fifty nine percent students did not like the teaching method of their teachers. Major reasons for this were – teacher cannot make teaching interesting, teacher explains very quickly, teacher does not provide sufficient practice in the classroom, teacher does not explain the topic on the blackboard.
- Forty one students responded that their teacher did not

provide guidance about the homework given and forty eight percent students told that teacher does not draw any attention to the errors committed.

- Students' responses regarding the questions related to examination showed tension and fear of mathematics.
- Sixty five percent students opined that more practice was required; thirty five students opined that slow teaching helped them to learn better while thirty percent students opined that more and more time for practice helped them. Ninety six percent students opined that practice of necessary prerequisite helped them.
- Forty seven percent students opined that they lost their marks in definitions and in fill in the gaps while seventy percent students lost their marks in theorems, riders and constructions. Sixty one percent students opined that their handwriting also caused for not getting good marks. Forty one percent students opined that they did not cultivate good method of writing answer book. Eighty seven percent students confessed that they could not recall and remember the things prepared.
- Sixty nine percent students opined that less practice of writing question paper at home was the cause of less marks in mathematics. Seventy nine percent students opined that less time was contributed for the subject was the reason of less marks. Forty four students confessed that the subject is tough therefore confidence is not developed while fifty one percent students opined that they did not know how to prepare the subject.
- Majority of the students opined following aspects were important to enhance the performance in mathematics – pattern of writing answer book, requirement to improve handwriting, to enhance concentration, recalling method, revision planning, goal setting, mini nap for relaxation, positive thinking, removing examination fear, hearing skill, speedy reading, writing and calculation, time management, how to study on the examination day,

planning of three hours of examination, preparation of charts for important topics, examination tips, formation of good study habits.

- Forty seven percent parents were unable to help their child in mathematics.
- The parents responded that their child did not sleep well on the day of examination, remained under tension till the paper was over. It clearly indicated that their child had examination fear.
- According to majority of teachers following type of help is needed to weak students who experienced difficulty in mathematics–providing additional help as and when needed, revision of each chapter, conducting unit test, providing remedial measures.
- Seventy six percent of teachers test the prerequisite knowledge for particular chapter not in a very planned manner, simply few questions were put before the class, while other teachers felt that no time is available for testing previous knowledge.
- All teachers responded that if the test was held after teaching each chapter and mistakes were corrected, definitely it was beneficial to the students who were getting fifty or less than fifty.
- In short, situation analysis clearly indicated that students are weak in basics and are not in clear prerequisite, teaching learning needs to be interesting. Motivation must be provided and study habits are needed to be cultivated.

Causes of Low Achievement

Major causes for low achievement according to the students in mathematics were learning difficulty in classroom teaching, difficulty in geometry and statistics, speedy teaching, insufficient time for teaching and learning of Mathematics in time–table, inability to solve homework without other's help, examination fear for the subject mathematics, examination stress, inability to remember due to stress in the examination hall, lack of basic concepts which become a potential cause of difficulty in learning higher concepts, lack of concentration and attention at the time of learning, lack of repetition, insufficient time provided by the teacher to solve the examples in the classroom, problems in understanding theorems, riders, constructions, etc., insufficient practice, lack of positive attitude for Mathematics, insufficient care for weak students by the teachers, lack of revision at the end of the year, negative attitude towards subject Mathematics, lack of inspiration from teachers and parents, slow recalling, difficulty in objective type questions of Mathematics like definitions and fill in the blanks, lack of knowledge regarding how to prepare Mathematics, lack of good study habits, were major causes for low achievement.

Major causes for low achievement of the students according to the parents were–confusion and difficulty in studying Mathematics at home, laziness in doing homework of Mathematics, lack of interest for Mathematics, confusion at the time of solving the examples at home and in the examination hall, parents were unable to help the students in the subject Mathematics, lack of guidance on the part of the teachers for Mathematics, negative attitude of the child towards the subject Mathematics.

Major causes for low achievement of the students in subject Mathematics according to the teachers were negative attitude of the students towards Mathematics, inferiority complex that Mathematics will not be understood, lack of enough practice, less attention to weak students in Mathematics, lack of explaining figures in geometry, theorems, lack of basic concepts.

Findings Based on Prerequisite Test and Unit Test

Mean of prerequisite tests showed poor performance of the students for prerequisite knowledge of previous standards. Performance of unit tests in respect of mean showed that teaching learning through developed programme enhanced their achievement to some extent. Counselling programme also reduced their teaching learning hurdles and enhanced their confidence and interest. Error analysis as well as remedial measures also helped the students to enhance their achievement to some extent.

Findings Based on Pre-test, Pilot-test and Post-test

The performance of the students has increased from mean of 39.17 in class IX (pre-test) to mean to 50.83 in Pilot Test. Thus, there is observed difference of 11.66. The mean achievement of pre-test (Class IX) was 39.17 and that of post–test (Final achievement test of class X) was 61.33. Thus, there is observed difference of 22.16.

Suggestions for Students, Parents and Teachers

- Students should develop good study habits for preparing the subject mathematics.
- Students should make charts for formulae and make notes for model sums which help them for fast revision and cultivating confidence in the subject.
- Students should create positive attitude towards the subject mathematics and provide positive auto suggestions to the self for getting enthusiasm.
- Students should work daily for two hours over and above the homework given by the teacher. They should not use ready reference material for solving the sums.
- Students should approach the subject teacher for their problems in mathematics and take help and guidance for improving their achievement.
- Parents should see that their child should study mathematics daily for two hours, and should see that the child should not copy the sums given in the homework from material in which solved sums are provided.
- Parents should contact the subject teacher of mathematics at least once a month for knowing the progress report of their child and if child is not working satisfactorily they

should take help of the subject teacher and work according to teacher's guideline.

- Parents should study the answer books of the test properly and find out the reasons of low achievement and take necessary steps accordingly.
- Parents should try to utilize the child's potential by providing enthusiasm, motivation, by giving surprise prize at the time of good achievement.
- Parents should take care about their friendship and their attitude towards the subject mathematics and parents should guide the child to make friends who are good at mathematics.
- Teachers should identify the areas of mathematics in which the students face difficulty and then should provide them remedial measures in those areas so that their weakness in reference to that area can be rectified.
- Teachers should conduct a test after the completion of each unit and errors committed by students should be identified.
- Teacher should conduct a test in the beginning of each unit to identify the weaknesses of the students in the area which they have already studied.
- Teachers must be aware of various correlates of achievement.
- Teachers should identify the errors committed by students and accordingly remedial programme be organized.

Suggestions for Further Study

- Similar studies can be conducted for other school subjects.
- Similar studies can be conducted for students having less than thirty five marks.
- Based on errors identified, a diagnostic test can be developed.
- Case studies of low achievers as well as high achievers can be conducted.

It is hoped that the present study will not only provide a

basis for further research but also give more effective guidelines to solve the problem of low achievers in mathematics by eliminating mathematical weaknesses and enhancing the achievement in mathematics of class X.

References

Ashar, R.R. (1972). "Construction and Standardization of the Diagnostic Test in Basic Algebraic Skills for the Pupils of Gujarati Medium Secondary Schools of Greater Bombay" (An Unpublished Ph.D. (Edu.) Thesis) In M.B. Buch (Ed.) Second Survey of Research in Educational. Baroda: Society for Research and Development, pp.379.

Aviles A.P. (1987) "An Environmental and Educational Characterization of Low Achiever's Experiences and Attitudes Towards Mathematics Performance Using Case Studies" (Doctoral Thesis, Fordham University, (1989), Dissertation Abstract International, 50(5), 1240-A.

Bhattacharya, A. (1982). "Diagnosis and Prevention of the Learning Disabilities of Primary School Students in Arithmetic" (Calcutta University, An Unpublished Ph.D. (Edu.) thesis) In M. B. Buch (Ed.) Third Survey of Research in Education. New Delhi: N.C.E.R.T, pp. 334.

Bruner J.S. (1962). On Knowing Essays for Left Hand, Harvard University Press.

Dandapani, C. (1992). "Dimensions of Effective Teaching of Mathematics" (Annamalai University, An unpublished Ph.D. (Edu.) Thesis) In Fifth Survey of Educational Research. New Delhi: N.C.E.R.T., pp. 1277.

Das, R.C. and Barua, A.P. (1968). "Effect of Remedial Teaching in Arithmetic, A Study with Grade IV Pupils" Assam. (An Unpublished ph. D. (Edu.) Thesis) In M.B. Buch (Ed.) Fourth Survey of Research Education New Delhi: N.C.E.R.T., p. 699.

Education and National Development: Report of the Education Commission (1964–66) Vol. 2, New Delhi: NCERT.

Gupta, R., Mukerjee, M., & Chatterji, S. (1993). "A Comparative Study of the Factors Affecting Academic Achievement Among Four Groups of Adolescents." Indian Educational Abstracts, Issue 3, July 1997.

Kothari, R.G. (1985). "An Investigation into Efficacy of Different Instructional Media in Teaching of Mathematics with Respect to

Certain Variables", Unpublished Ph.D. Thesis (Edu) V. V. Nagar, S. P. University.

Kumar, S. and Ratnalikar, D. N. (2003). Teaching of Mathematics, Anmol Publications Pvt. Ltd., New Delhi.

23

Entrepreneurial Education

Sarita Agrawal and Jyoti Achanta

Introduction

"Investments in terms of education of the people are critical for a country's economic and social development. Investment in human capital improves an individual's productivity." It also improves people's ability to acquire and use information, allowing them to deal more effectively with a rapidly changing environment. (Patrinos, 1999) "Governments around the world recognize the importance of education for economic and social development and invest large shares of their budgets to education. The provision of schooling is largely determined and financed by government. The main product has been the expansion of schooling. This is largely the result of supply-side growth." (Patrinos, 1999)

Skills and knowledge are considered as the driving forces of economic growth and social development. Countries with higher and better levels of skills adjust more effectively to the challenges and opportunities of globalization (GOI, 2006).The economy becomes more productive, innovative and competitive through the existence of more skilled human potential. The level of employment, its composition and the growth in employment opportunities are the critical indicators of the process of development in any economy. Increasing pace of globalization and technological changes provide both challenges and growing opportunities for economic expansion and job creation. In taking advantage of these opportunities as well as in minimizing social costs and dislocation, which the transition to a more open economy entails, the level and quality of skills that a nation possess are becoming critical factors.

The skill level and educational attainment of the work force determines not only the productivity but also the adaptability of the working class in changing environment. With the liberalization and globalization of the Indian economy, the rapid changes witnessed in scientific and technological world and the general need to improve the quality of life and to reduce poverty, it is essential that school leavers acquire a higher level of knowledge and skills than what they are provided in the 8 years of elementary education, particularly when the average earning of a secondary school certificate holder is significantly higher than that of a person who has studied only up to class VIII. (2006a). In addition, secondary Education is also a crucial stage in the educational hierarchy as it prepares the students for higher education and also for the world of work. The rigour of the secondary and higher secondary stage, enables students to compete successfully for education and for jobs globally. Therefore, it is absolutely essential to strengthen this stage by providing greater access and also improve quality in a significant way.

Secondary and higher secondary education are important terminal stages in the system of general education because it is at these points that the youth decide on whether to pursue higher education, opt for technical training or join the workforce. Whether General or Vocational education? This is a "tough choice" in many developing countries. In the human capital framework, general education creates 'general human capital' and vocational and technical education 'specific human capital' (Becker, 1964). The former is portable across one's life and from job to job, while the later one is not and hence many advocate general education, as more suitable to the flexible labour force that can change task and even the type of work; but the later one has an advantage, imbibing specific job-relevant skills, that can make the worker more readily suitable for a given job and would make him/her thus more productive. (Tilak, 2002).

Vocational Education

Educationists and experts have consistently recommended that education at these stages should be given a vocational bias to link it with the world of employment.

Leading social scientists have lent strong support for vocational education. Authors like Thomas Balogh (1969) were emphatic in arguing: "As a purposive factor for rural socio-economic prosperity and progress, education must be technical, vocational and democratic." The Kothari Commission felt that "it should be possible to divert at least 50 percent of the students completing class X to the vocational stream, reducing the pressure on the universities and also preparing students for gainful employment (GOI, 2002).

According to the Kothari Commission, the second level of skill the middle level supervisory and technician group is the responsibility of vocational and technical education system. The Commission stressed the responsibility of technical and vocational education for training not only those who will seek employment but also for those who will create employment (NCERT, 1970).

It was believed that the introduction of vocational education and training will help in solving many of the educational problems, like the rampant demand for higher education could be controlled, the financial crisis in education would be eased by reducing pressures on higher education budgets, and unemployment among college and secondary school graduates would be reduced. It was also believed that vocational education would contribute to economic progress of country, both by reducing unemployment and through creating employment opportunities in the fields of pre-vocational specialisation and self-employment. It will engender a higher propensity for labour force participation at the end of their secondary schooling, improving productivity, and correspondingly resulting in higher graduate earnings. And thereby vocational and technical secondary education can establish a closer relationship between school and work (Tilak,1988a).

However, in India the introduction and implementation of vocational education and training is far away from the success and has turned out to be a myth. Also, vocational and technical education is not necessarily favoured and welcomed by all. There are strong opponents to this as well. Foster (1965) exploded the vocational school myth and called it "vocational school fallacy." Foster(1965) and later Blaug (1973) clearly argued that vocationalisation cannot be a remedy for educated unemployment: it cannot prepare students for specific occupations and reduce mismatches between education and the labour market; academic streams promise higher wages than vocational streams; accordingly demand for vocational education might not exist, and Say's law that supply creates its own demand might not work. Furthermore, vocational schooling may create "a sense of second class citizenship among both teachers and taught which militates against effective learning" (Blaug, 1973).

Also, the social attitude towards the vocational education is not very encouraging in many parts of the country. Negative attitudes to manual work or blue collared work severely dampen the demand for vocational education. Further, VET is conceived as a system of education meant for the poor, and for those who belong to educationally backward sections that are not eligible for admission into higher education. This is viewed as one that perpetuates and deepens inequalities in the system. Low prestige attached to vocational education and its inherent inequities are somewhat a common phenomenon in many states. (Grubb, 1985) As a result, vocational education in countries like India did not take off on a sound footing.

Problem of Unemployment

Since independence the existence of high unemployment level has been regarded as one of the major economic problem confronting the Indian economy. The problem of educated unemployed is becoming more and more sensitive and complex over the period of time. The educated unemployment is rising alarmingly. Thus, the issue of educated unemployment needs consideration. (Naidu 1996).

According to the Economic Survey 2005-2006 the unemployment rate went up during 1993-94 to 2004. According to The Task force on Employment Opportunities, the number of job-seekers in the age group of 20 to 39 years, which was approx. 77 percent of the total number of job-seekers in the year 1991 has come down to 75 percent in the year 1999. On the other hand, the number of job-seekers in the age group 20-29 years decreased from 60 percent in 1991 to 51.5 percent in 1999. The number of job seekers in the age group of 30 years and above had increased during the period 1991 to 1999 from 18.5 percent in 1991 to 28.0 percent in 1999. There is a steady shift from the lower age (i.e. 20 to 29) to upper age (age 29 or more) from year to year, "which indicates that job-seekers face difficulty in securing suitable jobs at a younger age and continue in the register of the Employment Exchange" (GOI, 2001). The number of job seekers in the age group of 30 years and above had increased during the period 1991 to 1999 from 18.5 percent in 1991 to 28.0 percent in 1999. There is further a shift from the lower age (i.e. 20 to 29) to upper age (age 29 or more) from year to year, which indicates that job-seekers face difficulty in securing suitable jobs at a younger age and continue in the register of the Employment Exchange (GOI, 2001).

The unemployment rate for educated (secondary and above) persons in the age group 15-29 in 1993-94 was as high as 18.5 percent. For those who have any form of technical education, the unemployment rate is even higher at 27.3 percent in the age group 15-29 in 1993-94. Unemployment rates for educated youth in 1999-00 are still high at 14.8 percent for secondary education and above and 23.7 percent for all types of technical education.

The high rate of unemployment among educated youth is in many ways the core of the problem because it creates a sense of despair across a wide section of the population including not only the educated youth but their parents and families. It needs to be emphasised that the aspirations of this group cannot be met just by creating any employment opportunities. Indeed, the reason why this group has high unemployment is precisely because their aspirations are high and they do not just want to take up any employment that may be available (GOI, 2006).

Educated Unemployment

There are many causes of educated unemployment. The defective educational system, with its theoretical bias, lack of aptitude and technical qualifications for various types of work among job-seekers and maladjustments between demand and supply of workers are a few reasons. (GOI ,2005).

The Task Force on Employment Opportunities set up by the Planning Commission, noted that expansion in government employment is unlikely to be an important source of future employment growth. There is evidence of excessive employment in the government sector as a consequence of fiscal indiscipline in the past. Part of the problem is a strong preference among the young for general education over vocational training because general education has traditionally been seen as a route to acquiring government jobs which are highly valued. This has led to a low demand for vocational training courses.

However, there is also a problem with the supply side of vocational training. The physical capacity of the existing training institutes is limited and the quality of the training provided is also not up to the mark. Training courses in government run institutes are often not sufficiently reflective of market demand. There is also a perception among employers that the skill levels acquired by graduates of these institutes are inadequate.

A basic point which emerges is that the employment objective cannot be defined solely in terms of whether enough job opportunities are created for the projected increase in the labour force. "This purely quantitative approach ignores the very important issue of the low "quality" of employment which is the source of much of the current unhappiness with the employment situation." In this situation, an employment strategy which focuses on a mere creation of low quality job opportunities will not address the real nature of the problem (GOI, 2001).

Worsening unemployment now affecting young people in particular and the deteriorating competitive position of our enterprises is forcing people to be sceptical about the education system that produces so many unqualified youngsters." (Thatte1990). As mentioned earlier, the vocationalization of education at the secondary stage of schooling has also achieved only partial success.

Defective Education System

The educational system in India has not been able to cater to the needs. "Worsening unemployment now affecting young people in particular and the deteriorating competitive position of our enterprises is forcing people to be sceptical about the education system that produce so many unqualified youngsters." (Thatte, 1990) According to Myrdal (1968), India's educational policy does not aim at development of human resources. It merely produces clerks and lower cadre executives for the government and private concerns. With the expansion in the number of institutions which impart this kind of education, increase in unemployment is inevitable. It is also because education in arts, commerce and science will not ensure employment on account of its limited utility for productive purposes.

The data by Employment Exchanges and NSSO also narrate the same story. Myrdal (1968) considers all those who receive merely this kind of education not only as inadequately educated but also wrongly educated.

Entrepreneurial Education

In view of the situation of declining job opportunities, the challenge before the economy is to create conducive environment for employment. Entrepreneurial talent among individuals to work in increasingly productive and remunerative sectors of the economy is imminent (Agrawal and Patel, 2001). The Sixth Plan had also recognized since the bulk of the unemployed in the country are matriculates and the limited possibilities of employment in the organized sector, training in the ITIs which is mostly oriented to service sector should be refurbished to make it self-employment and production oriented.

"Entrepreneurship development has been accepted as a tool in the development process for over two decades in India (Mony, 1994). It was accepted in our country as a strategy for achieving twin objectives of rapid industrialisation and solving the problem of unemployment in the country. "Planning, implementation and evaluation are important aspects of making an EDP result-oriented if at all included in school curriculum". (Mali and Deka, 1994)

In the formal education, entrepreneurship is relatively a new discipline. "Entrepreneurship development was started in our country during the sixties in the form of industrial campaign. During the seventies systematic efforts were made for developing entrepreneurship. Gujarat followed by states like Andhra Pradesh, Karnataka and Tamil Nadu etc" was the first state to start planned and systematic efforts on entrepreneurship development. "Establishment of positive linkage between entrepreneurship and economic prosperity and emergence of strong planned effort were the two major contributions of 60s". (Akhouri, 1994).

It has been found by various studies that till the beginning of the 1990s entrepreneurship remained a topic of academics at undergraduate and post-graduate level. The innovations in these areas include motivating the target groups concerned to take up entrepreneurship courses at school level. New initiatives in formal educational system at school level can be:

- Motivating students at school level to seek self-employment as career option.
- Using consultancy as a method of teaching, there is a need to develop and enhance practical insight required to start new enterprise.
- Training teachers in entrepreneurship with real experience as students of entrepreneurship and spreading entrepreneurship development education to a large number of students at school level.
- There is need to combine entrepreneurial intensity and academic requirement in management education at school level.

Conclusions

Reforms in school education have been guided by a concern for (a) improvement in the quality of education through the dual process of energizing functioning of the system and its linkage with the development process in its all dimensions. "Education must subscribe to its definition of aiming at enriching the quality of human life and enhancing our capacity to cope with the challenge of change in a fast changing world order (Dubhashi, 1994). With the radical change of societies in social, political, economic, technological, and education spheres, there should be a change in the perspectives on the need for and nature of VET. New challenges have begun to emerge, and old ones to remerge.

In the given economic conditions, vocational education has not been able to solve many of the problems. The option would lie in merging entrepreneurship education with vocational education and training. This will also give a face-lift to the vocational education and training

References

Agrawal S. and Patel J. (2001), Self Employment of Women and Structural Reforms in Women and Employment edited by S. Murthy, RBSA Publishers, Jaipur.

Akhouri, M.M. P.(1999), Entrepreneurship Development in 1990s in Training for Entrepreneurship and self employment, Edited by D.D. Mali, Mittal Publications, New Delhi.

Anderson, C.A. and Bowman, M.J. (eds.) (1965) Education and Economic Development. Chicago: Aldine. Asian Development Bank (1991) Technical and Vocational Education and Training. Manila.

Balogh Thomas (1969) Education and Agrarian Progress in Developing Countries, In: Hufne, K. and Naumann, J. (eds.) Economics of Education in Transition. Stuttgart: Ernst Klett.

Becker G.S. (1964) Human Capital. New York: National Bureau of Economic Research, NY.

Bennell, P. (1995) General versus Vocational Secondary Education in Developing Countries: A Review of the Rates of Return Evidence. IDS Working Paper 23. Institute of Development Studies, Sussex, Brighton:

Bennell, Paul and Sergerstrom, J. (1998) Vocational Education and Training in Developing Countries: Has the World Bank Got it Right? International Journal of Educational Development 18 (4) (July): 271-87.

Blaug, M. (1973) Education and the Employment Problem in Developing Countries. Geneva: International Labour Office.

Boyd, T.F. and Lee, C. (1995) Educational Need and Economic Advancement: The Role of Vocational Education in the Republic of China, Requote from, Tilak (1988c).

Das. M, (1993), "Strategy for Excellence in Higher Education", "University News" June.

Dougherty, C. (1990) Unit Costs and Economies of Scale in Vocational and Technical Education: Evidence from the People's Republic of China, Economics of Education Review Vol.9

Dreze .J, and Sen, A. (1996), India: Economic Development and Social Opportunity, Oxford University Press, New Delhi.

Dubhashi, P.R (1994), "Indian System of Higher Education", "University News" February.

Foster P.J. (1965), The Vocational School Fallacy in Development Planning. In: Anderson and Bowman (eds.),

Ghanchi, D.A (1993), "Higher Education: Constraints and Strains", "University News", January.

Government of India (2002), Report of the Committee on India:

Vision 2020 Government of India Planning Commission, New Delhi.

Government of India (2005), Report of the Working Group on secondary and vocational education For 11th Five Year Plan (2007-2012), Government of India Planning Commission, New Delhi.

Government of India (2002), employment exchange statistics 1999-2000 Government of India, ministry of labour directorate general of employment & training, New Delhi, January.

Government of India, (2001) Report of the task force on employment, Planning Commission, Government of India, New Delhi.

Government of India, Planning Commission (2006), Report of the working group on skill development and vocational training, Planning Commission, Government of India, New Delhi.

Governments of India, Planning Commission, Tenth plan Report (20002-2007), Planning Commission, Government of India, New Delhi.

Grubb, W.N. (1985) The Convergence of Educational System and the Role of Vocationalism. Comparative Education Review 29 (4): 526-548.

Haq, M. and Khadija, H. (1998) Human Development in South Asia 1998. Karachi: Oxford University Press.

Jain, G.R and Gupta, D. (1994), "New Initiatives in Entrepreneurship Education and Training", EDII, Ahmedabad

Mony, S. (1999), Experiences with Entrepreneurship Development Programme in North East Region: NEITCO's experience, in Training for Entrepreneurship and self employment, Edited by D.D. Mali, Mittal Publications, New Delhi.

Mundle, S. (ed.) (1998) Financing Human Resource Development in the Advanced Asian Economies, World Development 26 (4) (April):

Myrdal, G., (1968), Asian Drama: An Enquiry into the Poverty in underdeveloped Countries., New York.

Naidu, K M (1996), "Unemployment: An Indian Perspective", Anubhav, September-October

OECD (2000) Education at a Glance: OECD Indicators. Paris: Organisation for Economic Co-operation and Development. July

Patrinos, H. A. (1999), "Market Forces in Education" retrieved on 29/12/07: //A:\ Market Forces.html.

NSSO, (1999), Sarvekshana Ministry of Statistics and Programme Implementation, government of India, Vol. XXIII, No. 1

Thatte, L. (1990), "Role of Educational Planning", "University News" Vol. XXVIII.

Tilak, J.B.G (2002), "Vocational Education and Training in Asia" in "The Handbook on Educational Research in the Asia Pacific Region", eds. John P Keeves and Rye Watanabe, Kluwer Academic Publishers)

Tilak, J.B.G. (1988a) Economics of Vocationalization: A Review of Evidence, Canadian and International Education 17 (1):

Tilak, J.B.G. (1988b) Vocational Education and Economic Growth. Journal of Educational Planning and Administration 2 (1-2) (January- April):

Tilak, J.B.G. (1988c) Vocational Education in South Asia: Problems and Prospects. International Review of Education 34 (2):

Tilak, J.B.G. (1994) Education for Development in Asia. New Delhi: Sage.

Tilak, J.B.G. (2001) Building Human Capital in East Asia. Washington DC: World Bank Institute.

Yang, J. (1998) General or Vocational? The Tough Choice in the Chinese Education Policy, International journal of Educational Development 18 (4) (July).

24

Academic Achievements of Tribal Students of Ashram Schools in Surat

Priti Chaudhari

Introduction

Education is a process, a long drawn out one, indeed a life long process. It has long been recognized as one of the corner stones of social and economic development. More recently with technological development and the changes in the methods of production, it has become even more important because the new technologies and production methods depend upon the human resource that is well trained and intellectually flexible. More than ever before, the development of nation today hinges on its capacity to acquire, adapt and then to advance knowledge. This capacity depends largely upon the extent to which the country's population has attained literacy, numeracy, communication and problem solving skills.

In the Indian education system education has a limited connotation. It is largely concerned with the existing formal structure of education and the institutionalized methodology of imparting knowledge to individuals. Within this very system exist many sub-groups of individuals with specific needs and tribals are one of them. In fact tribals form a large group of individuals in the Indian society. For several historical, economic and social reasons the scheduled groups have remained economically backward and socially retarded even to this day. This is true with respect to their educational levels also. India has the second largest tribal population in the world. This ST population is 8 percent of the total population of India and about 10 percent of all rural people. Twenty two of the twenty-six States of the country have about 90 percent of the ST population. There are 573 Scheduled Tribes living in different parts of the country, having their own languages different from the one mostly spoken in the state where they live. There are more than 270 such languages in India (Indian Education Report, 2002).

Meaning of Tribals

The term tribe or tribal is not defined any where in the constitution although according to the Article 342, STs represents the tribe or tribal communities that are notified by the president. Tribes are not part of the traditional Hindu caste structure. STs in India are more like the "indigenous" or "native people" in other parts of the world.

Tribals in India's Constitution

The constitution has devoted more than 20 articles on the redressal and upliftment of underprivileged following the policy of positive discrimination and affirmative action, particularly with reference to the STs. Recognizing the special needs of STs, the Constitution of India made certain special safeguards to protect these communities from all the possible exploitation and thus ensure social justice. While Article 14 confers equal rights and opportunities to all, Article 15 prohibits discrimination against any citizen on the grounds of sex, religion, race, caste etc; Article 15(4) enjoins upon the State to make special provisions for the advancement of any socially and educationally backward classes; Article 16(4) empowers the State to make provisions for reservation in appointments or posts in favour of any backward class of citizens, which in the opinion of State, is not adequately represented in the services under the State; Article 46 enjoins upon the State to promote with special care the educational and economic interests of the weaker sections of the people and, in particular, the STs and promises to protect them from social injustice and all form of exploitation.

Further, while Article 275 promises grant-in-aid for

promoting the welfare of STs and for raising the level of administration of Scheduled areas, Article 330, 332 and 335 stipulates reservation of seats for STs in the Lok Sabha and in the State Legislative Assemblies and in services. Finally, the constitution also empowers the state to appoint a commission to investigate the conditions of socially and educationally backward classes (Article 340) and to specify those Tribes or Tribal Communities deemed to be as STs (Article 342).

Education of tribals is an important task before the Government of India. Article 46 of the constitution talks about promotion of educational and economic interests of Scheduled Castes, STs and other weaker sections. To quote "The State shall promote with special care the educational and economic interests of the weaker sections of the people and in particular of SCs and STs and shall protect them from social injustice and all forms of exploitations." Many more other constitutional rights were available for tribal people.

One special educational input for tribal education is residential schools widely known as Ashram schools in India. These institutions are very special efforts in the direction of tribal education.

Rationale of the Study

Research in the area of tribal education has many vital and useful findings to report but the findings pertaining to the participation of tribal people in the school education programme have not been conclusive. It is a fact that tribal people are lagging behind in the sphere of education compared to other advanced sections of the population. This phenomenon has been witnessed by all of us both in the pre-independence and post-independent India. Even now education has not penetrated deep into the tribal life. Such a situation raises two pertinent questions. One, how far the tribal people have come forward and benefited from the prevailing education system? Second, what are the major stumbling blocks coming in their way? While the response to the previous question can be given through a large scale survey type studies (macro level studies), response to the latter can be given by a micro level in-depth study. Thus in the context of tribal education both the types of studies are essential. The macro level studies will provide valuable inputs for policy planning; micro level studies will be helpful in providing the needed educational inputs in the local specific context.

The existence of very few studies in tribal education in the Indian context bring to the forefront the need for conducting studies on tribal education in India, on any of its dimension. It has been found that the infrastructure in the Ashram schools in terms of buildings, teaching aids, hostel facilities etc are poor. The teaching learning process in these schools was not found to be satisfactory. Absenteeism, stagnation and wastage were high in the ashram schools. Ashram schools had perceptible impact on local communities. They had many positive effects. However, some negative effects were also seen (Raman, 1990). Thus, there is need to conduct studies to explore the empirical basis of tribal education in its different aspects.

A study of existing status will provide empirical base line about the status of tribal education. Such data also facilitates evaluation of tribal education programmes undertaken. From this point of view it would be worth while to know about the academic achievement of tribal students in the ashram schools. Also existence of such type of studies in primary education among tribals in Indian context will facilitate planners to design appropriate policies for the improvement of education among the tribal people.

Thus, an analysis into students academic achievement yield significant insight into the current situations of tribal education in ashram schools. It may give guidelines for curriculum renewal/development in education pertaining to tribals for making it more thorough, realistic and practical.

Thus there exists a need for investigating the academic achievement of tribal students in ashram school education in the Indian context.

Statement of the Problem

To study the academic achievement of Tribal students of Ashram schools of Surat district.

Objectives of the study

- To study the academic achievement of tribal students in all the subjects in terms of Girls, Boys and Total Students (Girls + Boys).
- To study the relationship between different subjects.

Explanation of the Terms: Tribals: according to the Article 342, STs represent the tribe or tribal communities that are notified by the President. Tribes are not part of the traditional Hindu caste structure. STs in India are more like the "indigenous" or "native people" in other parts of the world.

Academic achievement: Marks obtained by students in X standard Board examination of the academic year 2006-2007.

Delimitation of the Study: The study is confined to all the X standard students of Ashram schools of Surat District. Which are following Gujarat Secondary Education Board syllabus of 2006-2007 academic year.

Population: All the students of standard X studying in all the Ashram schools of Surat District following Gujarat State Education Board syllabus constitute the population. The students were of the academic year 2006-2007.

Sample: The sample has been selected using "Random Lottery Method". From all the ashram schools three schools were randomly selected. From these three schools, all the students of standard X were selected as sample of the study. The sample size was 221 (72 boys+149 girls) students of X standard studying in Amalsadi ashram School, Ambapardi ashram school and Vaghecha ashram school of Surat District.

Tools: Documents of results of X standard students.

Collection of Data: For the purpose of collecting data for the study, investigator had personally gone to schools constituting the sample. The investigator had personally approached the principals of the schools and explained the purpose of the study. The investigator had personally collected the documents of results of X standard students of sample schools.

Analysis of the Data: The data was analyzed using mean, median, mode, standard deviation, standard error of mean, quartile deviation, skewness and kurtosis. The data for objective two was analyzed by applying Pearsons Product – Moment correlation. The coefficient of correlation is a single value that tells about the extent to which two things are related and to what extent variation in one go with the variation in other.

Major Findings and Conclusion

1. The mean achievement of girls in Gujarati was found to be 51.7 out of the total of 100. The nature of distribution of scores of the entire sample was peaked than the normal i.e. leptokurtic. The fifty percent of the girls had scored 52 or more marks in Gujarati. Moreover, 10 percent of the girls had scored 64 or more than it.
2. The mean achievement of Boys in Gujarati was found to be 54.2 out of the total of 100. The nature of distribution of scores of the entire sample was peaked than the normal i.e. platykurtic. The fifty percent of the boys had scored 54 or more marks in Gujarati. Moreover, 10 percent of the boys had scored 67 or more than it.
3. The mean achievement of total students in Gujarati was found to be 52.5 out of the total of 100. The nature of distribution of scores of the entire sample was peaked than the normal i.e. leptokurtic. The fifty percent of the total students had scored 52 or more marks in Gujarati. Moreover, 10 percent of the total students had scored 66 or more than it.
4. The mean achievement of girls in English was found to be 37.5 out of the total of 100. The nature of distribution of scores of the entire sample was peaked than the normal i.e. leptokurtic. The fifty percent of the girls had scored 37 or more marks in English. Moreover, 10 percent of the girls

had scored 52 or more than it.

5. The mean achievement of Boys in English was found to be 46.5 out of the total of 100. The nature of distribution of scores of the entire sample was peaked than the normal i.e. leptokurtic. The fifty percent of the boys had scored 46 or more marks in English. Moreover, 10 percent of the boys had scored 59 or more than it.
6. The mean achievement of total students in English was found to be 40.5 out of the total of 100. The nature of distribution of scores of the entire sample was peaked than the normal i.e. leptokurtic. The fifty percent of the total students had scored 41 or more marks in English. Moreover, 10 percent of the total students had scored 55 or more than it.
7. The mean achievement of girls in Hindi was found to be 63.6 out of the total of 100. The nature of distribution of scores of the entire sample was peaked than the normal i.e. platykurtic. The fifty percent of the girls had scored 65 or more marks in Hindi. Moreover, 10 percent of the girls had scored 76 or more than it.
8. The mean achievement of Boys in Hindi was found to be 66.9 out of the total of 100. The nature of distribution of scores of the entire sample was peaked than the normal i.e. platykurtic. The fifty percent of the boys had scored 67 or more marks in Hindi. Moreover, 10 percent of the boys had scored 77 or more than it.
9. The mean achievement of total students in Hindi was found to be 64.7 out of the total of 100. The nature of distribution of scores of the entire sample was peaked than the normal i.e. platykurtic. The fifty percent of the total students had scored 66 or more marks in Hindi. Moreover, 10 percent of the total students had scored 77 or more than it.
10. The mean achievement of girls in Social Science was found to be 53.2 out of the total of 100. The nature of distribution of scores of the entire sample was peaked than

the normal i.e. platykurtic. The fifty percent of the girls had scored 55 or more marks in Social Science. Moreover, 10 percent of the girls had scored 69 or more than it.

11. The mean achievement of Boys in Social Science was found to be 60.8 out of the total of 100. The nature of distribution of scores of the entire sample was peaked than the normal i.e. platykurtic. The fifty percent of the boys had scored 61 or more marks in Social Science. Moreover, 10 percent of the boys had scored 72 or more than it.
12. The mean achievement of total students in Social Science was found to be 55.7 out of the total of 100. The nature of distribution of scores of the entire sample was peaked than the normal i.e. platykurtic. The fifty percent of the total students had scored 57 or more marks in Social Science. Moreover, 10 percent of the total students had scored 71 or more than it.
13. The mean achievement of girls in Science and Technology was found to be 42.7 out of the total of 100. The nature of distribution of scores of the entire sample was peaked than the normal i.e. platykurtic. The fifty percent of the girls had scored 44 or more marks in Science and Technology. Moreover, 10 percent of the girls had scored 63 or more than it.
14. The mean achievement of Boys in Science and Technology was found to be 59.1 out of the total of 100. The nature of distribution of scores of the entire sample was peaked than the normal i.e. leptokurtic. The fifty percent of the boys had scored 58 or more marks in Science & Technology. Moreover, 10 percent of the boys had scored 72 or more than it.
15. The mean achievement of total students in Science and Technology was found to be 48.1 out of the total of 100. The nature of distribution of scores of the entire sample was peaked than the normal i.e. platykurtic. The fifty percent of the total students had scored 50 or more marks in Science & Technology. Moreover, 10 percent of the

total students had scored 67 or more than it.

16. The mean achievement of girls in Mathematics was found to be 42.6 out of the total of 100. The nature of distribution of scores of the entire sample was peaked than the normal i.e. leptokurtic. The fifty percent of the girls had scored 41 or more marks in Mathematics. Moreover, 10 percent of the girls had scored 72 or more than it.
17. The mean achievement of Boys in Mathematics was found to be 62.7 out of the total of 100. The nature of distribution of scores of the entire sample was peaked than the normal i.e. platykurtic. The fifty percent of the boys had scored 64 or more marks in Mathematics. Moreover, 10 percent of the boys had scored 75 or more than it.
18. The mean achievement of total students in Mathematics was found to be 49.1 out of the total of 100. The nature of distribution of scores of the entire sample was peaked than the normal i.e. platykurtic. The fifty percent of the total students had scored 54 or more marks in Mathematics. Moreover, 10 percent of the total students had scored 73 or more than it.
19. The mean achievement of girls in Krushi Vigyan was found to be 80.4 out of the total of 100. The nature of distribution of scores of the entire sample was peaked than the normal i.e. platykurtic. The fifty percent of the girls had scored 81 or more marks in Krushi Vigyan. Moreover, 10 percent of the girls had scored 87 or more than it.
20. The mean achievement of Boys in Krushi Vigyan was found to be 81.7out of the total of 100. The nature of distribution of scores of the entire sample was peaked than the normal i.e. platykurtic. The fifty percent of the boys had scored 82 or more marks in Krushi Vigyan. Moreover, 10 percent of the boys had scored 87 or more than it.
21. The mean achievement of total students in Krushi Vigyan was found to be 80.78 out of the total of 100. The nature of distribution of scores of the entire sample was peaked than the normal i.e. platykurtic. The fifty percent of the total

students had scored 81 or more marks in Krushi Vigyan. Moreover, 10 percent of the total students had scored 87 or more than it.

22. There is moderate positive correlation ranging from 0.35089 to 0.670243 between scores of mathematics and Gujarati, Hindi, English, Social Science, Science & Technology and Krushi Vigyan scores of the students.

Conclusion

The academic achievement of tribal students was found average in Gujarati, Hindi, Social Science and Mathematics while below average in English and Science and Technology. The academic achievement in Krushi Vigyan was good. So there was a need to find out the reasons behind their different levels of achievement in different subjects.

References

Ekka, E.M. (1990). Development of tribal education in Orissa after Independence, Ph.D., In Buch, M. B. edited Fifth survey of Research in Education, New Delhi, NCERT

Panigrahi, S.C. (1992). A study of educational development of tribals in Kalakhadi district of Orissa, Ph.D. thesis, C.A.S.E., M.S.U., Vadodara

Raman, G.V. (1989). Problems of education among the tribal communities of Andhra Pradesh: A case study of Ashram schools, Ph.D., In Buch, M. B. edited Fifth survey of Research in Education, New Delhi, NCERT

Sathyabalan, V. (1993) Effectiveness of primary education in rural areas of Tamil Nadu, Ph. D. thesis, C.A.S.E., M.S.U., Vadodara

Educational problems of tribal children: www.nic.in/cd50years/2/51/7s/517soboi.htm

Effectiveness of various interventions for improving tribal education – A research study: www.education.nic.in/cd50years/2/5/17s/817soAo1.htm

Schedule Tribes: www.planningcommission.nic.in/plans/planrel/fiveyr/10th/volume2/v2-ch4-2.pdf

Tribal welfare and development-Draft paper: www.nac.nic.in/concept percent20papers/Tribalwelfare.htm

25

Innovation and Change in School Education

Priyadarshini S. Kelkar

"Survival of the fittest" said Darwin

The "fit" here should be taken as adaptive, wishing to change for better and being able to manage the change. Schools should modify their internal environment in such a way that they are able to handle the change that is inevitable and desirous by all. The world is changing at a rapid pace and each one of us needs to keep pace with the changes that are coming to stay. If this be the case, the entire concept of schooling will have to be transformed.

Rapid social economical and technological changes demand a new role from education. Education has to be concerned not only with promoting innovations in its own system, but also with helping to influence society in managing change. If education is to play this role effectively, it has to take a different approach to planning in order to promote both innovations and change management.

It is a truism that schools must change continually to keep up with the changing environment. The point that arises is whether there are ways to create conditions that change will happen naturally? Must we view change as something someone does to the other? Instead of thinking about change as an artefact of a strategy, management plan, or any other grant scheme, can culture of a school be reconstituted in such a way that change becomes natural?

Components to Manage Change in Schooling System

1. Leading successful change and improvement involves

developing and managing six critical components of schooling:

- a clear, strong, and collectively held educational vision and institutional mission;
- a strong, committed professional community within the school;
- learning environments that promote high standards for student achievement;
- sustained professional development to improve learning;
- successful partnerships with parents, health and human service agencies, businesses, universities, and other community organizations; and
- a systematic planning and implementation process for instituting needed changes.

2. A Clear, strong, and collectively held educational vision and institutional mission: Successful school improvement requires establishing a clear educational vision and a shared institutional mission, knowing how well the school is accomplishing that mission, identifying areas for improvement, developing plans to change educational activities and programs, and implementing those plans or new programs effectively.
3. A strong, committed professional community within the school: A school looking for successful change believes that all teachers have a potential that is needed and can be developed and fostered to make them into great teachers. And the great task that a school has to undertake is to provide a conducive environment which enables teachers to preserve and to use their creative instinct in what they do. Curriculum framers and implementers as well as the teachers, do make a critical difference in what, why and how students learn and in maintaining higher standards of student achievement. If the school has to be a change manager, it has to have teachers who are motivated, committed, enthusiastic, light houses of knowledge and who are individuals who believe impossible means "I am

possible".

4. Learning environments that promote high standards for student achievement: A school should be a learning laboratory where both its teachers and students are in a learning mode. In this great school teachers and students experiment, innovate, take joy in learning, take charge of their learning and where they are not bound by rigid, static environment. The school leader establishes a school culture which fosters cooperation, encourages professional risk taking, and empowers (creating a community of leaders), he/she promotes a philosophy of life-long learning among students, staff, and community, encourages high levels of participation in school level decision-making, monitors progress and creates a collaborative and proactive school culture which anticipates needs, initiates responses, and monitors progress.
5. Sustained professional development to improve learning: Today's teacher is well-informed, more equipped with materials and technology and is better read. Yet the importance of teacher in service training can not be undermined. Conventionally used short duration workshops help teachers to an extent, but do not help teachers to transfer new knowledge and practices to the classroom. Hence innovative practices with enlarged scope are required to be put to use. A school must have a very organized, planned and deliberate ongoing in-service training for professional growth of teachers. Professional development programmes should aim at developing (i) the knowledge domain, (ii) equipping the teacher with information technology (iii) empowering the teacher with newer & better educational technologies and more student cantered pedagogy and (iv) ensuring right attitudes & values to make them effective teachers. Professional development has become very imminent in the changed social, economic and technological environment. In

service training will be effective, only when it is need based and person specific and tailored after an induced self realization of shortcomings and strengths through appraisal of subject content, ability to deliver the subject content, emotional stability and attitude to teaching.

6. Successful partnerships with parents, health and human service agencies, businesses, universities, and other community organizations: It is essential that leaders of school establish and improve links to others outside the school and connect the school's goals to the broader and deeper mission of providing useful high-quality learning for all students. When developing and implementing change initiatives, leaders must ask themselves, whether a proposed program will improve access to higher-order learning tasks for marginalized students. For school improvement efforts to be successful, teachers, parents, community and business partners, administrators, and students must share leadership functions. The principal's role must change from that of a top-down supervisor to a facilitator, architect, steward, instructional leader, coach, and strategic teacher (Senge, 1990).
7. A systematic planning and implementation process for instituting the needed changes: Last but perhaps the most important component of successful change in school is the school leadership perception and style. If schools are to respond to the fundamental changes that are taking place in the social and economic terms, then it is necessary to re-conceptualize leadership. If a school or any organization is to be transforming itself, it has to be led by people who are capable of personal transformation. If the schools are to re-engineer themselves, then one of the starting points has to be re-engineering the perception of leadership. There is a tendency of expressing leadership as 'super management' i.e. leaders who are more competent to handle a wide range of tasks. Thus the model of leadership is one of omni competence; skilled classroom teacher plus a

curricular leader, plus a technical expert, plus all manifestations associated with a leader. The leaders must then be able to efficiently attend to wide range of tasks and create learning organizations.

Managing and Leading the Change

In the present context, schools have to function in the complexity of changing environmental factors. A leader therefore has to be a fundamental reorganizer and a perceiver of a new paradigm. The leader as an artist translates ideals into concrete outcomes. He/she needs to have vision, creativity and ability to communicate.

For schools to operate more as communities characterized by collaborative culture, a new vision of leadership is required. Principal's actions within the social, institutional and personal contexts, affect the instructional process as well as institutional climate. Students' outcome greatly depends upon the school climate for which the principal is responsible.

Visualizing the emerging issues and future challenges, school leaders need to adopt innovative strategies on both academic and administrative processes.

A collaborative school management is required wherein the principal, teachers, students and community at large become partners in the school affairs and contribute effectively for the growth and development of the institution. Learning organizations are participative and are powered by the synergy of people who work there. "The top thinks and the local acts" must give way to integrative thinking and acting at all levels. It calls for decentralization of activities, delegation of responsibilities, building of trust and ensuring accountability. In a learning organization, the leader's role differs dramatically from that of a charismatic decision maker. He acquires new skills, the ability to identify and develop a shared vision, to bring to the surface novel ideas to challenge and to replace the outdated mental models and foster more systematic pattern of thinking.

Managing school change and improvement is one of the most complex tasks of school leadership. As Fullan (1993), Sparks (1993), and others point out, school leaders need to understand the change process in order to lead and manage change and improvement efforts effectively. They must learn to overcome barriers and cope with the chaos that naturally exists during the complex process of change (Fullan & Miles, 1992). Principals and other key school leaders should help all stakeholders build effective teams by developing new organizational structures and creating a shared vision that focuses on authentic student learning (Newmann, 1993; Maeroff, 1993). Such inspired and informed leadership is critical to the success of schools.

The school leader encourages the learning communities within the school and outside the school to foster, grow and multiply by her/ his actions. A good leader senses a need for change within the school while responding to traditional cultural norms such as orderliness, respect and concern for others, academic achievement and co-curricular participation.

Plan of Action to Manage and Lead Change in School

Before beginning the change process, the leader must become familiar with the school improvement cycle, the stages of the change process, and change models associated with each. Leaders must be able to distinguish between the school improvement cycle and the change process, determine where the school is located within the change process, and identify appropriate next steps.

Therefore the schools and the school leaders must accept the change process as a positive experience to be understood and to be embraced, rather than a negative experience to be feared and to be avoided. For example, Fullan and Miles (1992) in "seven propositions for successful change". state.

1. Change is learning loaded with uncertainty.
2. Change is a journey, not a blueprint.
3. Problems are our friends.
4. Change is resource hungry.

5. Change requires the power to manage it.
6. Change is systemic.
7. All large-scale change is implemented locally. (Fullan & Miles, 1992)

When they are ready to begin the school improvement process, bring in change experts and facilitators to build the capacity of school staff to lead change efforts. It is important to draw upon the expertise and skills of university faculty, central Office personnel, external consultants, professional staff developers, and others. Fullan (1993) favours simply beginning the change process without necessarily planning every step in advance.

However, it is important to manage, guide, document, and learn from the change process which requires the following steps:

- Build a more collaborative school culture.
- Institute faculty study groups and a cross-grade or across department teams and provide time for collegial work.
- Build commitment and a collaborative culture to support the change process by being a "leader of leaders," having high expectations and communicating them, and demonstrating confidence in school staff and the surrounding community.
- Form partnerships with parents, businesses, and social service and community agencies to consolidate resources and meet the entire range of student needs emotional, social, and academic in order to improve student learning.
- Build new partnerships with other schools, using a carefully developed plan, organization and leadership, training, tools and processes, and monitoring and feedback loops to keep the new methods of teaching on course will enable schools to foster change.

Three Stages of Improvement Process

The school improvement process takes place in three stages described below: initiation, implementation, and institutionalization (Louis & Miles, 1990). Knowing about the challenges and problems as well as the success factors associated with each stage of the change process can increase the likelihood of success (Fullan, 1993).

Initiation: Without a focused effort to align and integrate school improvement initiatives, the probable result will be fragmented, uncoordinated programs and activities that may have conflicting objectives. It is up to school leaders to create a shared vision and mission for school improvement, to coordinate various change efforts so that they work together toward similar objectives rather than against one another, and to ensure that these efforts reach for the common goal of improved learning by all students.

Fullan (1993) points out that the change process can be chaotic and that leaders should not expect always to be systematic in their efforts. While planned change - including organized assessment and problem solving - can be useful, leaders often need to be able to cope with more informal, turbulent, and spontaneous change. To transform from a chaotic and poorly organized school, teachers should have regular workshops and seminars, classrooms be increasingly organized around cooperative learning, and teacher teams should develop, organize, and run most of the major programs and activities in the school. Staff and administrators will have to work collaboratively on the curriculum committees and school council to restructure the school. There has to be a combination of clear and shared mission, teamwork, a strong instructional program, and a well-developed improvement process, to become a successful school.

Through teamwork, staff development, and a continuous focus on student learning, the staff and principal should implement new instructional techniques. Schools should be able to develop a powerful collaborative, professional culture where teachers work together to improve instruction, learn new techniques, and value reflective dialogue on practice. The shared mission to serve all students with high-quality, interactive, in-depth, and engaging instructional approaches, regular reflective dialogue about new curriculum and instructional techniques that work and effort to incorporate new approaches in the classrooms will enable the schools to lead change in their organizations. There may be regular visits to each other's classes to observe, discuss, and give feedback in an informal form of peer coaching. Once a year, the entire staff could put on a daylong conference of instructional techniques and curriculum workshops for teachers in the region.

Implementation: If reforms are to improve learning for all students, leaders must find and implement meaningful curriculum and effective instructional programs for an increasingly diverse student population. To ensure that reforms do not overlook entire groups of students, leaders must understand the culture and needs of diverse students.

Institutionalization: A powerful vision for the school should serve all students by providing an intense, intellectually stimulating learning experience, by communicating high expectations for staff and students and supporting the development of quality instruction through a variety of symbolic actions.

Schools need to adapt to the multi-sensory world that students live in today and figure out how to take advantage of their students' ability to multitask and use different forms of media. Schools should have more team-based, open-ended classroom environments that allow students to help structure their learning. Technology motivates students and can help them be creative and tap into their curiosity. Teachers also need to be able to work with one another in a collaborative, team-driven environment, such as you find in businesses. Teachers need more time for planning, professional development, and community building that allows them to learn from one another. Professional development is very important, especially during times of change. Teachers are like physicians in that they are individual practitioners.

They should have the best tools so they can diagnose inherent shortcomings and prescribe and witness improvement. The principal may reinforce a strong collegial culture that is focused on students' academic achievement. A culture that reinforces shared ideas, sense of responsibility for change and improvement, and expectation of only the best from staff and students alike will enable schools to lead and anticipate change.

Conclusion

When the change is brought about systemically by adopting the above methods, it will sustain and will become a part of the school life. It will lead to qualitative improvement in the desired direction. Education will become more meaningful empowering the society. The schools should have collaborative culture, promoting school-home partnership, school-community partnership. When all stakeholders uphold the change, school education will become productive, responsive and a joyous experience for the learners.

Part III
Alternative Schooling in Education

26

Investigatory Projects in Educational Endeavours at Different Levels

A. Ramachary

Introduction

Learning is a continuous and multifarious process. Learning facilitators may have some limitations of their own, coming in the way of facilitating the learner to acquire knowledge, understanding, attitudes and skills. Yet, learners often seek the help of teachers to consolidate their knowledge through experience. It is a professional challenge to the teacher in identifying and offering the sequence of learning experiences suiting the learner for appropriate stimulation, motivation and educational enrichment.

In the constructivist perspective learners actively construct their own knowledge, by connecting new ideas to the existing ideas on the basis of materials/activities presented to them (experience). On the other hand learning takes place in a variety of ways through experience, making and doing things, experimentation, reading, discussion, asking, listening, thinking and reflecting and expressing oneself, in speech, movement or writing both individually and with others (NCF-2005). One of the least attended areas of learning experience being offered to the learner is project works, in its true sense. Even, when one finds some such project works take-up, they are restricted to making charts and playing with pieces of thermocol. Such project works may help in the process of construction of knowledge in a very routine and limited sense, without much of imagination, creativity, researching and reasoning etc.

National Curriculum Frame work (2005), in its

perspective, aptly identifies the key issues in this regard, as mentioned below:

- Connecting the knowledge to life out side the school.
- Ensuring that learning is shifted away from rote methods.
- Enriching the curriculum to provide for over all development of children rather than remain text book centric.

With a view to provide a better educational experience, which ensures the quality in education, one needs to look at the variety of co-curricular activities, which include project work. Project work call for the experiences designed for the learner in terms of knowledge and skills. These project works need not be restricted to a particular level of learner; on the contrary it can be for any and every level of learners. This is because of the fact that project work deals with application of knowledge and have the true potential of cognitive complement, besides enriching educational experience in the construction of own knowledge by the learner. In fact some of the projects at B.Ed, B.E, M.B.B.S and XII standard may be worth considering. As there can be a variety of projects, it is imperative to look at some kind of classification of these project works, prior to considering the investigatory projects, which are qualitatively different from other.

Types of Projects

Classification of project works can be based on different criteria and accordingly one may suggest different types of classification. Choosing one such way, following classification helps in finding the variety of project works. A simplistic division can be Confirmatory Type Projects (CTP) and Investigatory Type Projects (ITP). However, the results of ITP can also be used for suitable display, when required.

Confirmatory Type Projects (CTP): These projects are basically Confirmatory and display type, say for science exhibitions etc. These project works essentially confirm the concept/data/information available. Projects can be a static display type. That is data, photo, drawing, figure, material etc. displayed on a chart paper or pasted on a thermocol piece. Most of the works, in schools and colleges can be seen in this type. These can be of two dimensional or three dimensional types (cut-out). No part is meant for any movement in this type. Coin or rocks or stamp collection also can be displayed this way. These can be grouped as static display type of projects. Proper scaling in two dimensional (2-D) and three dimensional (3-D) models call for better understanding of metrics.

Dynamic display types of projects involve some movement in display of the data, say on the thermocol piece or a cut outs. A working model of any device, with some movement allowed in it can be a dynamic project work. Engine models, wind mills, with some movement, puppets with ability to move, Volcano demonstration model etc. can be of this type. Some of the working electronic circuitries also can be put under this type of projects. Essential difference between the static and dynamic projects is the working/demonstrating/moving character of the project components in its functioning pertains to dynamic and not so for static projects. Some of the biology projects say seed germination etc. without any investigation can also be treated as dynamic project.

Investigatory Type Projects (ITP): Investigatory type projects essentially differ from the above CTP, in the sense, ITP involve some investigation, search, probe, and finding. These types of projects follow the true scientific procedure in its methodology. Specific steps are to be followed in pursuing these projects. Critical elements of ITP are as follows:

- Identification and clear definition of the problem for investigation (PI).
- Choosing logical method for sampling and data collection (LM).
- Unbiased and systematic data collection (DC).
- Organizing data and critical analysis of it (DA).

- Listing out the results and findings (RF).
- Discussing the findings with reference to existing knowledge (DR).
- Drawing conclusions and making suggestions (CS).
- Reporting the investigation work suitably (RW).

Investigatory type projects certainly stand above the CTP, for its capacity to make scientific research process involved. Higher level abilities are called for in this process. Logical and creative thinking are much encouraged in this type of project work. Scientific temperament and spirit of enquiry are well nourished in such project works. Both individually and as a group these projects can be taken up. All most all the subjects like mathematics geography, language and history etc. can be considered for investigatory projects. Any level of student can handle these projects, under the suitable guidance of their teacher. Teacher can be cautious of the delimitations, level of the problem, cost, risk, time and feasibility factors can be assessed prior to engaging the student in such projects.

The degree of difficulty needs to be kept in view while assigning the investigatory project to students for a particular level. It is possible to identify the investigatory projects on different topics at different levels. Some of the investigatory projects, at school level, as an example are given here.

- A measuring glass jar can be used to investigate the water being wasted from dripping taps in an area, by collecting the samples from a number of taps on random selection basis.
- Period of germination and rate of growth of different seeds can be investigated.
- Salinity variation, if any, at a point near the sea cost area, over the period can be ascertained, using simple heating a unit quantity of water.
- Temperature variation in the class room, using a thermometer can be investigated for select period of time.
- Designing and building a bridge from a finite amount of thin wooden sticks, such as toothpicks or straw.

Competition consists of individuals or teams seeking to create the bridge that will bear undamaged the greatest load, with variations involving duration of loading, load motion or minimum structural weight.

- Calibrating the shadow lengths at a place and time for finding the heights of other objects like a pole or building or a person etc.
- Recording observations of an ant's behaviour in bright light and different coloured lights.
- Finding the ratio of optimum leaf length to optimum leaf width for a variety of leaves available and monitoring its variation with growth of leaves.
- Recording the rise in temperature of different materials, for a given period of exposure to sun light.
- Preparing the school map to the scale.

Similarly, at a different level, say, (in-service) at primary teachers level one may think of action research or intervention program like investigations. Investigating the reasons of failures or learning difficulties in a given subject topics and trying out remedial programs can be taken up by the in-service teachers. Following are the examples to consider a few.

- Investigating the effect of play way methods of teaching fractions, in contrast to routine classroom teaching.
- Investigating reasons for specific language difficulties of students at a given standard for both spoken and written form for boys and girls and analyzing them for evolving remedial measures.
- Trying out different methods to inculcate confident communication by students in the class, to investigate the most suitable one for a given social group of students.
- Investigating the effect of group activities in learning different subjects for a given standard.
- Investigating the common errors made by students in learning relatively difficult concepts and finding the effect of alternative methods of making learning easier.
- Investigating, by try out of, different application oriented

activities for teaching select curricular contents.

- Designing investigatory projects for any given subject and for a given standard, both for individual learners and as a group work.
- Investigating the difference in purely objective type testing, subjective type testing and mixed type of testing on select content unit for a given standard.
- Evaluating the influence of different methods of introducing a concept.
- Investigating the effect of dialogue approach in teaching a difficult concept.

Need and Scope

Need of Investigatory projects is acute, as it has a potential of learning by doing and has heuristic value. As the methodology involves specific scientific procedure in thought and action, it attempts to imbibe the scientific attitude and logical thinking in the learner. Starting from understanding the problem it carries the learner through cognitive, affective and psychomotor dimensions of learning, for finding solutions to real problems. While working in groups the investigatory project encourages the social interactions amongst the group members in finding solutions at every stage of project work. Having such a significant set of merits one can realize the need of encouraging the investigatory projects at all levels and for all subjects. Existing routine project work of making charts, cut outs with thermocol etc need to be intelligently replaced to the extent possible with real life and environmental problems suiting the learner needs. There is a clear need for developing investigative approach and ability to think critically and become good problem solvers. "The more accurately the students can describe their own thinking the more effective way they are able to control their decisions and actions during the process, and the stronger belief they have of their own abilities the better possibility they have to become expert problem solvers" (Schoenfeld, 1987).

Developing investigatory approach in students is needed to make them question their own knowledge and able to analyze the new problem. Tarja-Riitta Hurme and Sanna Järvelä (2002) observe: "Experts observe and question their own knowledge which is the main difference to novice problem solvers. The novices, the students, should learn to analyze and explore their existing procedural and declarative knowledge in a new problem solving situation".

One may find a lot of scope for taking up such a thought provoking projects, especially, when abundant source material is available in the websites offering due help. Teachers as guiding persons need to imaginatively raise questions to stimulate and motivate the learners to think, design and work out the investigatory projects. Curricular contents, environmental problems, day to day experiences, web site information, media and books may offer required material to enlist the investigatory projects suiting the level of the learners. Scope also ensures the broadening of the thinking horizons of the teachers and complements to their professional skills beyond text book centric existence. Teachers in their meetings or training can work on identifying the area specific problems for each standard as individual as well as group projects to be investigated over a period of time. It is ingenuity of the teacher to imaginatively think and connect the learning concepts to the investigations projects and provide appropriate opportunities to the learners. Learners as well as teachers get true benefit of application-oriented educational experience, in place of existing outdated content transmission by reading and talking ensuring just listening by learners. Scope of group participation in itself ensures lot of sharing and discussion. The discussion and negotiation help the students to make their thinking visible. According to the studies of thinking aloud (Chi & Bassok, 1989; Chi, DeLeeuw, Chiu & LaVancher, 1994) the students become aware of the existing knowledge and how to utilize it in new problem solving situations

Scope of the investigatory projects is sufficiently large

enough to enrich the educational endeavours. Even a student getting an opportunity to be involved in one such project per year certainly adds to the real potential of the student. Teachers in their planning for annual academic activities can chose to involve each student at least one investigatory project per year, on the recommendation of the sub-committee, which goes into the details of project works for students individually or in groups, subject wise and standard wise, annually. This meticulous planning obviously considers various aspects associated with project works, like, avoiding over loading the students and teachers, resource limitations, avoiding repetition, considering environmental relevance, feasibility and difficulty level etc. Each institution, over a period of time may become rich enough with these projects to go for sharing with other institutions, also maintain some evolutionary and developmental continuity in project works. Scope may also include organizing science exhibitions at school and regional level and encouraging the students to present their investigatory project's findings. Suitable awards can further motivate the students and teachers in quality learning. Teachers training programs can include these project related contents and methods.

Conclusion

Project works help learners to assimilate the concepts more so, when they them selves put their hands on. This further, enhances when the learner gets an opportunity to think, interact, investigate and find out the results related to learning concepts, relevant to their surroundings. Investigatory projects having the potential of inculcating and imbibing scientific spirit, logical and creative thinking, promoting scientific attitude in the learners, complementing their cognitive consumption.

Acute need and vast scope of implementation exists for the investigatory type projects at all levels of learning and for all content areas. Innovative embedding of this activity in to the curricular transaction, at different levels, remains with the practicing teachers. Hopefully, some teachers out of 55 lakh, spread over 10 lakh schools, educating 2025 lakh students in India may entertain educational investigations, in their educational endeavours, as a professional pursuit.

References

Chi, M. & Bassok, M. 1989. Learning from examples via self-explanations. In L.B. Resnick (Ed.) *Knowing, learning and instruction: Essays in Honour of Robert Glaser*, (pp.251-282). Hillsdale, NJ: Erlbaum.

Chi, M., DeLeeuw, N., Chiu, M-H & LaVancher, C. 1994. Eliciting self-explanations Improves understanding. *Cognitive Science, 18*, 439-477.

National Curriculum Framework (2005), NCERT, New Delhi.

Schoenfeld, A.H. 1987. What's all the fuss about metacognition? In A.H. Schoenfeld (Ed.) *Cognitive Science and mathematics education*, (pp.189-215). Hillsdale, NJ: Earlbaum Associates.

Tarja-Riitta Hurme and Sanna Järvelä 2002. *Metacognitive processes in problem solving with CSCL in Mathematics.* Department of Educational Sciences and Teacher Education, University of Oulu, P.O. Box 2000, Fin-90014 University of Oulu, Finland.

27

Grassroot Innovations for Quality Improvement at Primary Level

Satish Pathak and Sanjay Shah

It is an important fact that in the educational ladder the primary education is an important stage in helping the young minds to become responsible citizens of tomorrow. It is a base which needed to be strong enough so that the entire structure does not collapse. It is an important period that caters to the students the basic language knowledge, skills, values, attitudes and problem solving ability irrespective of what they are going to become later in life. These will help them in developing their full capacity of assessment, judgment, guidance, presentation and any kind of direction to improve the quality of their lives and to continue learning for the future.

The largest groups of human ability that are and must be the concern of education are human relations, cognitive skills and improvement upon abilities to perceive, to feel, to wonder, to intuit, to serve, to create, to fantasize, to imagine and to experience. Hence education from now on can no longer be defined in relation to fixed quantum of information which has to be assimilated, but must be conceived of as a process whereby human beings learn to discriminate, question and communicate their world of experience. For this, the education system has to relinquish the over emphasis on memorization of text-book knowledge by students. Instead, it must create and facilitate environment in and around the classrooms that fosters creativity in students. It is obvious that without some innovations, it is quite impossible. Looking to the fact that *creativity* alone can infuse the spirit of innovations and providing quality based education, it is a matter of growing concern that the creative spark in children be identified, nurtured and developed by all means.

Based on the above postulate Gujarat Council of Educational Research and Training (GCERT), Gandhinagar has initiated and organized some innovative programmes. GCERT is an apex resource organization catering to the quality of education under the Department of Education, Government of Gujarat. Twenty six (26) District Institutes of Education and Training (DIETs) are functioning under the direct control of GCERT. Research, training and innovative practices are the major focus areas to give thrust to the quality improvement in primary and secondary education. Innovations in education are supported and evaluated by need based research and monitoring. Such innovations are generally aimed at sustaining the spirit of innovation, encouraging experimentation and nurturing creativity at grassroots level. These are mainly for quality improvement using local wisdom and have direct relevance with the development of creativity in school children. The present paper highlights some of such grassroots innovations for quality improvement at primary level.

Grassroots Innovations

It is a fact that right action requires untiring patience for its success. Late Shri Gijubhai Badheka (1885-1939), the eminent educationist had proved this and mentioned in *Diwaswapana* (1931), the real story of a teacher who rejects the orthodox culture of education. He remains enthusiastic towards children and continues to experiment while consciously neglecting the traditions of teaching from prescribed textbooks. The theoretical background of his experiments lies in Montessori, but his preparation and implementation are thoroughly based on local wisdom. It is an original contribution to world-class pedagogy and establishes Gijubhai as luminary in the field of education. Based on his educational philosophy and the suggestions of the report on *learning without burden* by

Yashpal Committee (1993), the experiment of *Activity based and joyful learning* has been implemented in Std. I and II, in Gujarat.

Activity-based and Joyful Learning

In the present times of enormous changes all around, the education system needs to have a clear perception of the content, curriculum, transaction strategies and an evaluation of learners' achievements as these are critical to the quality and relevance of education imparted. The change in the curriculum, textbooks and instructional process need to be studied and analyzed continuously. Looking to the need, this experiment based on the approach *learning without burden* has been launched initially in early primary (Std.1 & 2) stage of education and then was extended up to the Std.3 & 4.

Under this, creative teaching and learning have been made possible with full of joyful experiences and activities in the textbooks and freedom from heavy school bags, mental stress, home-work, uninteresting additional information and formal examination. The separate teachers' handbook with abundant guidelines plays an important role in creating conducive climate using local resources. The teaching learning process is also being facilitated with school readiness programme, *Bal-Mitra Varg,* no cost/low cost Teaching Learning Materials (TLMs), use of simple spoken languages, songs, rhymes, stories, games, pictures, riddles, activities and continuous comprehensive evaluation.

The effectiveness of this experiment was studied by Ravi J. Mathhai Centre for Educational Innovation, Indian Institute of Management, Ahmedabad and some of the DIETs in their respective districts through qualitative research work. Not only this, but a number of action researches at school level have established the effectiveness of the approach under this experiment. On the basis of their recommendations, the curriculum and textbooks were revised.

For capacity building of teachers, they have been provided

six days residential intensive training regarding pedagogical aspects and preparation of TLMs. They have also been facilitated with modules, audio-video cassettes, Interactive Television (ITV) Programme, radio programme and guidance through *Jeevan Shikshan,* the monthly magazine published by GCERT. These aspects have fulfilled the requirements of teachers for making interesting and effective instructional process.

Bal Melas

Bal Melas are organized in the entire state at Cluster Resource Centre (CRC) level under the academic guidance of GCERT and DIETs. In these Bal Melas, the students of all primary schools under each CRC participate in various activities and competitions related to role play, action songs, reciting poems, patriotic songs, drawing, painting, preparing masks – puppets, *rangoli*, science experiments, mathematical games, classroom decoration, drama, group song, clay work, paper cutting, *origami*, making best out of the west and *Jadu Nagari* etc. Such activities provide them full opportunity and freedom to act or perform which inspire them to create innovative, imaginative and original ideas. There is a wide scope for the development of their hidden potentialities. Besides the limited government aid, the bounteous contribution of the local community helps a lot not only for rewarding the talents but also for over all success of the Bal Melas.

Ramatotsav (Sports Day at School Level)

Sport is a vital part of a nation's social fabric, and playing sport is every citizen's right. Keeping this in view, promoting sports for all students in the state is an attempt of reconstructing the school system and ultimately stressing tolerance and nation building. This also helps the students for the development of their physical and mental abilities. GCERT organizes *Bal Ramatotsav* every year at different levels like

School, CRC, Block, District, Zonal and State with the help of DIETs. The games selected for the *Ramatotsav* are generally based on local environment. GCERT also publishes the special issue of *Jeevan Shikshan*, on the same to provide better guidelines for organizing *Ramatotsav* at various levels.

Eco Club

Considering the role of school cleanliness, health and hygiene, developing fertile land, plantation, using natural resources with proper awareness and environment conservation etc. as some of the norms or indicators for quality education, GCERT has implemented the concept of Eco Club in selected 4000 schools of Gujarat state during 2005-06. Each school was provided Rs. 600 grant for Eco Club activities. With full involvement of the teachers, students and community this programme has become successful. Now all the schools of the entire state have been joining this movement.

Anandshala

Anandshala was a collaborative project of GCERT, Centre for Environment Education (CEE) and Directorate of Primary Education funded by UNICEF-Gujarat, for 14 months during 2003-04. This was based on an integrated approach of school cleanliness and Environment education. The project attempted to evolve and demonstrate the concept of an ideal school in 30 selected schools from Vadodara, Dang and Valsad districts of Gujarat with the following objectives:

- To initiate a process of upgrading the quality of educational environment.
- To develop a demonstrative model of Anandshala by improving existing school infrastructure facilities.
- Revamp and enable 'shalas' to impart socially oriented sustainable education, creating child-friendly environment where every child loves to come, learn and be able to translate his/her learning into action.
- To develop a methodology to establish and sustain a

replicable Anandshala model in other schools / districts of Gujarat.

- To involve community, other departments of state govt., allied institutions ,and individuals to facilitate a better quality of education to internalize and support Anandshala on a long-term basis.

The major thrust areas like; *improving quality of education in schools* (through some interventions viz. Teachers' training on better classroom teaching techniques, Exposure tour for teachers, Creation of subject corners, Greening activities, Science experiment tour for children, conducting Bal Melas, Establishing library, Bulletin board activities etc.), *improving school infrastructure facility* (includes development of school master plan, Sanitation unit, Roof rain water harvesting tank, Hand pump, school fencing, shaping the land etc.) and *developing an Anandshala module as a guidebook for replication* have developed the school climate and established each school as a brand name. These schools are qualitatively better in all aspects than the others, even today. SSA, Times of India and National TV Network(in its programme *Bhumi*) have also mentioned Anandshala as one of the best need based and research based approach as far as quality improvement at primary level is concerned.

Looking to the success of this project, all the districts have started this movement in the state. Many school teachers have visited these schools under exposure tour and motivated towards adopting this approach. There are more 400 schools added in Vadodara district so far. Also the states like Madhya Pradesh, Bihar, Rajasthan and Kashmir have shown interest in implementing such a project.

Science-Mathematics Exhibitions (SMEs)

NCERT has been organizing Pandit Jawaharlal Nehru National Science Exhibition every year since 1971 on different themes. In this connection, at state level in Gujarat, GCERT organizes Science-Mathematics Exhibitions at different levels starting from CRC level to State level.

Studying any concept or event systematically provides scientific knowledge. This is the fact, very well associated especially with teaching-learning in Science and Mathematics. Looking to this, GCERT has initiated SMEs as it continuously strives to improve the quality of education at primary and secondary level. SMEs enable children to participate from interior village schools and CRC level to Block, District, State and even at National level. SMEs create not only interest in Science and Mathematics, but also develop curiosity, a sense of inquiry, reasoning ability, logical thinking, decision power, problem solving skill, a sense of appreciation for great scientists and mathematicians and scientific attitude among the students. The educational value of SMEs can be realized by observing the progressive trend of the same in Table 27.1.

Table 27.1: Progressive Trend of SMEs in Gujarat from 2000-01 to 2005-06

Year	No. of SMEs	No. of Participant schools	No. of Projects	No. of participated students
2000-01	031	1800	2170	4340
2001-02	327	19315	22890	45780
2002-03	3732	35448	52950	105900
2003-04	3570	42335	65357	109400
2004-05	3626	45790	67172	134344
2005-06	3668	46508	68443	142992

Contd...

Year	No. of participated teachers	No. of visitors	No. of projects selected for National level
2000-01	2170	15500	05
2001-02	22890	1335000	07
2002-03	52630	2237613	10
2003-04	65224	2264506	08
2004-05	67172	4337008	16
2005-06	68443	6595666	07

Gujarat Achievement at Primary (GAP – I to IV)

Rapid global changes in educational outlook and sense of competitiveness necessitated the quality improvement in education. In this context, India amongst several other developing countries has embarked upon far reaching reform programmes (namely Minimum Levels of Learning i.e. MLLs and DPEP – SSA) which aim to improve the quality of education such that the country would build a skilled work force and a manpower base that would enhance its competitive capacity world-wide.

Deep concern for educational standards also necessitated the continuous monitoring of students' achievement and assessment of educational progress on standardized tests. GCERT had realized the need of continuous monitoring of students' achievement. Hence GCERT has sponsored a series of research projects, named *'Profiles of Academic Achievement of the Primary School Children of Gujarat'* since 1998-99 under the frameworks of MLLs. Up to the date, four research projects(GAP I, II, III and IV) have been conducted by GCERT and DIETs with the academic guidance and support of Department of Education, Bhavanagar University(DEBU) and Department of Education, Saurashtra University(DESU), especially to integrate and synthesize the district level studies for preparing the profiles of achievement at state level. These research projects have been carried out with a view to achieve the following objectives:

- To explore the profiles of academic achievement of the primary school children (Std. 3 to 7) of Gujarat for the academic year 1998-99/2000-01/2002-03/2004-05 in the context of the MLL programme.
- To compare the academic achievement in the academic years 1998-99, 2000-01, 2002-03 and 2004-05.
- To find out the relationship of students' academic achievement to their gender in GAP – I/GAP – II/GAP–III/GAP – IV.
- To find out the 'Hard points' of the syllabi of the subject

areas (Gujarati, Maths, Science, Social Studies, Hindi, English and Health & Physical Education) of selected standards of primary education in the context of MLL programme.

The summary of the above mentioned research projects with regard to covered districts, sample, standards, subjects and overall average achievement at state level can be seen from Table 27.2.

Table 27.2: Gujarat Achievement at Primary

[

Project	Year	No. of Districts	Sample (No. of students)	Standards
GAP- I	1998-99	19	32232	3 to 6
GAP- II	2000-01	18	96886	3 to 7
GAP-III	2002-03	23	120160	3 to 7
GAP-IV	2004-05	23	72379	5 to 7

Contd...

Project	Year	No. of subjects	Average Achievement Percent
GAP- I	1998-99	18	47
GAP- II	2000-01	27	49
GAP-III	2002-03	27	54.15
GAP-IV	2004-05	21	55.84

The above table shows the gradual improvement in average achievement of the students. Also it is to be noted that the knowledge about the hard points of the syllabi can be useful for improving the quality of education, useful to policy makers as well as parents. Such information is directly useful to teachers in several ways. The research based knowledge about the hard points of syllabi can make qualitative changes in curricula, textbooks, teacher training and evaluation. GCERT has already put into practice the above probable implications of the GAP series at various levels like teacher training, curriculum reformation, evaluation system etc. This is an example of the fruitful relationship between Research and Training. Thus, with this planned efforts, GCERT highlighted Research and Training in its very own name.

Looking to the above, it is realized that GCERT has implemented a variety of innovative programmes from grassroots level, especially for quality improvement at primary level. But still Gujarat is at 12th position as far as the Education Development Index (EDI) is concerned. Still it requires more and more planned efforts to achieve the goal of quality improvement at primary level.

References

Chand, S & Amin, V.G. (2004). *Reformulating the early primary curriculum: implementing a 'progressivist' approach.* Gandhinagar: GCERT.

GCERT. (2006). Souvenir: State level Science – Maths Exhibition, Gandhinagar.

Joshi, H. (2005). *Profiles of academic achievement of the primary school children of Gujarat : 2004-05 [Gujarat Achievement at Primary 4 (GAP 4)].* The report of GCERT sponsored research project, Department of Education, Saurashtra University, Rajkot.

Mehta, A.C. (2007). *Elementary Education in India – Progress towards UEE Analytical Report 2005-06.* New Delhi. : NUEPA

28

Deep Approach of Learning

Mahesh Narayan Dixit

Introduction

Education is a providing and receiving process of knowledge, experiences and good habits. The quality of education not only depends upon the provider, organizer or instructor of education like the government, principal or teacher but it also depends on the habits and learning style of students. There are many burning issues which are closely related with our education system and calling proper attention to solve it. Among these issues our examination system is one of them. It is often said that students are learning for obtaining good marks in examinations and not for knowledge, good thought or good habits.

We know that secondary education is the foundation for higher education. Giving the proper picture of primary and secondary education, Biswas (2007) says in his article, "unfortunately in India, the standard of primary and secondary stage is far from satisfactory in most of the government and private schools barring few good schools. As a result, students do not pay adequate attention to studies and generally, resort to short cut methods, mainly, cramming to pass examination without understanding the basic concept of subject.

It is a frankly stated fact that today's secondary education is not satisfactory. There many causes and issues related with this condition. It is important to search for all causes with the proper evidence. In this scenario, this paper is an attempt to draw out the present picture of deep approach of learning among higher secondary students.

Approaches to Learning

There are three approaches of learning which are directly associated with the quality of teaching- learning process in a positive or a negative way. These approaches are the deep approach, strategic approach and surface approach of learning.

The deep approach of learning is associated with those learners who are serious about their learning. These types of learners want to know the meaning of the content what they have to learn and they are actively interested in the search of new ideas and knowledge. They always relate new knowledge with their previous knowledge and ideas. They have a tendency to examine every knowledge and theory before accepting. They regularly read reference material too. These learners are strongly, internally motivated rather than externally motivated.

Another approach is the strategic approach of learning. The main goal of this type of learning is achieving high marks or grade in the exam. The learners, having this approach, are regulated by the examination system and prepare themselves, how to write the accurate answers of the questions .These learners are strongly externally motivated to learn.

One more approach of learning is the surface approach of learning which is related with the tendency of obtaining passing marks. They have no interest in learning. They try to memorize every thing without proper understanding. They are externally weakly motivated.

Objectives of the Study

The basic objectives of the study are given bellow:

- to know the present level of the deep approach of learning among HSC students,
- to know the relationship between the deep approach of learning and gender;
- to find out the relationship between the deep approach of learning and medium of instruction.

Methodology of the Study

Sample: For the purpose of collecting data for the study, three hundred sixty seven higher secondary students were taken from three Gujarati and three English medium schools in Ahmedabad city. There were 139 girls and 228 boys students out 367 students in the sample. There were 136 students who were English medium and 231students belonging to Gujarati medium. The stratified random cluster sampling method was used to collect the data.

Tool: The scale entitled 'What do you say?' was used in the study. It was adapted and scientifically validated by Dixit and Joshi (2007). The scale is based on the 'Understanding Approaches to learning and studying', originally developed by Bournemouth university (2005). The scale has 36 items for three subscales, namely Deep approach scale, Surface approach scale and strategic approach scale.

Collection and Analysis of the Data: In the present study the deep approach scale (DAS) was administered for the purpose of collecting data. The responses from every respondents to each item were scored on the four point scale i.e. agree, partially agree, partially disagree and disagree. The responses were scored by 3, 2, 1, 0.There were ten items in DAS. The researcher used descriptive statistics for analyzing the present level of deep approach of learning among the higher secondary students. To test the hypotheses t-test was used. The data was analyzed using the SPSS package.

Findings

There were 10 items and maximum score for each item was 3. For each student it was possible to score from 0 to 30. The score on DAS ranged 10 to 30. The mean and SD of the score were 23.30 and 3.70, respectively. It means the level of deep approach of learning among the higher secondary students was fairly high. This can be seen in figure 1.

Figure 1: Frequency histogram for

Deep Approach of Learning

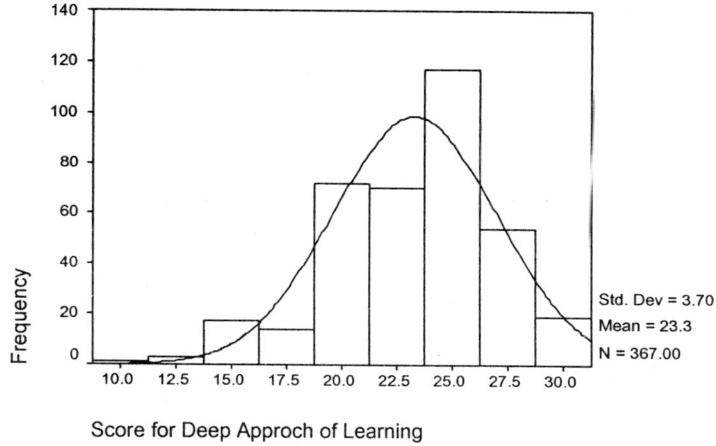

The observation of Table 28.1 shows that there were 139 girls and 228 boys in the sample. The mean and SD of the scores of the girl respondents were 23.19 and 3.19, respectively and that of boys respondents were 23.32 and 3.99, respectively. The t-ratio for the mean difference was 0.17, which was not significant even at 0.05 levels. So the null hypothesis was not rejected. The gender of the students was not related with their deep approach of learning.

Table 28.1: Mean, SD, and t-ratio in Reference to Gender

Gender	Number of students	Mean	SD	t-ratio
Girls	139	23.26	3.19	0.73
Boys	228	23.32	3.99	

The observation of Table 28.2 shows that in the sample there were 231 and 136 students of Gujarati and English medium students, respectively. The mean and SD of the scores of the Gujarati medium respondents were 23.41 and 3.54, respectively and that of English medium respondents were 23.11 and 3.97, respectively. The t-ratio for the mean difference was 0.70, which was not significant even at 0.05 levels. So the null hypothesis was not rejected. The medium of instruction of the students was not related with their deep approach of learning.

Table 28.2: Mean, SD, and t-ratio in Reference to the Medium of Instruction

Medium	Number of students	Mean	SD	t-ratio
Gujarati	231	23.41	3.54	0.70
English	136	23.11	3.97	

Conclusion

The level of deep approach of learning was fairly high among higher secondary students. About 85 percent students have scored above 80 percent on the DAS. The study shows that gender and medium of instruction were not associated with deep approach of learning among higher secondary students. The results of the present research should be interpreted keeping the limited scope and resources of the study in mind.

References

Biswas, K..K. (2007). Indian Higher Education at Crossroad. *University News weekly journal of higher education*, Vol.45, No.50, December 10-16, 2007.p.4.

Bournemouth university.(2005). *Understanding: Approaches to learning and studying.* Retrieved December10, 2007, from http://pdp.bournemouth.ac.uk./documents/u_approaches_to learning_and_studying.doc.

Campbell, E. (1998). Teaching Strategies to Foster "Deep" versus "surface Learning, *Teaching options pedagogiques* ,Vol.2 No.3, November 1998, Retrieved August 1-2007,from http://www.uottawa.co./academic/cut/options/nov 98/teaching strategies,en.htm.

Dixit, M.N. & Joshi, B. H. (2007). *Validation of a scale to measure approaches to learning*. Unpublished manuscript. Department of Education, Gujarat Vidyapith, Ahmedabad-14

Najar, R.L. *Approaches to learning and studying in psychology: A revised perspective* retrieved August 1-2007 from http://www.aare.edu.au/01pdp/Naj01247.htm.

29

Innovations in School Education

Lakshmi Venugopal and Indu Kataria

Education from Ancient Times

India has a long history of organized education. The gurukul system of education is one of the oldest on earth but before that the guru-shishya system was existing, in which students were taught orally and the data would be passed from one generation to the next. Gurukuls were traditional Hindu residential schools of learning; typically the teacher's house or a monastery

The first millennium and the few centuries preceding it saw the flourishing of higher education at Nalanda, Takshashila University, Ujjain, and Vikramshila Universities.

Each university specialized in a particular field of study. Takshila specialized in the study of medicine, while Ujjain laid emphasis on astronomy. Nalanda, being the biggest centre, handled all branches of knowledge, and housed up to 10,000 students at its peak.

The current system of education, with its western style and content, was introduced & funded by the British in the 19th century, following recommendations by Macaulay. Traditional structures were not recognized by the British government and have been on the decline since. Gandhiji is said to have described the traditional educational system as a beautiful tree that was destroyed during the British rule.

After independence, education became the responsibility of the states. The Central Government's only obligation was to co-ordinate in technical and higher education and specify standards. This continued till 1976, when the education became a joint responsibility of the state and the centre.

The Indian Education System is generally marks-based. However, some experiments have been made to do away with the marks-based system which has led to cases of depression and suicides among students. In 2005, the Kerala government introduced a grades-based system in the hope that it will help students to move away from the cut-throat competition and rote-learning and will be able to focus on creative aspects and personality development as well.

Modern education in India is often criticized for being based on rote learning. Emphasis is laid on passing examinations with high percentage. Very few institutes give importance to developing personality and creativity among students. Recently, the country has seen a rise in instances of student suicides due to low marks and failures, especially in metropolitan cities, even though such cases are very rare. The presence of a number of education boards (SSLC, ICSE, CBSE, IB, IGCSE) leads to non-uniformity

Many educational theorists discussed and implemented radically different forms of education. Rabindranath Tagore's Shantiniketan and Mahatma Gandhi's ideal of "basic education" are prime examples. In recent years many new alternative schools have formed, such as Sarang, Palakad Kerala; Adharshila, Saakad MP; Poorna Learning Centre and Sita School, Bangalore; Kanavu, and Timbaktoo Collective, Andhra Pradesh.

Innovative Approaches in Education

Steiner, Montessori and Piaget methods of pre-school education are based on freedom from coercion. The child is encouraged to learn at his pace.

Jean Piaget was a Swiss scientist, educationist. His Cognitive Development theory or stage development theory had a sensory-motor stage (0-2 years); pre-operational stage (2-7); concrete operation stage (7-11) and formal operation stage (11 years onwards).

Maria Montessori was a physician in Italy, created the first

"'House of Children'" in Rome. Montessori believed children should be allowed to "move, touch, manipulate and explore." Montessori classrooms have children of mixed ages. The rooms are filled with colourful objects, tiny chairs, tables, low-washbasins, meant to create a living room for children.

Dr. Rudolf Steiner was a highly respected and well-published scientific, literary and philosophical scholar who was particularly known for his work on Goethe's scientific writings. Rudolf Steiner's philosophy, shown through his Waldorf schools, was also based on appreciating the needs of a child at various stages.

Waldorf (Steiner) Education

Waldorf Education (also known as Steiner or Steiner-Waldorf education) is a pedagogy based upon the educational philosophy of Rudolf Steiner, the founder of anthroposophy. Learning is interdisciplinary, integrates practical, artistic, and intellectual elements, and is coordinated with "natural rhythms of everyday life". The Waldorf approach emphasizes the role of the imagination in learning, developing thinking that includes a creative as well as an analytic component. The education's overarching goal is to provide young people the basis with which to develop into free, moral and integrated individuals and to aid every child in the unfolding of his or her unique destiny. Schools and teachers are given considerable freedom to define curricula within collegial structures.

The first Waldorf School was founded in 1919; there are now more than 1000 independent Waldorf schools and 1400 independent Waldorf kindergartens located in approximately sixty countries throughout the world, making up one of the world's largest independent educational system. Waldorf methods have also been adopted by significant numbers of teachers within traditional state and private schools.

Definition of Steiner Education

Rudolf Steiner believed that education should be designed

to meet the changing needs of a child as they develop physically, mentally and emotionally. He believed that it should help a child to fulfil their full potential but he did not believe in pushing children towards goals that adults or society in general, believed to be desirable.

His approach was systematic, and appears to have been based on his own extensive experience of working as a tutor, and on his study of 'anthroposophy' or 'spiritual science'.

Here are some of its key points:

- Up to the age of seven encourage play, drawing, story telling, being at home, nature study and natural things.
- Do not teach children younger than seven to read.
- Teach a child to write before you teach them to read.
- Do not keep changing a child's teacher: allow one teacher to carry on teaching the same class for seven years.
- Allow children to concentrate on one subject at a time - do history two hours per day for several weeks and then do geography for two hours per day etc.
- Find links between art and science.
- Engage with the child and make sure that they are enthusiastic about the material being covered.
- Give a moral lead but do not teach a particular set of beliefs.
- Encourage learning for its own sake. Do not just work for exams.

He made specific curriculum suggestions for history, geography, mathematics, languages, literature, science, handwork, gymnastics, painting, music, shorthand and many other subjects that were taught in the school in Stuttgart. Obviously, some of these are more appropriate than others to today's conditions.

Some distinctive features of Waldorf education include the following:

- Academics are de-emphasized in the early years of schooling. There is no academic content in the Waldorf kindergarten (i.e. pre-class 1) experience (although there is a good deal of cultivation of pre-academic skills), and minimal academics in class 1. The letters are introduced artistically in class 2, with the children learning to read from their own writing in class 2 or 3.

- During the primary school years (classes 1-8) the students have a class (or "main lesson") teacher who stays with the same class for (ideally) the first eight years of their schooling.
- Certain activities which are often considered "frills" at mainstream schools are central at Waldorf schools: art, music, gardening, and foreign languages (usually two in primary grades), to name a few. In the younger grades, all subjects are introduced through artistic mediums, because the children respond better to this medium than to dry lecturing and rote learning. All children learn to play recorder and to knit.
- There are no "textbooks" as such in the first through fifth grades. All children have "main lesson books", which are their own workbooks which they fill in during the course of the year. They essentially produce their own "textbooks" which record their experiences and what they've learned. Upper grades use textbooks to supplement their main lesson work.
- All children learn a stringed instrument from class 3 onwards. This often includes one-on-one tuition as well as orchestra.
- Learning in a Waldorf school is a non-competitive activity. There are no grades given at the primary level; the teacher writes a detailed evaluation of the child at the end of each school year.
- The use of electronic media, particularly television, by young children is strongly discouraged in Waldorf schools.

Philosophy of Waldorf Education

Consistent with his philosophy called Anthroposophy, Steiner designed a curriculum responsive to the developmental phases in childhood and nurturing of children's imagination. He thought that schools should cater to the needs of children rather than the demands of the government or economic forces, so he developed schools that encourage creativity and free-thinking.

The term "Anthroposophy' comes from the Greek "anthropos-sophia" or "human wisdom". Steiner expanded an exacting scientific method by which one could do research for her/himself into the spiritual worlds. The investigation, known also as Spiritual Science is an obvious complement to the Natural Sciences we have come to accept. Through study and practiced observation, one awakens to his/her own inner nature and the spiritual realities of outer nature and the cosmos. The awareness of those relationships brings a greater reverence for all of life.

Steiner and many individuals since, who share his basic views have applied this knowledge in various practical and cultural ways in communities around the world. Most notably, Waldorf schools have made significant impact on the world. Curative education, for mentally and emotionally handicapped adults and children, has established a deep understanding and work with people who have this difficult destiny. Bio-dynamic farming and gardening greatly expand the range of techniques available to organic agriculture.

Anthropomorphically medicine and pharmacy, although less widely known in Australia, are subjects of growing interest.

It should be stressed that while Anthroposophy forms the theoretical basis to the teaching methods used in Waldorf schools, it is not taught to the students.

Anthroposophy has its roots in the perceptions, already gained, into the spiritual world.

Yet these are no more than the roots. The branches, leaves, blossoms, and fruits of Anthroposophy grow into all the fields of human life and action.

Various Studies

A UK Department for Education and Skills report noted significant differences in curriculum and pedagogical approach between Waldorf/Steiner and mainstream schools and recommended that schools in the state sector could benefit from the following elements of Waldorf education.

An Australian study comparing the academic performance of students at university level found that students who had been at Waldorf schools significantly outperformed their peers from non-Waldorf schools in both the humanities and the sciences.

A survey in U.S. on Waldorf schools found that parents overall experienced the Waldorf schools as achieving their major aims for students and describe the education as one that "integrates the aesthetic, spiritual and interpersonal development of the child with rigorous intellectual development", preserving students enthusiasm for learning so that they develop a better sense of self-confidence and self-direction.

The Education Renaissance Trust, which runs Shloka in Hyderabad, is guided by the thoughts of Rudolf Steiner. Anandhi left her job in a mainstream school to teach in Shloka.

"Childhood years," she notes, "are vital to our total existence. Overloading children early, with too much memory-oriented learning and formal writing, can cripple a child's sense of wonder."

Tina Bruinsma, a specialist in Steiner methods, contends that learning is as natural to a child as flying to a bird. It comes at the right time if the right stimuli are provided. Too-early imposition of formal skills will harden a child's soul, she says. "Steiner learnt so much from India," she reveals. "He drew inspiration from your sacred books. It is wonderful that his ideas should come back to India."

Conclusion

The best overall statement on what is unique about

Waldorf education is to be found in the stated goals of the schooling: "to produce individuals who are able, in and of themselves, to impart meaning to their lives".

It is important to note that Waldorf schools honour and protect the wonder of childhood. Every effort is expended to make Waldorf schools safe, secure and nurturing environments for the children, and to protect their childhood's from harmful influences from the broader society.

Secondly, Waldorf education has a consistent philosophy of child development underlying the curriculum. All subjects are introduced in an age-appropriate fashion.

Finally, Waldorf schools produce graduates who are academically advantaged with respect to their public school counterparts, and who consistently gain admission to top universities.

At present schools are considered as knowledge shops and teachers information mongers.

Educational institutions are also becoming profit oriented. We need to emphasize the basic objective of education which is to develop four fold skills in young children.

We should encourage alternate education system based on ancient Indian education system & modern methods as detailed above, especially in primary education, to help the child to develop his intellectual, aesthetic, emotional, moral, spiritual being and his communal life and impulses out of his own temperament."

30

A Study of *Navprerna* as an Alternative School

R.L. Madhavi and M. Rajendran

Providing education to all is one of the millennium goals of the world now. The Indian government with its aim of providing education for all has made education a fundamental right through its constitutional amendment. With this responsibility now it is the responsibility of the government to provide for the education of its citizens. Many ideas have been put forward to achieve this goal, of which alternative education is one. The present paper focuses on one such alternative school established in Baroda city.

Education in India

With the attainment of independence the process of education has attained a more democratic approach, with ideas of universalization of education and providing equal opportunities of education to all. A constitutional provision for free and compulsory education up to the age group of six to fourteen has opened new avenues for the marginalized, underprivileged sections of the society. With these social goals, India has come up a long way from an illiterate society to a literate society where awareness, knowledge and skills form the basis of life for present citizens. Still a long way has to be travelled in terms of achieving full literacy.

Alternative Education

An alternative education is an educational approach with a curriculum and methods that are non-traditional. This approach follows a special curriculum offering a more flexible program of study than a traditional school. Many forms of alternative programs have been worked out basing several philosophies and approaches. Home Education is also one form of alternative education. The idea came into being with compulsory education at primary and secondary levels. Most of the educational thinkers felt that education at this level has to be offered in more than one ways.

Alternative Education in Indian Context

Alternative education in the Indian context is mostly related with a non formal form than formal establishment. Particularly where governmental efforts are involved, there are many programs planned and implemented concerning the educational opportunities of marginalized sections. Efforts of non- governmental organizations are also involved in this aspect. Some of the important points to be mentioned here are establishment of National Open School; Mobiles in rural India; Education Guarantee Scheme and Alternative and Innovative Education Scheme.

Navrachana Education Society

Navrachana Education Society is established with an aim to provide quality education to citizens of Baroda city. It started with initial establishment of a senior higher secondary school Navrachana. The society is now flourishing with institutes: Navrachana Senior Secondary School, Sama; Navrachana Vidyani Vidyalaya, Sama; Navrachana International School, Bhaili; Navprerana, Sama; and Navrachana Sports Academy.

Navprerna School

Navpreprna School was founded on 14th November, 2002 with an intention to provide quality education to underprivileged children of Sama Village, Baroda. Initial funding for this school was provided by Navrachana Education Society and donations by individuals and parents of the students of Navrachana School.

Objectives for establishing this school are:

- To provide education less privileged children in Sama Village
- Almost free education with all related material and infrastructure
- Giving holistic and quality education
- Focus on health hygiene and personality development of students
- Vocational Training (Earning while learning): Tailoring, Machine Embroidery, paper Craft and Screen Printing
- Focus on individual development than mere academic scoring
- Appreciation and nurturing of individual talents and abilities of each child
- Progress in small stages

The mission of the school is to empower children by encouraging them to view education as a journey of discovery and learning of the world around and more importantly the talent and strengths within. Apart from academic progress the emphasis is on Personality Development, Value Education and Skills Development.

Classes are conducted in the premises of the Navrachana School from 2:00 p.m. to 5:30 p.m. Around 350 children of various age groups have been enrolled and are taught by fifteen teachers who are employed. Now regular classes are being conducted from Nursery to Std. X. for age groups of 3 to 16 years. Children pay Rs.50 per month as fees. There are no grants from MHRD.

Children enrolled in the school are with minimum academic knowledge and training. So, in the initial stage they were trained to accustom to the conditions of a formal academic environment. The initialization program was Abodh-Prabodh-Subodh, through which child is made known about reading, writing and related skills. After initial six months training based on the level attained by the child, he is placed in the relevant class and trained.

Promotion from one class to another in an academic year is not the goal. Promotion will be given on the basis of academic progress shown by student and through periodical assessments; promotion may be given 2-3 times a year also. A flexible course design is made available for this. The aim is to provide an education leading to competence to write the Higher Secondary Examination of National Open School. To make a child understand his or her inherent potentials and competence in order to improve upon self and surroundings through wholesome development is the objective behind this approach.

The medium of instruction is Gujarati. The teachers make lesson plans and try to implement them at the level of the students. For computer training English and Gujarati languages are used and time is provided for students to make them feel comfortable with using computers. Some take more time to become familiar with the things. The teacher has to be flexible in the implementation of the teaching- learning looking into the situations.

In addition to academic activities extra-curricular activities include Yoga, Athletics, Dance, theatrics/Dramatics, Computer Skills Development, Collateral visits/Excursions, Wholesome nutrition, Vocational training. Vocational training is provided for students in tailoring, machine embroidery, paper craft and screen printing. The products being made are sold and the money collected is deposited into the bank accounts opened in their respective names. This will provide the impetus for them to continue their academic further and feel self- sufficient. Most of the children are self-employed and come to school after attending the work.

Many changes have been brought in from initial flexible teaching environment to an organized educational activity in the five years of its establishment. Now students are provided with uniforms. The academic progress of the students is being assessed through tests, conducted at regular intervals. The students from fifth standard onwards are being trained in computer skills. Various competitions are held in patriotic singing, rangoli, garba competition. etc. Picnics are organized with the help of donations. Regular medical check-ups are done by doctors at frequent intervals and required actions are made known to parents. The school takes part in annual concert of Navrachana and has its own annual day and prize distribution function.

Because of their employment before school hours, children take leave more. Parents give more importance to earning than studying. So teachers have to go for rounds in the village and explain to parents about importance of education and sustain the efforts of child in learning. Initial training of children in behaviour, greeting, speaking, body cleanliness, maintenance of health and hygiene are to be taken care of. They are made responsible for conducting programs in school to make them learn leadership qualities and to develop managerial abilities Some times peer-teaching is also emphasized. Extra- curricular activities are regularly provided to make learning joyful.

The School has been accredited as a Study Centre of Open Schooling (NIOS) for Open Basic Education. Under this program students will get academic certificates from NIOS for Std. III, V, and VIII. With these certificates they can gain entry into any government school in India. Twelve students had appeared for 10th Board through NIOS and cleared three subjects for which they have given exams. They can clear the remaining subjects in nine chances to gain certificates. These certificates will help them to gain employment or to pursue higher education. To develop a trust fund and gain more self-sufficiency in organizing various activities of the school is another plan.

Conclusion

Within the four years of its existence Navprerana School has emerged into an organized educational institution for under privileged children of Sama Village. Children with little academic exposure are being groomed into enthusiastic children with interest academic and extra-curricular activities. The dream of the school is to develop students with confidence and knowledge and to lead a life with responsibility and pride.

31

Relevance of Alternative Schooling

Geetha Dinker

Introduction

Education can reflect the world in which it exists and also help to change and develop that world. Education has a major and a critical role to play in the updating and honing skills in our society both in terms of economic and societal pressures and as a response to individual needs. Education, in the true sense, is the understanding of one self for it is within each one of us that the whole of existence is gathered. Recognizing the importance of education, the governments vide Article 45 of the Constitution which states, "The state shall endeavour to provide within a period of 10 years from the commencement of the constitution for free and compulsory education for all Children until they complete the age of 14 years." Universalization of elementary education has therefore been accepted as a national goal and set before itself the goal of "Education for All" by 2010.

According to the latest estimate of the Planning Commission, out of approximately 200 million children of the age group 6-14 years, 42 million children of this age group do not attend schools. There are problems relating to high drop out rates, low levels of learning achievement, low participation of girls and marginalized segments of the society, remote and far flung areas of the country. In such a scenario, alternative schooling with innovations and experiments in education needs to be explored to improve the quantitative and qualitative aspects of the school system particularly to the large portion of the children for whom education remains unreached. The paper focuses, particularly on pre- school and

6-14 age group children.

Concept of Non Formal Education (NFE)

Non-formal modes of education such as correspondence education open and distance education run by the Government and non Government agencies, come under the arrangement of Alternative schooling. In such an arrangement flexibility is the key word. Open learning, like most aspects of education and training, has its own set of terms and phrases with particular meanings in given context. Broadly, of the different kinds of learning—open-learning, distance-learning, flexible-learning, individual-learning, resources-based learning, independent-learning, student-cantered learning, computer-assisted learning, interactive-learning—the umbrella term 'open learning' tends to be the one which includes all the rest.

Open learning as a process, focuses on access to education opportunities and a philosophy which makes learning more student-oriented. Open learning is when decisions about learning are taken by the learners themselves. These decisions may be over a number of different aspects of the learning process including.

- Whether or not to learn
- What to learn (Selection of content, skill)
- How to learn (Methods, media)
- Where to learn (start and finish, pace)
- Who to turn to for help. (Tutors, Trainers, friends, colleagues)
- How to get learning assured (nature of feedback provided)
- What to do next (other courses, career direction)

Open learning caters to the educational needs of individuals, often disadvantaged by their lack of pre-educational qualifications and are habitant of far flung remote rural areas. The need is to establish an equitable, coherently planned and resourced public and low cost provision, open learning can be carried out at a distance and is called distance education.

Genesis of National Open School (NOS)

The Central Board of the Secondary Education (CBSE) set up the first open school of the country under its aegis in the form of a project in 1979. It was converted to National open school in 1989 when as a result of the project report, became an autonomous organization of the Department of Education, Ministry of Human Resource Development. National Open School (NOS) is now known as the National Institute of open Schooling (NIOS) since July 2002.

The NOS was set up to design, develop and offer a flexible, life oriented programme through distance education in 1989 by the Government of India in pursuance of the National Policy on education 1986. The primary mission of NOS is universalization of education, achievement of social equality and justice, creation of learning society. Subsequently in 1990, NOS was vested with the authority to conduct its own examination and grant certifications NOS started with academic courses at secondary, senior-secondary levels. Today the focus of the National Institute of open learning covers right from the elementary education to courses at the pre degree level, both academic and vocational. NIOS has shown a steady growth in student enrolment, number of courses and study centres. It has developed into the largest open school in the world with 1427 thousands students on its roll. It attempts to reach out to physically, mentally, socially and geographically disadvantaged groups through suitable learning material and delivery mechanism. It uses new technologies for training and teaching purpose mainly to increase access and ensure quality. In order to systematize the interaction between NIOS and the state open schools and other agencies, it was considered appropriate to establish a forum under the NIOS in the form of Consortium.

The National Consortium for open schooling (NCOS) was launched in September 1997, with a view to facilitating better cooperation, collaboration and expansion of activities in the open learning system.

Special Features of NIOS

- Self-paced learning.
- Flexibility in choice of subjects.
- Credit accumulation.
- Part admission.
- Readmission and transfer of credits (TOC).
- No age bar.

Training Courses in Open Schooling

The Ministry of Human Resources Development, Government of India and The National Institute of open schooling India, have in collaboration with, and/or the support from the Commonwealth of learning Canada, have established an International centre for training in open schooling (ICTOS) at NIOS to address to the training needs of the functionaries involved in open schooling and open basic education.

The Government of India has launched EGS and AIE schemes to reach the unreached children.

Education Guarantee Scheme (EGS) and Alternative Innovative Education Scheme (AIE)

The main aim of the scheme is to cover the non-formal education sector with a more holistic and flexible approach. It is actually a modified version of the centrally sponsored Non Formal Education (NFE) scheme initiated in 1979-80 on a pilot basis with a view to supporting the formal education system in providing education to all children up to the age of 14 years as enunciated in the Directive Principles of the Constitution. The National policy on Education, i.e. NPE (1986), recognized that the school could not reach all children and a large and systematic programme of non -formal education would be required for school drop -outs, for children from habitation without schools, working children and girls who could not attend schools throughout day.

Thus NFE became an important component of the overall strategy for achievement of universalization of elementary education (UEE). The NFE scheme was revised in 1987-88. The concept of the "Non-formalized School" proposed by the Ramamurti Committee (1990). "All essential resources, both financial and intellectual, should be made available to the school to enable it to "reach out to" the children outside the school, at least two thirds of whom are girls. The school should open up and non -formalize in creative ways. According to Ramamurti Committee, this would be preferable to building up an exclusive parallel system of non formal education for the poor and working children. The school could be non- formalized by:

1. Shifting school timings to early morning hours, afternoons or late evenings as per requirements of the community.
2. Adjusting school calendar to agricultural activity and other local needs to maximize attendance.
3. Holding classes twice in the day for written and oral traditions and using upgraded classrooms.
4. Providing for flexible entry points for first generation learners and girls.
5. Providing freedom to question, inquire, explore, and enjoy through group learning and peer- teaching.
6. Introducing environment based content and formative evaluation, community participation, and internship model of teacher training.

The Programme of Action (1992), outlined strategies for strengthening of NFE school A major portion of the NFE Scheme is run by the state governments which set up NFE Centre. One component of the scheme provides grants to Voluntary Agencies (VAs) directly from the Central Government for running of NFE centres and a third is for projects of experiential innovative nature of VAs. The current status of NFE scheme is:

- Total coverage of children under NFE scheme is about 74 lakh
- 2.38 lakh Primary and 6800 upper primary centres are presently anchored in the state sector.

- 58000 primary and 1000 upper primary centres are run by VAs.
- 41 Experimental and innovative education projects are being implemented by VAs.

The NFE scheme till now has functioned largely, as a separate intervention for 'out of school' children resulting in poor linkages with the formal system, inadequate emphasis on mainstreaming of children from the NFE system and duplication of enrolment between formal and alternative system. Thus a reorientation was necessary the effort to provide access to 'out of school' children and ensure their regular participation and completion of primary/elementary level of education with satisfactory levels of learning had to form a part of the overall effort for achievement of UEE. The challenges before the nation to, therefore to evolve such a strategy that the goals of universalization of education and full literacy are achieved within the time frame now stipulated under Sarva Shiksha Abhiyan (SSA). The Educational Guarantee Scheme (EGS) and Alternative and Innovative Education scheme (AIE) have evolved out of major concerns and learning experiences.

EGS and AIE are important component of Sarva Shiksha Abhiyan (SSA) to bring 'out of school' in the fold of elementary education. The scheme envisage child wise planning undertaken for each 'out of school' child and the possibility to enrolment of 'out of school' children into formal schools is explored first before deciding on the alternative approaches that are necessary.

The EGS and AIE would cover children in the age group of 6-14 years, however for children with disabilities; it would cover children up to the age of 18 yrs. The salient features are:

- The EGS and AIE should have three components such as: (i) state run/EGS schools or different types of schools or school camps run by other Government Agencies (ii) Learning centres alternative schools run by voluntary Agencies (iii) Experimental projects for innovative pedagogical strategies and DRUs run voluntary agencies.

- The scheme should form a part of the Sarva Shiksha Abhiyan (SSA) and be merged at the beginning of the 10th plan with the SSA programme.
- Preference would be given to the ten educationally backward states. The scheme would set up schools in the small, scattered and unserved habitations and this alternative educational facility would be meant for specific categories of highly deprived children.
- In project districts EGS and AIE would support interventions for out of school children under some prescribed conditions.
- The scheme would give priority to establishment of alternative (EGS schools) in unserved habitations where schools are not available within the radius of 1 km and at least 15-20 children in the age group of 6-14 year are available.
- Micro planning would be conducted including house to house surveys and taking community demand as well as commitment into account with preference and priority.

Academic Inputs

The EGS and AIE would provide recruitment of educational volunteers to transact teaching- learning activities and the minimum qualification for appointment of the volunteers would be Matriculation (Class V) at primary stage and graduation or class XI at upper primary stage.

Duration and Management

Centres under the scheme would function for a minimum of four hours a day and timing should be suitable for the learners, may be evening or night time. There should not be any rigidity about the duration and timing and the EGS schools would function for several years till their up gradation or till the out of school children in that area is covered. There should be separate management structure for EGS and AIE till the

SSA becomes fully operational.

Concept of Alternative School

Many schools, which were often founded by persons with a strong interest in what education means, attempt to provide quality holistic education to children from poor economic backgrounds, far flung remote rural areas. These schools seek to explore different alternatives is education and therefore come under a special category called alternative schools because their approach is learner oriented with emphasis on nurturing the child's interest and learning. This encourages children to think independently and become more responsible. Some parents felt that mainstream schooling was not giving their children what they needed. They feel that learning did not go beyond reading, writing and stuffing children with mindless facts and did not help them to build a relationship and bonding with nature was having a detrimental effect on their development.

This attempt to return to the basics where children can explore and begin to understand the entire gamut of human existence and bring meaning to the process of learning is possible through alternative schools which are mostly engaged in creating and using innovative teaching methodologies that ensure that rote learning does not happen. Some schools use excellent language teaching methodologies, some others use games and experiments to explain difficult concepts in Mathematics and Science to kindle interest in the children. They also try to address the inadequacies in the conventional system. Many of the schools assist children in taking the main stream government examinations. Alternative schools today caters to a larger number of students who have either not enrolled in schools or dropped out due to social, economic or geographical disadvantages.

According to the Education Commission (1964-66), "But in view of the immense difficulties involved such as lack of adequate resources, tremendous increase in population, resistance to the education of girls, large numbers of children of the backward classes, general poverty of the people and illiteracy are apathy, it was not possible to make adequate progress in primary education and the constitutional directive has remained unfulfilled." The initiatives/salient features of some of the groups working in this area namely Anugriha, Auroville educational centre, Rural Litigation and Entitlement Kendra… are detailed below:

Anugriha Charitable Trust

A school named Shikshyatan, commenced operation in mid 1994 admitting 15 children aged 3 to 3.5 years to the first class. All these children were drawn from low income scheduled caste families in which they are the first generation to receive any education. Their educational philosophy was – education is the process by which centuries of knowledge can be transferred in the shortest possible way. Seven stages of learning was evolved which take the children to this point by the time they are 14 yrs. All the methods employed in the school are based on the philosophy that the children whatever profession they may choose, she/he will be a good person. To start with, physical condition of the children is given utmost importance then only the child will be able to read well and think with the mind. When the child is 5-6 years, they are given yogasans, evening games etc. The reading and math program are the next introduction to the children. Programs which make the word and object familiar and use of words familiar are also introduced. The math programme is based on a dot card system. The philosophy of the school is based on the fact that the school need only merely help the child to articulate what she/he already knows. Children over 14 years go to Government school, 4 kms from the village.

Auroville Educational Resource Centre

Isai Ambalam is one of the several schools run by Auroville; a township near Pondicherry According to

Aurobindo and Mother, education should bring out the divine element in all human beings. This divine element expresses itself qualities as strength, love, beauty, delight, knowledge and many aspects contributing to a better life. Physical part in our body should be strong and enduring enough to support this endeavour. Education should aspire to improve on this with full consent of the child. The school applies the principle that everything is within the child .The school only helps to bring out the best. An environment is created where action involvement in learning, curiosity and thinking power is encouraged. These help the child to grow in a natural spontaneous way. The school uses the thematic project methods to increase their awareness and general/subject knowledge. The school also uses spiritual methods. Learning aids are used to bring out the child's learning. The teachers in the school are trained on an ongoing basis. Because of this, the teachers are well versed with adapting/creating learning aids based on the needs of the children with modern tools including the computer, print outs etc. Teachers are helped to create their own aids. Audio tape method is a bilingual method which uses the mother tongue and English for learning English .Another method, which has great potential in education is the design method. Students do not learn subjects as separate units, but in an integrated manner. They are given challenges or problems and find answers for these. The uses of spiritual methods are also explored. They make the mind silent and help identify with the divine.

Rural Litigation and Entitlement Kendra (RLEK)

Education was one of the first programme of Rural Litigation and Entitlement Kendra (RLEK) initiated with Van Gujjar Community who reside in deep forest areas and lead a nomadic lifestyles. They had been deprived of the benefits of any education programme of the government. Another significant fact was that the community migrates to the higher Himalayas for six months in a year. RLEK therefore came up with an innovative education programme wherein the teacher volunteers of the organization, migrated with the community members to the highlands and continued the education programme. Both the community members and teacher volunteers built a good rapport amongst themselves and the programme thus made significant progress. For enabling quick and easy assimilation of knowledge, books and material for the literacy programme are context specific i.e. examples from their day to day life has been used. It goes to the credit of Van Gujjars that within a short span of time the community has been able to utilize the skills acquired through the literacy programs to address some of the most critical issues confronting them. Two hundred primary and upper primary centres are being run for Van Gujjars in many districts in Himachal Pradesh.

Suggestions

Choice in education is finally emerging on the educational landscape, and it is gaining momentum. Alternative learning, democratic decision making, new learning environments, restriction of time, community- parental involvement, project-based learning, sensitivity to learning styles and small size of learners are just a few of the features that characterize alternative schooling. For enhancing quality improvement in Alternative schooling to sustain the teacher/students interest and motivation with constructive and meaning learning experience, can be given encouragement as follows.

- Mobilization campaign for universal enrolment by way of street plays, drama, songs, house to house visits.
- Creating a pleasant environment in which children can study and feel comfortable.
- Provision of teaching aids, spring balances, models of human body, mathematical boards which run on electricity, charts and models to teach Mathematics.
- Children should be given affection and caring attitude on the part of teacher, which will remove fear from the mind

of children and they will enjoy to attend school and to learn. Group singing also will remove shyness and fear from the minds of children.

- Flexibility of attending the schools as per the convenience of children should be allowed because of their requirement at home for work.
- Textbooks, writing materials and breakfast are very important and items contributing to children's motivation
- Inclusion of teachers to be part of policy making processes so that such policies are likely to have greater relevance to the actual situation in which teachers find themselves.

Philosophy underlying the Alternative Education is to create a healthy environment for a joyful learning so as to retain the students in the school for pursuing their education. Alternative Education recognize and celebrates cultural pluralisation and the need for all to be included in meaningful ways. This means equal opportunity for each student, regardless of ethnicity, gender and ability. EGS and AIE supports flexible strategies including schools in unserved habitants for migrating children, bridge courses, residential camps, drop in centres for street and slum children. Alternative schools is thus a blessing to reach the unreached, school drop outs, neo-literates, girls and women marginalized groups, scheduled caste and scheduled tribes, first generation learners and those who want to pursue their interest in sports/music/dance, have been benefited from these schools.

References

Ministry of Human Resource Development, (1964-66). Report of the Education Commission (1966), Government of India, New Delhi.

Ministry of Human Resource Development, (1986). National Policy on Education (1986), Government of India, New Delhi.

Ministry of Human Resource Development, (1990, December 26). Ramamutri Review Committee (1990), Government of India, New Delhi.

Ministry of Human Resource Development, (1992) .Programme of

Action (1992), Government of India, New Delhi.

Ministry of Human Resource Development, (1992). National Policy on Education (1986), revised policy Formulation (1992), Government of India, New Delhi.

Ministry of Human Resource Development, (2001, December). Report of the Steering Committee of Elementary and Adult Education for the 10th Five year Plan (2002-2007), Government of India, New Delhi.

Paine, N. (1989). Open Learning in Transition: An Agenda for action. London: Kogan page Ltd.

.Patel, R. and Geetha, D. (2007). Teacher Education in open schooling system in India presented at National Seminar on Emerging scenario of Teacher Education (22-23 March, 2007).

Ramalingam, S. (2005). Open Distance Learning. Jaipur: ABD publisher

Rao, V.K. (2005). Alternative Education. New Delhi: APH Publishing.

Index

Index